# CRIMINAL AND CITIZEN
# IN MODERN MEXICO

# CRIMINAL AND CITIZEN
# IN MODERN MEXICO

ROBERT M. BUFFINGTON

UNIVERSITY OF NEBRASKA PRESS

LINCOLN AND LONDON

Chapter 4 originally appeared in *Mexican
Studies/Estudios Mexicanos* 9, no.1, © 1992 by
the Regents of the University of California;
reprinted with permission. Additional
acknowledgments of the use of previously
published materials can be found
on pages 201 and 205.

Library of Congress Cataloging-in-Publication Data
Buffington, Robert, 1952–
Criminal and citizen in modern Mexico /
Robert M. Buffington.
p.   cm.
Includes bibliographical references and index.
ISBN 0-8032-1302-6 (cloth : alk. paper).—
ISBN 0-8032-6159-4 (pbk. : alk. paper)
1. Crime—Mexico.    2. Criminal justice,
Administration of—Mexico.
3. Nationalism—Mexico.    I. Title.
HV6812.B84    2000
364.972—dc21          99-38716
CIP

# Contents

# ILLUSTRATIONS

# Acknowledgments

During the course of this project I incurred many debts. Some were intellectual, some not. A few of these debts are acknowledged here:

For intellectual stimulation, practical suggestions, and encouragement, especially in the formative phases of this manuscript, I thank Michael Meyer, Donna Guy, and Kevin Gosner. For their insightful critiques of the final drafts, I thank the anonymous readers who commented on the manuscript for the University of Nebraska Press.

For invaluable suggestions on individual chapters I thank Carlos Aguirre, Dan Balderston, Katherine Elaine Bliss, Marcus Daniel, Bob Dean, Martha Huggins, Alan Knight, Leisa Meyer, Ricardo Salvatore, Lynn Stoner, Laura Tabili, and the participants in Crawford Young's 1997 NEH summer seminar on "Nation, State and Cultural Pluralism" at the University of Wisconsin, Madison. For scholarly generosity and good advice I thank Bill Beezley, Pablo Piccato, and John Sherman.

For unflagging courtesy and many useful suggestions I thank the staffs of the Archivo General de la Nación, Hemeroteca Nacional, Biblioteca Nacional, and the University of Arizona Library, and the archivists at the Reclusorio del Sur and Reclusorio Oriente. For enthusiatic support and quiet professionalism, I thank the staff of the University of Nebraska Press.

For keeping me and my family well housed (among other kindnesses) during the graduate-school phase of this project, I thank Robert and Sandy Buffington, Charles and Alice Proctor, and Nancy Howard and Dick Mello. The rest of my extended family, for favors too numerous to list here, I thank as well.

Thanks can't begin to express the debt I owe my wife, Megan, and children, Sam, Owen, Celina, and Frances. This book is for them.

# Introduction

"And which do you regard as the greatest force for peace, the army or the schoolhouse?" I asked.

The soldier's face flushed slightly and the splendid white head was held a little higher.

"You speak of the present time?"

"Yes."

"The schoolhouse. There can be no doubt of that. I want to see education throughout the Republic carried on by the national Government. I hope to see it before I die. It is important that all citizens of a republic should receive the same training, so that their ideals and methods may be harmonized and the national identity intensified. When men read alike and think alike they are more likely to act alike."

"And you believe the vast Indian population of Mexico is capable of high development?"

"I do. The Indians are gentle and they are grateful, all except the Yaquis and some of the Mayas. They have the traditions of an ancient civilization of their own. They are to be found among the lawyers, engineers, physicians, army officers and other professional men."

Over the city drifted the smoke of many factories.

"It is better than cannon smoke," I said. – James Creelman interviewing Porfirio Díaz

Unlike news of his projected retirement and his cordial welcome to an opposition party, the announcement that Porfirio Díaz preferred schools and factories to cannons provoked little response in Mexico. Cynics might have questioned the strength of his commitment, but none would have doubted the sincerity of his vision. After the 1867 execution of Maximilian, liberal political dominance ensured that secular public education, integration of the "Indians," and industrial development would represent the acknowledged pillars of official social policy.[1] Few among Mexico's ruling elites would have argued with Díaz's imperative that "all citizens of a republic should receive the same training, so that their ideals and methods may be harmonized and the national identity intensified." Nor would they have disputed his declaration that "when men read alike and think alike they are more likely to act alike." Effective nation building required perceptual conformity—a common sense of purpose and a common goal. And General Díaz blushed with good reason; the question was more than a little condescending. He understood perfectly well that modern societies were not disciplined by cannons, even if, in still modernizing Mexico, there were "times when cannon smoke [was] not such a bad thing."[2]

In *Imagined Communities: Reflections on the Origin and Spread of Nationalism*, Benedict Anderson analyzes the development of the modern nation-state: an inexorable historical process rooted in Enlightenment epistemologies and capitalist political economics. According to Anderson the modern nation is an imagined cultural artifact: "limited" in extent (having spatial boundaries), "sovereign" in itself (outside the dynastic pretensions of divine-right monarchy), a "community . . . conceived as a deep, horizontal comradeship" (in spite of actual inequalities).[3] Thus he places the dichotomous principles of exclusion (spatial boundaries) and inclusion (community or comradeship)—ideologically reconciled by the "popular" sovereignty of an imagined citizenry—at the root of modern nationhood. Anderson also argues for the tremendous adaptability of modern "nation-ness." "The creation of these artifacts toward the end of the eighteenth century was the spontaneous distillation of a complex 'crossing' of discrete historical forces," he notes, "but . . . once created, they became 'modular,' capable of being transplanted, with varying degrees of self-consciousness, to a great variety of social terrains, to merge and be merged with a correspondingly wide variety of political and ideological constellations."[4] What had begun as a distinctly Western European and North American phenomenon during the formative period of the American and French Revolutions, he insists, quickly became an international model of political organization.[5]

Mexico, with longstanding colonial and cultural ties to Europe, aspired early to modern nationhood.[6] Since independence and despite nearly a century of fratricidal battles for political domination, most

Mexican elites defined modernity—political, economic, and social progress—in nationalistic terms.[7] After 1821 the kingdom of New Spain (and various peripheries) became simply Mexico, the Nahua name signifying both the new nation's separateness from the colonial metropolis and its historical roots in precolonial antiquity. By extension, a wildly heterogeneous population became the Mexican "people," at least in the official imagination, and policymakers implemented a broad range of social policies to facilitate the development of loyal national citizens.[8] Disagreements there were—devils in the details— but, with the significant exception of the much contested issue of the Catholic Church's proper role in the new nation, Mexican elites shared a remarkably consistent vision of the new requirements for national citizenship.

Breathing fresh life into their imagined community, Mexican nationalists recognized, required the reconstruction of the colonial subject.[9] Strong corporate ties to crown, church, village, hacienda, confraternity, guild, extended family—the bulwarks of colonial society—undermined loyalty to the nation-state. Liberal nationalists in particular argued that only universal, secular (state-controlled), public education could effect the spiritual reconquest of the Mexican masses, converting them from superstitious, lazy colonial subjects into the loyal and productive citizenry vital to a soon-to-be modern nation. Conservatives were less eager to break colonial ties to church education but, except for a few unreconstructed monarchists, most favored similar ends. Moreover, after 1867 their ability to subvert liberal means diminished considerably (although the Cristero revolt of the 1920s and 1930s demonstrated that liberal ascendancy had muted but not silenced the conservative agenda). Regardless, on issues of citizenship and social reconstruction, consensus was most often the rule.

As Porfirio Díaz did, scholars have noted the importance of state activities like secular public education to national consolidation. In her pioneering study of nationalism and education in Mexico, for example, Josefina Vázquez de Knauth focuses on educators' deliberate and persistent efforts over nearly a century and a half to inculcate modern values and to foster a sense of national identity through a reconstruction of the past that stressed (Anderson would say "imagined") the common historical experience of all Mexicans. Presented in this light, differences between the turn-of-the-century liberal education policies of the Díaz administration and the socialist bent of Cardenismo in the late 1930s, for example, seem incidental to their common vision of an educated, productive citizenry united by the strong, if imaginary, bonds of shared experience.[10] And, as William Beezley and others suggest, public education extended far beyond the schoolhouse to include everything from patriotic festivals and parades to statuary and baseball.[11]

Public education, however, was only the most visible part of a more comprehensive civics. Clearly, not all Mexicans qualified for full citizenship. Some were excluded because of age, sex, or mental incompetence, others because they had broken the law. And it was this last exclusion—based on criminal *acts* rather than on "natural" *condition*—that provided elite policymakers the flexibility needed to *legally* delimit the all-too-inclusive (if still male) category of citizen. So, while public education proselytized the virtues of citizenship, the criminal-justice system identified and disciplined the transgressors—those who would not or could not conform to new national standards. Just as exploitation and dispossession tainted the accomplishments of capitalist economic development, criminal courts, penal codes, and penitentiaries functioned as overtly coercive institutional corollaries to the obvious benefits of public schools and festivals. The exclusive function of criminal justice nicely complemented public education's essential inclusiveness.[12] The opposition of criminal and citizen thus became the fundamental dichotomy within modern Mexican society—a dichotomy that shaped and legitimized the more obvious (but *illegal*) exclusions of race and class. (The exclusion of adult women, on the other hand, *was* legal even if ideologically suspect.) Imagined social boundaries divided the national community internally just as political boundaries separated it from other nation-states; categorical criminalization served—especially after independence, when legal segregation no longer could—to legitimate those boundaries.

The Mexican state—blunt instrument though it often was—had an important role to play in determining national and individual identity. In their exploration of the cultural revolution that underlay English state formation, Philip Corrigan and Derek Sayer note that:

> Out of the vast range of human social capacities—possible ways in which social life could be lived—state activities more or less forcibly "encourage" some whilst suppressing others. Schooling for instance comes to stand for education, policing for order, voting for political participation. Fundamental social classifications, like age and gender, are enshrined in law, embedded

in institutions, routinized in administrative procedures and symbolized in rituals of state. Certain forms of activity are given the official seal of approval, others are situated beyond the pale. This has cumulative, and enormous, cultural consequences; consequences for how people identify . . . themselves, and their "place" in the world.[13]

This formulation presupposes a relatively stable, institutionalized state. The forgers of the Mexican fatherland, however, traveled a rockier road than their English counterparts did. For two centuries after the conquest, church institutions, like schools and the Inquisition, played an important role in constructing the identities of colonial subjects; by the late eighteenth century modernizing Bourbon reformers had transferred much of this authority to the secular state. Independence and the break with royal authority (and especially royal "legitimacy") interrupted and altered the process.[14] Reaching consensus among elites and legitimizing "state activities" in an era of political chaos—with only the deceptively peaceful Porfirian interlude separating post-independence civil wars and revolution—required imaginative acts of the first order. It was these imaginative acts that would provide the basis for public policy and thus for state-sponsored social engineering. In post-independence Mexico, then, many elites saw in discourses like criminology, penology, and anthropology the ideological ballast they needed to stabilize the lurching ship of state.

Acts of imagination, however sincere, do not necessarily produce cultural revolution (never mind state formation). This is especially true of nations struggling to shrug off the coils of colonialism. Clifford Geertz has argued that "the peoples of new states are simultaneously animated by two powerful, thoroughly interdependent, yet distinct and often actually opposed motives—the desire to be recognized as responsible agents whose wishes, acts, hopes, and opinions 'matter,' and the desire to build an efficient, dynamic modern state." The tension that inevitably results, he adds, "is one of the central driving forces in the evolution of the new states; as it is, at the same time, one of the greatest obstacles to such evolution."[15] This double bind was (and is) the still-unresolved paradox at the heart of Mexican state formation in which a centralist authoritarian liberalism seemed (and seems) the only solution to popular sectarian violence.

Moreover, discourses like criminology, penology, and anthropology were, for the most part, the imaginings of well-educated, internationally oriented elites—imaginings through which they hoped to conceive, construct, and legitimize a new order of things in Mexico. Although couched in nationalistic terms, these discourses were popular only in the sense that they represented what social theorists in the Marxist tradition of Antonio Gramsci have identified as dominant or "hegemonic" ideologies. Gramscian hegemony, which is too complex to do justice to here, is distinguished by its insistence that effective domination requires, at best, the consent of the governed and, at least, their acceptance of the terms and conditions under which power is contested.[16] One of the consequences (or in a more paranoid vein, intentions) of discursive hegemony was (and is) to generate considerable status anxiety, especially among upwardly mobile sectors of marginal social groups. Once generalized to include entire social groups, criminality became the operational equivalent of collective disenfranchisement. As a consequence, the pressure on members of marginal groups to distinguish themselves in obvious ways—to be perceived at the very least as "worthy," in classic Victorian usage—was immense. Any acknowledgment of the problem, however, meant acquiescing to the normative values of dominant elites.

Florencia Mallon and others have noted that the larger liberal discourse (which subsumed criminology, penology, and anthropology) held out considerable promise for certain groups within Mexico's marginalized classes and often served to structure their resistance to state formation.[17] And, indeed, popular resistance to elite social engineering, especially its more violent manifestations, precluded any sense of complacency and often forced radical changes in public policy. Elite attention to the popular voice, however, carried inherent and significant limitations. "What hegemony constructs," William Roseberry asserts, "is not a shared ideology but a common material and meaningful framework for living through, talking about, and acting upon social orders characterized by domination."[18] This study explores the discursive contribution of Mexican elite intellectuals and policymakers to the construction of "a common material and meaningful framework" on criminality and citizenship. It also respects Roseberry's caveat: it was a hegemonic process "characterized by domination." Popular resistance frequently goaded elites into action—the independence wars and the Revolution were especially important in this regard—but they responded to these pressures mostly on and in their own terms. The "people" might have a voice; the elite imaginary set the discursive parameters.

This study follows in the wake of a vast and still-growing literature that critiques the pretensions of liberal capitalist development and the populist rhetoric of institutionalized revolutionary nationalism.[19] It is intended to complement the better-developed historiographies of Mexican nationalism, education, and political ideology (i.e., liberalism, positivism, revolutionary nationalism). All of these fields touch on and are touched by the issue of criminality. All are currently incomplete, in part because they have failed to examine what is, admittedly, their dark and often deliberately hidden side.[20] Revealing the exclusions embedded in these various efforts to forge a Mexican national identity and nation-state may, in fact, help explain the insuperable obstacles—often the result of internal contradictions of a practical and ideological nature—that their practitioners faced (face) as they struggled (struggle) to realize their initial promise.[21]

The failure to recognize the important role of criminality in the imagining of modern Mexico is hardly surprising; historical works on crime and criminality in Mexico are few and far between. Four excellent dissertations: Gabriel Haslip-Viera's "Crime and the Administration of Justice in Colonial Mexico City, 1689–1810," Michael C. Scardaville's "Crime and the Urban Poor: Mexico City in the Late Colonial Period," Laurence J. Rohlfes's "Police and Penal Correction in Mexico City, 1876–1911: A Study of Order and Progress in Porfirian Mexico," and Pablo Piccato's "Criminals in Mexico City, 1900–1931: A Cultural History," along with Teresa Lozano Armendares's *La criminalidad en la ciudad de México, 1800–1821*, Sergio García Avila and Eduardo Miranda Arrieta's *Desorden social y criminalidad en Michoacán, 1825–1850*, and Paul Vanderwood's study of the *rurales*, *Disorder and Progress: Bandits, Police, and Mexican Development*, comprise the essential historiography.[22] These efforts provide a solid foundation for integrating criminality into the larger frameworks of Mexican history; nevertheless the lack of a well-developed historiography renders any attempt at systematic synthesis premature.

This study adopts instead a thematic approach that examines the dialectic between criminality and citizenship in Mexico as manifested in the intertwined discourses of criminology, penology, and anthropology. These purportedly rational, even scientific disciplines devoted to the study of crime, punishment, and human social evolution, respectively, developed synchronistically during the course of the nineteenth century. Each discipline logically addressed the common concerns of the historical milieu, and taken together they represented in many respects a common discourse. Individually, however, each disciplinary discourse also served a distinct, if related, function in explaining different aspects of Mexican society and consequently in delimiting internal social boundaries.

Mauricio Tenorio-Trillo has argued that "if we were to be fair with history when writing it, our narratives would approximate more that of *The Book of Thousand and One Nights* without abandoning our linear monographs."[23] This polyphonic study attempts, then, to be "fair with history." The inevitable redundancies that result are thus intended to unify seven semiautonomous essays on the general topic of criminality and citizenship. In practice, disciplinary distinctions, especially between closely related fields like criminology, penology, and anthropology, were semantic at best. The requirements of effective nation building concerned all alike, and the consolidation of a dependent capitalist development model directly affected both discourse and public policy. It is to be hoped that this interconnectedness is a source of strength rather than of tiresome repetition.

In the final analysis this is a study in exclusion. Generally, it examines criminality in modern Mexico—how elite notions of crime and criminal behavior developed and changed during the nineteenth and early twentieth centuries, the formative years of state formation. Specifically, it focuses on what Benedict Anderson calls the "social terrain," especially the delimitation of the boundaries of national citizenship. In Mexico elite constructions of crime represented contested areas of the social terrain, places where generalized notions of criminality transcended the individual criminal act to intersect with larger issues of class, race, gender, and sexuality. It was at this intersection that modern Mexican society bared its soul. Attitudes toward race mixture and *indios*, lower-class lifestyles and *léperos*, women and sexual deviance, all influenced perceptions of criminality and ultimately determined the fundamental issue of citizenship: who belonged and who did not. The liberal rhetoric of toleration and human rights, the positivist rhetoric of order and progress, the revolutionary rhetoric of social justice and integration, sought in turn to disguise the exclusions of modern Mexican society behind a veil of criminality—to proscribe as criminal certain activities that were clearly linked to marginalized social groups. This study is an attempt to lift that veil and to gaze, as José Guadalupe Posada did, at the grinning *calavera* that it shields.

# 1. Classic Criminology

Forging the
Criminological
Paradigm

The element most necessary to the prosperity of a people is the good use and exercise of its reason. – José María Luis Mora, "Revista política de las diversas administraciones que la República mexicana ha tenido desde 1837"

Oh mother of mine! Judging by the scorn with which gentlemen treat us, it seems to me that we are the worst of the world and incapable of anything good; and truly, that calling us poor is the same as calling us demons come from hell. What I see is that those-that-have flee from us as though we were the devil. – José Joaquín Fernández de Lizardi, "La ciega y su muchachita"

The foundations of modern criminology in Mexico were laid during the era of Mexican independence from Spain. The connection between these seemingly unrelated events was far from coincidental and was very closely tied to changes in the European intellectual climate. From the eighteenth century on, the works of Enlightenment thinkers gave succeeding generations of social analysts and policymakers confidence in the ability of human reason to order their seemingly disordered societies. This confidence in a brave, new, and reasonable world inspired Mexican revolutionaries Fathers Miguel Hidalgo y Costilla and José María Morelos, as well as the Creole elites that ultimately controlled post-independence politics, to free Mexico from arbitrary (politically unreasonable), impractical (economically unreasonable), and backward (socially unreasonable) Spanish colonial rule.[1]

Enlightenment-inspired works on crime and punishment also found a sympathetic ear in Mexico. In his world-renowned 1764 essay, *Dei delitti e delle pene* (On crime and punishment), Italian jurist Cesare Beccaria suggested a rationalization of criminal justice that English legal philosopher Jeremy Bentham would later develop into a utilitarian moral calculus—"the greatest happiness of the greatest number"—and a notorious but influential protopenitentiary, the panopticon.[2] As "enlightened" Bourbon reformers and post-independence Mexican policymakers struggled with the perceived increase in crime that accompanied political and economic modernization, the classic criminology of European social reformers like Beccaria and Bentham played an important role in informing the educated public imagination and consequently in determining public policy.

But the rationalism and utilitarianism of classic European criminology, with its widely trumpeted universalist pretensions, was only part, albeit the officially sanctioned part, of a considerably more complex and more specifically Mexican discourse on crime and criminality. Deeply concerned about the effects of crime on their rapidly changing society, Mexican legal scholars, policymakers, and social critics eagerly engaged the new ideas and technologies being developed by foreign criminologists and penologists. However, they brought to that task the cultural baggage of three hundred years of Spanish colonialism, a heritage they often rejected but never denied. The resulting Mexican criminology included elements that were both modern and traditional, imported and domestic—a hybrid criminological discourse that addressed local concerns in universalist terms, and vice versa.

Some discursive strategies were less compromised by local concerns than by others. The legal experts that produced officially sanctioned texts usually took great pains to maintain an overtly rationalistic, utilitarian approach to crime. Nevertheless, elite prejudices about the perceived criminality of the racially mixed lower classes persisted as an unacknowledged subtext, glimpsed obliquely through the overlay of Enlightenment egalitarianism.[3] Elitist class prejudice also informed public policy from the mid-eighteenth into the nineteenth century. In this case the intersection of class and criminality was obvious; administrative policies and arrest records clearly connected official definitions of crime and lower-class lifestyles. Social critics also explicitly linked class status and criminality even as many fought vigorously to change the social structures that they insisted were responsible for crime in the first place.

These overlapping but distinct visions of crime and criminality addressed different audiences—although often the same individuals—and served different social functions. Written ostensibly for reform-minded policymakers, officially sanctioned texts presented the official story, an ideologically charged representation of criminality confident in its rationalism and pious in its egalitarianism. Public policy, directed and implemented by elites, logically reflected their concerns about social order and about Mexico's potentially disruptive lower classes. Social criticism, intended to arouse educated public opinion, also fueled the class prejudices of Mexican elites even as it sought to create a more equitable society in which these classist concerns would have no place.

Taken together, these different elite visions comprised late-eighteenth- and early-nineteenth-century Mexican criminological discourse. A product of a society in transition, that discourse was necessarily complex and frequently contradictory. The tension in Enlightenment thought between the promise of liberation and the need for greater social control (usually of the liberated) became even more convoluted in Mexico, where class and racial hierarchies persisted long after independence despite the rhetorical aspirations of liberal social engineers. The conservative nature of Mexican independence, fears of lower-class violence raised by the Hidalgo and Morelos revolts, and ongoing political turmoil exacerbated the typical liberal tendency to liberate the middle classes at the expense of more marginal social groups.[4]

Given its dispersed nature, the complexity of Mexican criminological discourse is best understood intertextually—by taking into account the interaction of its different constituent elements or branches. In *The Archeology of Knowledge and the Discourse on Language*, Michel Foucault insists on the disorderly nature of discourses like criminology and argues that "one must characterize and individualize . . . the coexistence of these dispersed and heterogeneous statements; the system that governs their division, the degree to which they depend upon one another, the way in which they interlock or exclude one another, the transformation that they undergo, and the play of their location, arrangement, and replacement."[5] Although meant as a general rule, Foucault's program is especially important for deconstructing the early stages of ideological formation in new nation-states like Mexico. Elite attitudes toward crime and criminality were (and would remain) too inconsistent and too contested, both inside and outside elite circles, to constitute a coherent ideological position. Taken as a discursive system of "dispersed and heterogeneous statements," however, these attitudes played a crucial role in the imagination and construction of the new nation.

Officially sanctioned texts, public policy, and social criticism each contributed essential, distinct, and sometimes contradictory ingredients to early Mexican criminological discourse. For classic criminology, which was ideologically committed to Enlightenment rationalism and liberal egalitarianism, blatant class prejudice was a potential embarrassment. Although central to the larger discourse, blanket indictments of lower-class criminality had no acknowledged place in a rhetoric of universal "human" rights. This discursive schizophrenia, finally reconciled with the advent of scientific criminology in the late nineteenth century, made textual dispersion a desirable as well as a logical solution. Attitudes toward criminality expressed in public policy and in the press complemented the official story by appealing to the "common sense," cultural expectations, and prejudices of a generally elite audience. Textual dispersion minimized the obvious contradictions between official and unofficial visions of criminality, and increased its explanatory power. Thus, in spite of its inherent schizophrenia, the intertextual discourse that comprised early Mexican criminology was more convincing, more functional, and ultimately more influential than any of its individual components.

### Officially Sanctioned Texts (and Subtexts)

Enlightenment rationalism permeated officially sanctioned texts about crime and punishment in Mexico from the late eighteenth century until the advent of scientific (as opposed to "classic" legalistic) criminology in the 1880s. In 1776, more than a decade after the publication of Beccaria's pathbreaking if sketchy essay, a royal decree charged Mexican-born jurist Manuel de Lardizábal y Uribe with reviewing Spanish criminal jurisprudence.[6] Six years later Lardizábal produced his *Discurso sobre las penas*, a detailed analysis of Spanish criminal law. Like his Italian counterpart, Lardizábal insisted that harsh and arbitrary criminal laws were outmoded and counterproductive. Humanity, he suggested, "having broadened its understanding, also softened and moderated its customs; and after learning the value of life and the liberty of man . . . could no longer avoid the indispensable necessity of reforming criminal laws."[7]

Lardizábal's argument, like Beccaria's, revolved specifically around humanity's increased capacity for rational behavior. Even crime, he argued, was a logical by-product of an irrational society; most people committed crimes through ignorance, out of desperation, out of disgust with the administration of justice, because they could get away with it, or (most often) because crime did in fact pay. Thus, although Lardizábal as a devout Catholic recognized the passion-dominated, selfish side of unregulated human nature, he nonetheless argued that under the right conditions even criminals could behave rationally and learn to modify their behavior.[8]

Lardizábal's solutions for crime reflected this abiding faith in humanity's capacity to be or to become reasonable. The principal social causes of crime—ignorance, and idleness—could thus be overcome by that great Enlightenment panacea, public education, which would instruct previously oppressed social groups in the virtues of hard work and the obligations of citizenship. He argued further that just as education relieved ignorance (and thus poverty), rationalized penal codes could actually prevent crime by advising potential criminals of the consequences of transgression. In order to ensure deterrence, Lardizábal advised, penal codes should be straightforward and accessible; punishment should be public, prompt, proportionate to the crime, impartial, and certain.[9] "If one wishes to keep public order," he advised, "it is necessary to seek out criminals [los malos], persecute them unflinchingly, and punish them quickly."[10]

Prison reform was a central component of rationalized punishment. Existing prisons, according to reformers like Lardizábal, actually encouraged criminality. Employing a medical metaphor that would become ubiquitous in the nineteenth century, he declared that in most prisons "bad examples more contagious than epidemic diseases, spread like cancer, perverting those who were not [perverse], and consummating in their perversity those who already were."[11] Well-ordered prisons, on the other hand, could serve to rehabilitate prisoners through a system of rewards and punishments that made good behavior the only logical choice.

Great confidence in the social potential of human reasonableness clearly underlay all these assertions. Even before the advent of scientific criminology, the rationalist view of human "nature" provided a discursive paradigm eagerly pursued by penal reformers like Lardizábal.[12] For classic criminologists crime was the unfortunate but inevitable result of a disordered society. Their cure reflected their new faith: rational laws and well-ordered institutions would render criminal activity unproductive and even (in the jargon of Lockean materialist psychology) "displeasing." A profound confidence in the underlying rationality of human behavior characterized officially sanctioned attitudes toward crime and punishment for more than a century after the publication of Beccaria's essay.[13]

This distinguishing characteristic, however, disguised (often deliberately) fundamental continuities with more traditional notions of human depravity and late-nineteenth-century criminology, especially the latter's supposedly unique obsession with punishing the criminal rather than the crime. In fact, even exponents of the official story, like Lardizábal, included a contradictory subtext about the nature of criminality that subtly undermined the rationalist premises of classic criminology. Practical considerations, in particular, encouraged an eclectic approach that often subverted Enlightenment logic.[14]

The principal subversive issue was "mitigating circumstances," the basic criteria used to determine sentencing, always a concern to practicing magistrates like Lardizábal. His extensive list of mitigating circumstances included everything from time and place to damages, motivation, and "the bad example set by the crime."[15] Many of these circumstances could be determined by police or court inquiries; those related to the criminal's motivation and character, however, required considerable judicial interpretation. Lardizábal noted, for example, that criminal intent, age, sex, drunkenness, and recidivism all played a crucial role in sentencing.[16] By themselves these categories hardly precluded a rationalist reading—drunkenness, femaleness, youth, and bad habits often signified the inability to reason effectively—but determining intent could be tricky. "Who alive," Lardizábal asked, "is capable of fathoming the deep and infinitely variable malice of the human heart, in order to determine its punishment?"[17] The rhetorical question reflected perhaps the Catholic religious training of a conservative courtier of Charles III; it also cast doubts on classic criminology's rationalist foundations.

Beneath these practical concerns about criminality lurked a subterranean world of elite prejudices and stereotypes that belied the egalitarian presumptions of Enlightenment criminal justice.[18] Likely influenced by French magistrate Baron de Montesquieu's *The Spirit of the Laws*, Lardizábal remarked on the need to adapt legal systems to specific circumstances, including climate. "A wise and prudent legislator," he warned "should always take into account the religion, character, customs and genius of the nation. . . . Even the location and climate of the country ought to influence penal laws regarding certain crimes . . . because without a doubt, climate influences the physical organization and consequently the morality of mankind."[19] Although it exhibited the concern about milieu that characterized most Enlightenment social thought, postulating the influence of geography and climate on human physiology and the presumption of a direct link to morality suggested an existing and possibly permanent inequality between nations and geographically distinct races. Lardizábal noted, for example, that "barbarous, ferocious and ignorant" nations still required "severe and rigorous" laws to control their savage inhabitants.[20] God might have created all men equal in the mythical past, but climate and geography could presumably bless a nation with civilization or doom it to barbarism.

This protonationalistic chauvinism was often (but generally covertly) extended to include barbarous, ferocious, and ignorant social groups within the nation itself. Lardizábal, for instance, singled out two traits considered typical of lower-class lifestyles—idleness and begging—as "the most fecund sources of crime and disorder."[21] And, although drunkenness served all classes as a mitigating circumstance, perennial concerns about the links between drunkenness and criminality focused on the violent street crimes that elites invariably connected to the lifestyles of the racially mixed lower classes.[22]

Within this general context of lower-class criminality, recidivists came to symbolize a separate, degenerate subclass that required special punishment. "Recidivism," Lardizábal wrote, "supposes a soul most perverted and obstinately bad sometimes to the extent that the delinquent becomes incorrigible, in which case public utility requires that the punishment be intensified."[23] Because of their incorrigibility, he banned recidivists from his reformed prisons and suggested that they be consigned to public works or the army.[24] Recidivists were thus presented as *gente sin razón* (literally "people without reason"), a traditional social type that enlightened opinion had rejected as a racial category but that effectively served to stigmatize habitual criminals as irrational and consequently unable to resist temptation. Lardizábal's Augustinian sense of human depravity and enlightened concern with irrationality linked to a class of offenders and directed principally (although obliquely in this case) at the lower classes persisted as an increasingly prominent subtext in the officially sanctioned texts of classic criminology.

Classist and racist subtexts were especially striking in the reports of Bourbon reformers in Mexico not intended for a general literate audience. Prominent Mexico City judge (*alcalde mayor*) Hipólito Villarroel's "Enfermedades políticas que padece la capital de esta Nueva España" (Political diseases that afflict the capital of New Spain), written some ten years (1785–87) after Lardizábal's *Discurso sobre las penas*, condemned the rampant criminality of Mexico City's lower classes (*plebe*)—"the most insolent in the world."[25] The Indian was a particular problem because "he is stubborn and does nothing of his own free will, that he isn't forced to do; he is extremely malicious, enemy of the truth, untrustworthy, friend of novelty, disturbances, and riots; he is not at all loyal to the Catholic religion and too much given to superstition, idolatry, and other detestable vices; he is inhuman, vengeful and cruel among his kind, and his life is spent submerged in the vices of drunkenness, theft, robbery, homicide, rape, incest and other innumerable evils."[26] And Indians were only the most egregious offenders of public morality. In Villarroel's apocalyptic vision, the city itself—"an impenetrable forest of evils" where filthy inhabitants inhabited "pig sties rather than the habitations of rational beings"—generated, in his deliberately racialized metaphor, "all imaginable castes of vice."[27]

But in spite of his hyperbolic descriptions of lower-class poverty, degradation, and criminality, Villarroel stressed both the rational causes and the classless nature of crime. "I have tried to make known," he noted, "the character of the immense people [*pueblo*] that bury this capital, its nudity, its voluntary poverty and debasement, its dissipation, its perverse inclinations and blind adhesion to robbery, pillage and all the other types [*castas*] of vices, due to the lack of instruction, correction, and application necessary to make these people useful."[28] A devout Catholic like Lardizábal, Villarroel expected very little of a naturally sinful humanity left to its own devices; the real problem was poor (irrational) public administration, and especially a venal, permissive judicial system that failed in its duty to instruct, correct, and make useful its clientele. "Of what use is a law . . . that says *that justice is the life and maintenance of the people*," he inquired, "if here [in Mexico City] it is more properly the death of those that solicit its help and the life, extravagance and propagation of those that carry it out."[29] In the same vein, he devoted an entire chapter to the problem of "lujo" (extravagance) especially among the city's upper classes; in this chapter he denounced their "excessive use of that which is unnecessary for sustenance and basic comforts of life" and "the shocking freedom of men and women without regard to distinctions of class, employment, and station [*facultades*]."[30] Likewise, his chapters on drinking and gambling, while especially attentive to the degraded lower classes—"deprived of reason and judgment, with an aspect more proper to brutes than rational beings"—stressed their pernicious effects on all classes of Mexico City society and carefully documented the vested economic interests of Mexican and Spanish elites in nurturing these vices.[31] Again, as Lardizábal suggested, the solution was a reformed, rationalized criminal-justice system that would instruct the lower classes, protect the public interest, and ensure the continued legitimacy of Spanish colonial government.

Nor did these "enlightened," paternalistic concerns disappear with independence from Spain. In 1830 Mexican historian Carlos María de Bustamante republished a serialized, edited version of Villarroel's text in his newspaper, *La Voz de la Patria* (The voice of the fatherland). In his preface, the republican Bustamante logically stressed the colonial corruption exposed by Villarroel that "reminds us to bless the generous hand that in Dolores broke our chains." In the conclusion, however, he recommended the author's "perfect knowledge of this country" that might serve the "citizen legislator . . . to better existing institutions that are formed for the most part on those [Villarroel's] bases."[32] Once divorced from its colonial context, Bourbon legal and social reform found a sympathetic audience among Mexican Creole elites.

Not surprisingly then, officially sanctioned texts of post-independence Mexico echoed many of Lardizábal and Villarroel's arguments. In 1831 Mexico City's *Registro Oficial* ran installments of Mexican government agent and future president of Ecuador Vincente Rocafuerte's "Ensayo sobre el nuevo sistema de carceles" (Essay on the new system of jails).[33] Focused specifically on prison reform, Rocafuerte's essay lacks the breadth of his predecessors' work, but the basic themes of classic criminology persisted. These included his eclectic approach. "I do not pretend to say anything new," he magnanimously declared, "nothing that has not already been written, known, recommended and published by the philanthropists Howard, Buxton, Lord Suffild [*sic*], Lyncour, Villarme, Bentham, Fry, Guerney y Cuningham [*sic*]."[34]

Like his royalist predecessor, Rocafuerte noted the importance of an enlightened criminal-justice system to the legitimacy of the nation-state even if as a revolutionary he attempted to co-opt the issue for the liberal cause. "If we examine all the rights that the liberal system promises to man," he noted, "we will see that they are based on justice," adding that "liberty, security, and equality are the inestimable benefits that form the essence of free governments, and they cannot exist without the fair administration of justice."[35] According to Rocafuerte the fair administration of justice particularly benefited the common people, "the most numerous class of society," ensuring their "happiness" and loyalty, an essential ingredient to a free society based on citizenship rather than corporate privilege.[36] In Mexico criminal-justice reform and liberal nation building would become inextricably linked during the course of the nineteenth century.

Aside from Rocafuerte's efforts to co-opt penal reform for the liberal cause, however, his vision remained remarkably close to Lardizábal's enlightened ideals. Like his predecessor, Rocafuerte blamed "ignorance and the furor of the passions" for "all" crime and suggested typical rationalist solutions, especially education and prison reform.[37] Thus he denounced the "cruel" punishments of despotic governments (Spanish colonial administration, for example) as counterproductive because they "irritated and exasperated" rather than rehabilitated the criminal.[38]

For liberals like Rocafuerte rationalized punishment meant reformed prisons. (Political conservatives like Lardizábal showed much greater tolerance for public punishment and forced labor than did doctrinaire liberals like Rocafuerte.) With extensive, firsthand knowledge of the latest European and North American experiments in prison reform, he proposed a detailed reform program designed to prepare prisoners to reenter society by providing them with useful skills and inculcating in them the good habits necessary for effective citizenship.[39] An insistence on straightforward, accessible prison rules and a proposed early-release program to reward good behavior further reinforced the rehabilitation effort. As Lardizábal's did, Rocafuerte's reforms emphasized Enlightenment confidence in human reasonableness: rationalized laws and institutions could inculcate rational behavior even in criminals.[40] The astounding success rates reported in Europe and the United States seemed to support his optimism.[41]

Although Rocafuerte generally upheld the rationalist and egalitarian spirit of Enlightenment social reform, he too allowed subversive elements to creep into his text. For example, he singled out idleness encouraged by the "dismal" Spanish colonial government, "because it was in the interests of the metropolis to keep us ignorant of the arts and suffocate the progress of industry" as a principal cause of vice.[42] But the vices of idleness that became actual crimes and encouraged other kinds of criminal behavior—vagrancy and unlicensed begging—were decidedly lower class. Rocafuerte also recognized recidivists as a separate class of criminals—"those hardened in evil, accustomed to robbery, homicide and other infamous crimes that entail a perversity of heart"—and insisted that they be separated from those prisoners "that conserved sentiments of honor."[43] Again, since most recidivists engaged in petty crimes like public drunkenness, theft, or brawling, the onus of recidivism was shifted primarily to lower-class criminals. Thus in the enlightened, rational world of Rocafuerte and Lardizábal perverse irrationality became the stigmata of the lower-class criminal, separating, in the Victorian sense, the worthy from the unworthy poor.

The purest exponent of Enlightenment ideals in classic Mexican criminology was influential liberal theorist José María Luis Mora.[44] In pieces he wrote sporadically during the late 1820s and 1830s Mora reiterated many of the themes developed by Lardizábal and Rocafuerte. Not surprisingly, given his theoretical bent, he stressed in blatantly utilitarian terms the crucial role of the criminal-justice system in legitimizing the political system and arbitrating social tensions. "The greatest good of the people is to obey the law," he advised; "the greatest good of government is the fortunate necessity to be just."[45] Derived from both Beccaria and Bentham, this moral calculus required a rationalization of the arbitrary criminal justice that liberal reformers typically ascribed to various ancien régimes.[46] For Mora it also required drastic structural reforms, especially an end to the "corporate spirit" that operated contrary to the public good by discrediting the criminal-justice system, because "the corporation believes itself offended and dishonored when one of its members appears delinquent and thus is determined to hide the crime or to save the criminal."[47] Only prompt, certain, and impartial justice, he reiterated, could effectively claim the loyalty of Mexico's recently formed but still divided citizenry.

Even more than his predecessor Lardizábal and his contemporary Rocafuerte, Mora exhibited an abiding faith in the power of rational reforms to reduce criminal behavior and foster good citizenship. Nevertheless he still acknowledged a class component to most crime, which he attributed primarily to the pernicious influence of the lower-class milieu. "Accustomed from the earliest age to crime and profoundly impressed by the most detestable scenes," he noted, "the child surrenders and succumbs to the contact of a corruption, which none could resist."[48] According to Mora the principal culprits were negligent parents that "have provided neither education nor position [estado], and who have in many cases encouraged [their children] in vice either through advice or example." Crime, like begging, he warned, was "hereditary" among the degraded lower classes.[49]

Public, secular education, designed to inculcate modern values and counteract the church's pernicious hold on the superstitious lower classes, was the obvious preventative for future crimes. In the meantime, however, Mora supported extensive prison reform along the lines suggested by Rocafuerte. And, in a repressive vein, he observed that "if all the criminals of the present generation could be apprehended and incarcerated, the youth to be reformed and the adults to spend the rest of their lives, the following generation would probably have very few criminals."[50] Like his colleagues, then, Mora upheld a rationalist interpretation of crime and criminal behavior while also reinforcing concerns about "hereditary" lower-class criminality. Irrational society might be responsible for crime, but lower-class criminals would bear the brunt of repression.

The identification of criminality with the Mexican lower classes was made even more explicit in the works of liberal jurist Mariano Otero.[51] As his predecessors did, Otero borrowed openly and eclectically from foreign sources. He concurred that harsh penal codes and corrupting prisons contributed to crime, and he strongly advocated their immediate reform. And his programs, although more up-to-date, still reflected his predecessors' confidence in the reformative powers of rationalized institutions. Otero, however, far more even than Mora, stressed the role of milieu in fostering lower-class criminality. In a Rousseauesque romantic style typical of the mid-nineteenth century, Otero chronicled the "fall" of the lower-class criminal:

> Who has not at sometime witnessed the career of a man of this class? Scarcely born, when all the physical and moral causes that can degrade a human being surround him and determine his fate: badly fed, badly dressed and badly lodged, once able to feel and compare, he finds himself sunk in misery, mired in meanness, and made an object of scorn for those who ought to respect him, and those on whom his miserable luck depends. The example of a temperate family should reveal to his tender soul the first notions of morality, and the soft caresses of the paternal home should open his heart to the soft and enchanting emotions of love and gratitude: but instead of this, he sees a family of debased sentiments, overwhelmed with unhappiness and given over at least to abjection and misery, if not to crime and prostitution; and victims of foolish caprices and inhuman treatments, these sacrosanct re-

lations that nature has established between parent and child, find themselves, so to speak, trampled upon and despised. He grows then, and with already debased heart, to the time the tempestuous passions develop, when the
circle of individual needs is widened and begins to operate by itself, being the
master of his actions, then the germ of evil develops with each occasion in
which he finds it impossible to satisfy his needs and direct his passions in an
orderly fashion; and the example of evil and of criminality that has grown
extraordinarily with the number of his relationships, finally perverts his
soul, and crime is the inevitable result.[52]

In many ways Otero's depressing scenario merely realized the implications of his predecessors' recognition that an irrational, oppressive
society encouraged crime. In others ways his extreme environmentalist
approach broke important new ground. By spelling out in melodramatic detail the social processes behind crime, Otero highlighted the
desperate need for immediate social reforms and clarified some of the
specific issues that these reforms entailed. Popular education had been
the hallmark of earlier proposals; like Mora, Otero took a more comprehensive position, stressing the crucial role of the supportive family in
forming individual character and thereby ensuring social harmony.

But, while sympathetic to the plight of the *léperos* (literally "the
lepers"), the most denigrated, if ill defined, of Mexico's lower classes,
Otero nonetheless powerfully reinforced elite perceptions of the degenerate nature and innate criminality of Mexican society's least-privileged
social group.[53] That *lépero* criminals were likely victims of their degraded lifestyle or of corrupting Mexican prisons did little to dispel
these fears or to correct deeply ingrained prejudices. Lardizábal, Villarroel, and Rocafuerte had stigmatized the recidivist as an incorrigible
subclass within the lower classes; Otero suggested that all *léperos* were
potential recidivists, thus stigmatizing them as a "class" in advance of
any actual criminal act. For Otero the principal culprit was an attribute,
criminality, that he associated with a certain group: *léperos*; the crime
and the individual criminal became secondary. Perversity and irrationality he considered group traits rather than the attributes of a single
offender. The progression was both logical and portentous.

### Crime and Public Policy

By the late colonial period public policy had begun to reflect the concerns of Enlightenment reformers. Reminded by critics like Villarroel
of the legitimizing potential of an equitable criminal-justice system,

Bourbon-era courts in Mexico City eschewed what they considered the harsh, erratic punitive practices of the Hapsburg era in favor of a more moderate and consistent judicial system. In some cases judicial reforms were quite successful. In the informal courts that handled the bulk of minor criminal cases most trials were prompt, judgments fair, and punishments lenient.[54] This remained the case until after 1810, when Mexico City judges responded to concerns about the Hidalgo and Morelos insurrections by sentencing able-bodied male prisoners to military service.[55]

As this quick shift in policy indicated, despite judicial reforms, elite concerns about Mexico's "dangerous" classes were never far from the surface. Subtexts aside, officially sanctioned texts were generally circumspect about linking class and racial status to criminality. This was not necessarily the case in public administration, where this linkage often became quite explicit. For instance, 1786 regulations for the *alcaldes de barrio* (government-appointed neighborhood watchers) established throughout Mexico City empowered them "to rigorously persecute drunkenness and gambling [and] to frequently exhort the debased lower classes [*gente de la ínfima plebe*] to make good use of what they earn."[56] Just four years later, in 1790, Viceroy Conde de Revillagigedo issued a decree ostensibly directed at "all citizens and inhabitants regardless of estate, age or condition; without distinction of class or person" that nevertheless ordered the arrest and confinement of specifically lower-class offenders, "in order to prevent the extremely indecent abuse by the plebians of both sexes who foul themselves in the streets and courtyards."[57] Lawmakers thus sanctioned lower-class behavior as criminal while often ignoring similar activities by privileged elites.[58]

The rapid urbanization that accompanied Bourbon modernization efforts had made colonial authorities extremely sensitive to the issue of public order; the swelling lower classes in particular represented a potentially dangerous source of criminal activity.[59] Rising lower-class criminality, authorities feared, would threaten continued economic development, the raison d'être of Bourbon administrative reforms. In fact economic development often made things worse. *Campesinos* (country people), many dispossessed by the expansion of commercial agriculture, migrated in increasing numbers to the cities. Most lived in the streets or in makeshift housing, and even those who managed to find factory jobs contributed, in the eyes of some public administrators, to social disintegration. One inspector asked rhetorically: "Who will prevent the perverse and dangerous conversations of a licentious people? . . . Who can stop the pernicious damages that result from the gangs of young men and women that although they leave from different doors, get back together as soon as they turn the corner?"[60] Ironically, then, economic modernization efforts accelerated social change, which exacerbated elite anxieties about a perpetually troublesome underclass. And these concerns persisted into the post-independence era. An article on population in the first edition (1839) of the *Boletín de la Sociedad Mexicana de Geografía y Estadística* (Bulletin of the Mexican Geographical and Statistical Society), for example, still recognized a direct link between crime and urbanization, noting that in "populous cities . . . the inducements to crime, idle people, and the opportunities for corruption abounded."[61]

Under these circumstances the obsession with public order translated quickly into increased repression, especially of lower-class lifestyles. Accordingly, during 1798 over 75 percent of all Mexico City arrests were for public-order crimes committed principally by young lower-class men—the usual source of public disorder, political or otherwise.[62] Arrest patterns also reflected the ethnic and racial makeup of the lower classes; the percentage of mestizos and Indians arrested exceeded their percentages of the total Mexico City population. In 1796, for example, mestizos represented 19 percent of the population and 24 percent of the arrests; Indians accounted for 24 percent of the population but 37 percent of the arrests.[63]

These policies and attitudes clearly reveal the repressive, classist (and probably racist), assumptions of independence-era criminal justice. One official from Mexico City's Sala del Crimen, which represented the formal criminal-justice system, labeled the poor "licentious people of ruined customs from which result thefts . . . and other excesses."[64] His attitude was hardly unique. As colonial officials became increasingly concerned about threats to public order and thus to economic development, they declared many public aspects of lower-class life illegal and implemented campaigns to reclaim the streets, especially of Mexico City's outlying barrios.[65] This obsession with public order and the policing pattern it engendered characterized the last two decades of colonial administration and persisted into the national period as well.[66] In 1838 the Junta del Departmento de México (city council) created round-the-clock patrols of *vigilantes* and *rondines* "to persistently guard over the policing of the city and the conservation of order, apprehending scandalous drunks, bearers of arms, brawlers, vagrants, gamblers, wounded, deserters, thieves, and in general all criminals."[67] Given the nature of the specified crimes, most of these criminals were undoubtedly lower-class "*plebes*."

Placing "scandalous drunks" at the beginning of the above list was hardly an accident. The dangers of public drunkenness obsessed authorities, who saw it inhibiting worker productivity and contributing substantially to crime and political unrest.[68] This obsession made an early mark on Bourbon public policy. A 1784 report to viceroy Matías de Gálvez notes that there were "not enough judges . . . to cover the innumerable abuses of the pulquerías, which are the true center and origin of the crimes and public transgressions with which this numerous population is flooded."[69] And a 1788 report on Mexico City policing made the classist subtext explicit. It remarked that "those that are seen in pulquerías are all of the infamous plebian *or the lowest class* [*más extragados*] of artisans," adding ominously that "the lower class [*bajo pueblo*] from birth lacks any education, receiving from its parents only the outrageous customs that it inherits *through example and tradition*."[70] Not surprisingly then, by 1798, 44 percent of all arrests involved either public intoxication or violations of drinking ordinances.[71] To make matters worse in official eyes, drunkenness was directly implicated in other common crimes, especially violent quarrels (*riñas*), which often resulted in serious injuries and even homicide.[72] Worried urban officials responded with several unsuccessful anti-alcohol campaigns targeting pulquerías, *viñaterías*, and the illegal stands of *cuberas* (women selling alcohol without a license, often out of their homes), all establishments patronized primarily by the lower classes.[73]

Gambling was another source of official concern because, like drinking, it encouraged interpersonal violence, discouraged industrious behavior, and further impoverished the poor. Although all classes of Mexican society gambled, regulatory efforts again focused principally on lower-class gamblers. Again, these efforts failed miserably.[74] That these repeated attempts to control public drunkenness and gambling invariably floundered testifies to the insuperable difficulties involved in large-scale social engineering. Not only did the lower classes persist in the face of repression, but the economic interests of powerful, landed elites, especially those invested in pulque production, and the crucial role of sin taxes in the colonial economy, made failure inevitable.[75]

Mexicans of all classes indulged in gambling and alcohol consumption; social critics also accused all strata of Mexican society of laziness (*holgazanería*) and idleness (*ociosidad*). The do-nothing attitude of most Mexicans, which post-independence reformers generally blamed on Spanish colonialism, discouraged entrepreneurial behavior, which inhibited economic development, which in turn prevented national consolidation. But, although critics felt that all classes of Mexicans were lazy, the crimes associated with idleness, especially vagrancy and begging, were strictly lower class. Just as official repression of drinking and gambling did, then, repression of idleness focused principally on its lower-class manifestations.[76] And, as before, given the lack of employment opportunities in the Mexican urban economy and the migration pressures exerted on rural peasants by various modernization efforts, official repression had little effect.

State efforts to regulate lower-class lifestyles also extended into the private sphere as reformers increasingly linked family morality and national prosperity. Thus, consensual unions (informal marriages), common and practical among the financially strapped and transient lower classes, became sex crimes and were at times actively prosecuted by the criminal-justice system. Authorities saw a direct correlation between consensual unions, domestic violence, and abandoned children, all of which, they argued, encouraged criminality and thus increased crime.[77] This official concern about the private lives of marginal social groups, a usurpation of former church prerogatives, would remain a hallmark of future discussions of lower-class criminality even though efforts at repression again ran quickly aground.

Elite anxieties about public order and the potentially subversive characteristics of lower-class lifestyles—public drunkenness, gambling, vagrancy, begging, consensual relations—dominated nineteenth-century criminological discourse in large part because of the failure of both reforms and repression. Public criminal policy, then, contributed significantly to a generalized discourse about criminality in Mexican society by reflecting and reinforcing the classist subtexts of officially sanctioned texts like those of Lardizábal, Villarroel, Rocafuerte, Mora, and Otero. Unsuccessful efforts at reform and repression kept these issues in the public eye and thus perpetuated the elite biases they invariably evoked.

### Crime and the Popular Imagination

Popular writings on crime also contributed essential ingredients to criminological discourse. This was especially true in the post-independence years, when political turmoil and economic constraints precluded serious efforts to develop and implement public policy. With little hope of immediate action, nineteenth-century social commentators took a more speculative approach to the ongoing problem of crime in Mexican society. It was in these unofficial texts that the issue of criminality (as opposed to crime) received its fullest treatment.

The ambiguous, even schizophrenic nature of liberal social reform was especially evident in the works of Mexico's preeminent independence-era journalist and novelist, José Joaquín Fernández de Lizardi.[78] The plot of his great picaresque novel, *Periquillo Sarniento* (1816), for example, centers around the fall and redemption of Pedro Sarmiento, the educated son of loving and respectable parents.[79] Thus, rather than focusing exclusively on lower-class criminality, Fernández de Lizardi juxtaposed his portrayal of the degenerate Mexican underworld with the criminal behavior of his *gente decente* (respectable) hero. In an 1813 essay he declared that "everyone knows that all men have their vices and virtues," adding rhetorically that "just because I have been robbed by a black man, does that mean all blacks are thieves?"[80] A typical enlightened liberal, Fernández de Lizardi's commitment to education, family values, and the regenerative power of work (especially having a trade), as well as his corresponding condemnation of alcoholism, gambling, and idleness, was clearly demonstrated by endless didactic interludes in his novels. And in an 1825 "Political constitution for an imaginary republic," one of the "privileges of the citizen" convicted of a minor crime ("que no irroguen infamia") was to "be conducted to a decent prison."[81] Not surprisingly, he also agitated for straightforward, accessible penal laws and severely sanctioned judicial corruption.[82]

But, like Mora, Fernández de Lizardi had a repressive side as well. "Beggars can be divided into two groups," he noted, "those legitimately prevented from working . . . and those lazy rascals, who not wishing to dedicate themselves to a profession, are *content to live off the streets* [*la carrera de tompiate y de la ollita*] . . . the first are deserving of our compassion, the second of our righteous anger; the former require the help of the pious, the latter the vigilance and punishment of the magistrates."[83] His imaginary constitution decreed the death penalty for premeditated homicides and for robberies over ten pesos, and transportation to isolated penal colonies for recidivists committing petty crimes like public drunkenness, illegal gambling, indecent exposure, and vagrancy. He even suggested that neighborhood "wardens" [*celadores del orden*] be placed every four square blocks to "investigate the employment or manner of living of all the citizens [*vecinos*] under his jurisdiction" and provide monthly reports to the "government."[84] Thus, while Fernández de Lizardi clearly recognized and explored the universal nature of criminal behavior, he nonetheless advocated the ruthless suppression of what were typically lower-class crimes.

His successors were generally less subtle. Like the independence-era works of Fernández de Lizardi, later social commentaries owed a debt to the Bourbon reformers. Alcoholism, gambling, and idleness were roundly condemned for their role in fostering crime. An 1857 analysis of crime in Durango, written for the prestigious *Boletín de la Sociedad Mexicana de Geografía y Estadística*, estimated that drunkenness accounted for nearly all the crimes against the police (i.e., resisting arrest) and public order and played a role in more than three-fifths of all crime. The author added that "the influence that this unfortunate vice exercises on the morals of our society does not stop here, but spreads through all its veins, making its wickedness especially felt in that which society and man hold most sacred, personal security." The author even embellished Montesquieu's argument correlating climate and behavior with the argument that alcoholic beverages in the tropics "acquire a corrosive quality that annihilates the intelligence and poisons the sources of life."[85]

The stereotype of the lazy Mexican was a favorite, especially among self-conscious social critics who often saw Mexican society through the eyes of potential foreign investors. In his widely disseminated and much praised 1808 *Political Essay on the Kingdom of New Spain*, Prussian geographer Alexander von Humboldt remarked on the carts used in Mexico City "to collect the drunkards to be found stretched out in the streets" and "swarms [of] . . . from twenty to thirty thousand wretches of whom the greatest number pass the night *sub dio* [exposed to the elements] and stretch themselves out to the sun during the day with nothing but a flannel covering."[86] Independence brought no relief. In 1822 North American ambassador Joel Roberts Poinsett estimated that at least 20,000 of Mexico City's 150,000 residents were *léperos*, adding that "they issue forth in the morning like drones to prey upon the community, to beg, to steal, and in the last resort to work."[87] A few years later Swiss naturalist Jean Louis Berlandier remarked on the "disgusting picture" presented by the Mexico City rabble, "remarkable for its laziness and number."[88] And in 1834 the British consul, offended by the *léperos*' relaxed style, remarked sarcastically that:

> the general facility of obtaining a livelihood, the high rate of wages compared with the necessaries of life, indifference to comfort and decency of appearance, a consequence of the fineness of climate which may be said to render the lower orders independent of clothing, fuel and shelter, all tend to produce in the Mexican population habits of idleness, profligacy, and improvidence beyond what is observable in most countries—accordingly their industry is limited only to that which is necessary to providing basic subsistence, the only stimulus to greater exertion being the desire to find means of gratifying their vicious propensities.[89]

Mexican elite critics generally concurred. In an 1852 article, "De la mendicidad y de los medios que deben adaptarse para hacerla desaparecer" (On begging and on the methods that should be adopted to make it disappear), written for the aptly titled *La Ilustración Mexicana* (Mexican Enlightenment), the author denounced the practice of *hacer san lunes* (taking an extra day off work on Monday) because for the common laborer it amounted to "nothing more than giving himself over to drunkenness and prostitution, squandering the fruits of his labor, and contracting debts beyond his ability to pay."[90]

Mexican "selfishness" [*egoísmo*] as demonstrated by the lack of private philanthropy was a related critique. The selfishness of Mexican elites, critics argued, discouraged the development of modern charitable institutions to counteract the idleness of the poor.[91] In their eyes national vices seemed to compound each other. One critic even rejected the classic criminologists' demand for reform of criminal laws. He insisted that existing laws were more than adequate and charged that "the indolence, selfishness, and idiotic economy of large landowners . . . the inertia of urban judges, and the ignorance, corruption and venality of rural judges," perpetuated crime in Mexican society.[92]

As these concerns demonstrated, this new generation of liberal social critics, like their distinguished contemporaries Mora and Otero, showed considerably more interest in the underlying causes of crime than did Bourbon administrators or even earlier experts like Lardizábal and Rocafuerte. And, like Mora and Otero, they were willing to consider the structural causes of criminality. The same article that condemned workers for taking off *san lunes* commented that "while there are no small landowners, and while parochial rights continue to be excessive, it is inevitable that there be no good customs, nor love of work, nor the moral need for family living."[93] Thus, while many of their proposed solutions, especially education and prison reform, were typical of their predecessors, they integrated these specific recommendations into the larger liberal attack on colonial institutions—corporate privilege and the traditional hacienda in particular. The implication was that a more just (liberal) political and economic structure combined with public education and modern prisons would significantly reduce lower-class criminality.

As Otero's was, this willingness to implicate social structures was generally linked to heart-rending but ultimately degrading portrayals of lower-class existence. Again, elite critics focused on the lower-class family or, more precisely, on the lack of family structure. One author noted that "while these proletarian classes fail to live in families, and procreate only to satisfy their brute instincts; children will have no parents, women will have no husbands, and the corruption of customs will cause misery, barbarism, and vice."[94] In contrast to this depressing spectacle, another writer extolled the virtues of "the domestic hearth," adding that "the husband and the wife, the father and the son, the mother and children, are nothing more than a community of happy beings, that in adversity as in prosperity, unites together to suffer or enjoy, augmenting the pleasures and diminishing the pains."[95]

The lack of family life among the lower classes, critics argued, undermined national well-being. Writing only five years after Mexico's disastrous war with the United States, one commentator remarked that "they cease being productive, inhibit population growth, give a very unfavorable impression of our civilization, offend morality, and finally provide bad soldiers for our army." He added that in "creatures so miserable and so ignorant, the germ of patriotism cannot germinate." The end result was a weakening of moral fiber that could only lead to national degeneration and further embarrassment at the hands of foreign aggressors.[96] Thus, the lower classes were not only portrayed as criminally inclined but also as unpatriotic and at least partially responsible for Mexico's devastating territorial losses.

Linked to social analysis that blamed criminality on irrational social structures, lack of education, inadequate prisons, and the debilitating effects of the milieu, these devastating portrayals of lower-class criminality were intended to evoke sympathy and to convey the desperate need for reform. Thus the works of mid-nineteenth-century social critics complemented the reformist tendencies of officially sanctioned texts and earlier public policies. But at the same time, embedded in all three sources was a classist subtext that perpetuated elite preconceptions and prejudices about the Mexican lower classes. In social criticism, as in public policy, that subtext often superseded the reformist purposes of the text itself.

Less constrained by the ideological requirements of liberal egalitarianism than were the writers of officially sanctioned texts, mid-nineteenth-century social analysts also reintroduced the subject of race into Mexican criminological discourse. In spite of enlightened pretensions, Bourbon social policy had made no serious effort to challenge Mexico's complex class and racial hierarchies. Official colonial crime statistics routinely (if often inaccurately) noted the race or race mixture of the criminal.[97] After independence, however, this category was deliberately discarded in official documents as unbefitting an enlightened modern Republic.

With the emergence of scientific statistics later in the nineteenth century, racial statistics reappeared in conjunction with crime. An 1851 article entitled "Necesidad de la estadistica" (The need for statistics), in the Boletín de la Sociedad Mexicana de Geografía y Estadística, advocated the collection of statistics, including racial comparisons, on the morality of Mexico's population.[98] Following these guidelines, the writer of an 1852 statistical report on Yucatán proudly noted "the separation we have made between indigenous, white, and mixed-race [casta] prisoners, for the interesting opportunity this comparison offers for judging their respective morality." The author attributes the fact that the indigenous population committed significantly fewer crimes to their humility, a product of "either natural inclination or degradation." In spite of their passivity, however, they were "thieves" and "pickpockets . . . always and without exception," even though the relative insignificance of their crimes kept them out of court. On the other hand, dominant whites and castas were "more excitable, more impetuous and more resolved in their passions . . . which produces immediate conflicts that are quickly resolved."[99] Another statistical report on Acapulco noted that blacks (los de la Africana) were "inclined to gambling, drunkenness . . . [and] vengeance to which they sacrifice all humanitarian sentiments."[100]

This implied linkage between race and criminality, typical of the colonial period, represented yet another breech in Enlightenment ideology. Inherent racial characteristics ran counter to both universal human rationality and liberal egalitarianism. One author remarked that "the wise policies and regulations of our government have proscribed forever the odious distinctions between whites, blacks, coloreds [*bronceados*] and mestizos [*mistos*]" but excused the collection of racial statistics on the grounds that "without the practical knowledge of the races [*pueblos*] one cannot calculate their civilization, their morality, their wealth, nor their needs."[101]

The assumptions of mid-nineteenth-century Mexican statisticians thus clearly realized the racist subtext of Lardizábal's comments (via Montesquieu) on climate and criminality.[102] These assumptions, endorsed by evolutionary science, would later pass unmolested into the scientific criminological paradigm. Linked to elite concerns about lower-class criminality, this reemerging racist subtext would, in the works of later "scientific" criminologists, naturalize Mexican society's traditional social categories and justify continued repression of the racially mixed lower classes.

### Criminality and the Liberal State

The official texts of the liberal Restored Republic, ironically, represented a return to the relative ideological purity of early reformers like Lardizábal, Rocafuerte, and Mora. As minister of justice and public instruction under Benito Juárez, Antonio Martínez de Castro, in particular, steered clear of the overtly classist implications of mid-nineteenth-century Mexican social critics.[103] The moving force behind Mexico's first post-colonial penal code, Martínez de Castro recognized the ideological importance of criminal-justice reform and its crucial role in restoring public confidence in liberal government. "The state of anarchy in which we have lived for so long," he reasoned in his introduction to the 1871 Penal Code, "has sown distrust among the citizenry, has engendered hatreds; and breaking social bonds, has resulted in mutual isolation, in the selfish pursuit of private interests, and in disregard for the public good."[104] In this formulation, Mexicans of all classes contributed to political unrest, economic underdevelopment, social dissolution, and, by extension, to increased crime.

Martínez de Castro's historical explanation, an updated version of liberal attacks on the legacy of Spanish colonialism, also stressed the role of irrational social institutions in encouraging crime. In typical post-Enlightenment fashion he argued that convoluted criminal laws, lackadaisical enforcement, and unreformed prisons fostered criminal behavior because criminals "will not be intimidated by legally imposed punishments, regardless of how harsh or terrible they might be, and even less by a prison where they will live in idleness, if they convince themselves that the punishment will not be applied or will be considerably delayed." This apparently rational response on the part of criminals, he insisted, reflected a typical "human reaction" [*conforme con los sentimientos del corazón humano*] to an inefficient and often corrupt criminal-justice system.[105] Not surprisingly, his reform agenda included proportionate, prompt, and certain punishment; a straightforward and accessible penal code; well-trained police; and modern penitentiaries; complemented, as his official title suggested, by public education.

In Martínez de Castro's works, then, the rationalist, utilitarian assumptions of classic criminology predominated. As official texts—rather than just officially sanctioned texts—these works sought to reflect the *puro* liberal ideology of the Juárez regime and thus tended to submerge elitist subtexts beneath a rhetoric of universal human rights. And, unlike the more speculative works of midcentury social critics, the cracks in this ideological edifice were few and far between. In a report to the Mexican Congress on the need to reform criminal procedures, Martínez de Castro noted that "he who lacks the requirements of life because he does not want to work, necessarily seeks them in fraud, forgery, theft, robbery, uprisings, and revolutions," and denounced public punishment for unnecessarily humiliating "decent" people.[106] But, although these remarks betrayed obvious concern about the moral lassitude of the rabble and about the sensitivities of the emerging middle classes, he assiduously avoided deliberate indicators of class, thus preserving the ideologically essential appearance of equality before the law.

As before, however, contemporary social critics showed considerably less reticence, drawing clear connections between class and criminality. In an 1875 article for *El Federalista*, a young Justo Sierra echoed the earlier sentiments of Fernández de Lizardi, remarking that "the beggar is generally an immoral and corrupting individual; . . . his motto is resistance to work." "Indigence is holy," he concluded; "begging is criminal." And, like earlier social critics such as Otero, Sierra portrayed Mexico City *léperos* as degenerate and probably incapable of forming moral judgments. Only the literary style had changed. His description of a visit to a Mexico City tenement house (*una de esas sórdidas casucas de vecindad*) mimicked the naturalist tones of late-nineteenth-century French novelists like Emile Zola or Mexico's own Federico Gamboa: "We approach a room inhabited by four women. A mother and her three daughters. The mother led us into a nauseating room in which there was a sleeping mat and a blanket. This was all the furnishings and, with the dress and shawl of the mother, all the clothing in the apartment. The three girls, in order to avoid appearing naked before us, had been forced to raise the floorboards and hide underneath them. From the hole that they had left to breath through, stuck their faces, pallid with hunger and shame." Little wonder, Sierra remarked, that "the majority of the young girls that wander through the streets have an astonishing precocity for vice."[107] Under these appalling conditions, he implied, a generalized lower-class criminality was probably inevitable. The naturalistic combination of realist narrative and sensationalism forcefully conveyed his ultimately denigrating message.

This critical view of lower-class lifestyles persisted into the Porfirian era. In regular editorials for *El Monitor Republicano*, Enrique Chávarri (a.k.a. "Juvenal") and Enrique M. de los Ríos perpetuated the liberal tradition of exposing lower-class degradation and criminality in order to encourage social reform. In a report on a Mexico City press campaign to investigate the "alarming" rise in homicides among the lower classes (*el pueblo inferior*) instigated by *Hijo de Ahuizote* editor Daniel Cabrera, De los Ríos identified pulque drinking, vagrancy (a product of *ociosidad*), gambling, and "bloody spectacles" like bullfights as the underlying causes of most urban violence.[108] His colleague Chávarri also stressed the link between lower-class pursuits, especially pulque drinking ("one of the principal causes, if not the principal cause of penal infractions"), and endemic violence. He explained that "since time immemorial we have seen in our barrios, especially in the pulquerías, in the tenement houses [*casas de vecindad*], because of a misunderstood word, a rejected or unoffered drink, a gesture, or for no reason at all, two men or even two women resort to knives . . . and fight ferociously, like savages, until one of the combatants is unable to continue."[109]

According to both authors, rising criminality pervaded urban life. "When we see only the surface of our society," Chávarri warned ominously, "we cannot even conceive of the miserable multitudes [*pobredumbre*] hidden in its bowels." In typical liberal fashion both authors lobbied hard for a reformed criminal-justice system that would include speedy trials, modern penitentiaries, and a larger, more professional police force.[110] Repression of the "idle" lower classes was justified, Chávarri argued, by the need to protect the larger society. "We are zealous defenders of individual rights," he disingenuously insisted, "and would never advocate their abuse, above all as regards the class that suffers all the rigors of destiny; but we do understand that vagrants, those that defraud their neighbors by invoking public charity, those that in the name of misfortune dedicate themselves to petty thievery, deserve the vigilance of the police."[111]

By the last quarter of the nineteenth century the *puro* liberalism of a Martínez de Castro had become somewhat anomalous in social-reform discourse, although it would remain the rhetoric of choice for official texts. Anxiety about Mexico City's burgeoning lower classes was clearly eroding liberal scruples about individual human rights. Social critics responded by drawing the typical Victorian distinction between worthy and unworthy poor. Unproductive, politically volatile, and potentially criminal vagrants, in particular, drew their ire. A compelling desire for order had replaced idealistic promises of liberty even among Porfirio Díaz's political opponents like De los Ríos and Chávarri. The productive, "worthy" members of Mexico's lower classes represented the foundation of a modern workforce and merited benefits like public education and public health; idle, alcoholic vagrants undermined national development and therefore deserved severe repression.[112] The needs of the larger society and the fledgling Mexican nation required immediate attention even at the expense of the (generally lower-class) individual.

In many ways, however, social critics like Chávarri and De los Ríos were nearly as out of date as Martínez de Castro, harking back to the mid-nineteenth-century attitudes of Mariano Otero or even to late-eighteenth-century Bourbon public policy. The rising prestige of evolutionary science during the second half of the nineteenth century had brought an impressive new perspective to criminological discourse. That perspective would finally resolve the discursive schizophrenia of *puro* liberalism that was still in evidence during the Restored Republic and the first decades of the Díaz regime.

In 1878, just two years after the Revolution of Tuxtepec brought Porfirio Díaz to power, Justo Sierra invoked the natural science of Charles Darwin to explain "this social disease called crime."[113] He observed that "the two great factors in crime are essentially the same ones that serve as the basis of Darwinism in biological studies: heredity and milieu [*la influencia de los medios*]." He also added portentously that "this explanation more than any other authorizes severity towards delinquents." For Sierra, Mexico's notorious political instability and economic underdevelopment coupled with weak educational and penal institutions made repression an unattractive but necessary response. "It is a disgrace," he concluded, "but . . . it is the unavoidable law of self-preservation that imposes this harsh duty; and those that have failed to comply, men or nations, have disappeared."[114] The acceleration of capitalist development begun during the Restored Republic and intensified under the Díaz regime was, for social critics like Sierra, a matter of national survival. Lower-class criminality, whatever its cause, threatened vital economic development and demanded a vigorous response—a new war on crime uninhibited by unrealistic liberal abstractions.

Evolutionary science thus justified, as Enlightenment-inspired liberal ideology could not, elite anxieties about lower-class criminality. According to the biological metaphors of Social Darwinists like Sierra, criminal behavior was no longer a rational response to irrational social institutions but an epidemic disease that threatened to destroy a still young and vulnerable Mexican nation. And, although Sierra himself demonstrated some concern about rural poverty, for most analysts that disease was most prevalent among the growing urban underclass.[115] This medicalized discourse implied that elite concern was only "natural," as were class-specific strategies for dealing with the problem of crime. Thus a new generation of self-proclaimed positivists advocating "scientific" politics disparagingly dismissed Enlightenment egalitarianism as idealistic "metaphysics" and the rationalism of classic criminology as inappropriate and unworkable.[116] During the Porfiriato, elite anxieties about lower-class criminality, an unacknowledged subtext in officially sanctioned classic criminology, would become a recognized element of mainstream criminological discourse.

The legacy of classic criminology in Mexico is schizophrenic. Its intellectual basis in Enlightenment rationalism contrasted sharply with its unacknowledged classist subtext. Officially sanctioned texts carefully preserved their theoretical and ideological purity by submerging elite prejudices within a framework of universalist reform proposals that ostensibly benefited all of humankind. In public policy and in the unofficial texts of social critics the inherent biases of criminological discourse were more readily apparent. The result was quite effective and very functional. Educated "consumers" of these different texts were reassured by the legitimizing potential of Enlightenment rationalism and liberal utilitarianism, while their preconceptions and prejudices regarding the Mexican lower classes were simultaneously integrated into what touted itself as a "new" vision of crime and criminality.

This integration was gradual. But by the mid-nineteenth century even officially sanctioned texts clearly reflected a growing anxiety about innate lower-class criminality that superseded earlier rationalist assumptions about the nature of criminal behavior: criminal behavior was no longer a rational response to an irrational society but a category of lower-class "unreason" that inhibited rational social development. With the notable exception of the official texts of Martínez de Castro, the classist subtext of classical criminology had nearly become a full partner in the larger criminological discourse. Only a unifying principle was needed to bind them together. The emergence of evolutionary science would provide that bond.

Scientific criminology benefited from its predecessor in more specific ways, as well. Mexican criminologists never ceased to link crime to ignorance, alcoholism, gambling, prostitution, and even idleness, and they continued to recommend public education, prison reform, and rationalized criminal laws as solutions to crime. And the eclecticism of classic criminologists remained a hallmark of later Mexican criminology, as practitioners borrowed and adapted haphazardly from their European and North American colleagues.

Even the theoretical concerns of late-nineteenth-century European criminology were foreshadowed in the works of these earlier social critics. Environmentalism, of course, was central to classic criminology, and its explanatory role expanded further in the mid-nineteenth century in the works of Manuel Otero and other social critics. The role of heredity in determining human behavior was also recognized. In 1813 José Joaquín Fernández de Lizardi noted matter-of-factly that "some people are ignorant by nature and some are ignorant through education," and that "those ignorant by nature are the ones whose comprehensive ability is so obscured or confused, perhaps by the organization of their brains, that they scarcely understand even the coarsest and most material things."[117] The irrational, "born criminal" of early scientific criminology was clearly just around the corner. Classical criminology, which privileged reason and criminalized the irrational, provided the missing link. Evolutionary science would forge the chain.

The last word, then, rightly belongs to Fernández de Lizardi's bumpkin (*payo*), who, taking leave of the sacristan, remarked: "You're very right to say that it's through following the old routine that men are most easily subjugated. So long, see you Saturday."[118]

# 2. SCIENTIFIC CRIMINOLOGY
## Consolidating the Criminological Paradigm

Of what use is intellectual progress without moral progress, of what use are our marvels of mechanization, if we haven't added to the chalice of human life even a single drop of harmony and of justice? – Justo Sierra, "Discurso de clausura"

Our work, I understand, will be at first timid, vacillating, indecisive; but little by little it will strengthen itself and with time we also will give to science elements that others will know how to take advantage of, without doubt, to the benefit of the classes that need it most. – Carlos Roumagnac, Los criminales en México

The coup d'état that brought General Porfirio Díaz to power in 1876 inaugurated an era of unparalleled modernization in a country whose outward-looking elites thirsted for "progress." During the thirty-five-year Porfiriato the Mexican cult of modernity would achieve its purest expression: until the Porfirian edifice began to crumble in the first decade of the new century, national policymakers seemed confident that the tumultuous nineteenth century would soon become a distant, unhappy memory. To that end they introduced their now admirably stable nation to all the wonders of modern technology, from a modern rail system and urban electrification to bicycles and moving pictures.[1] They even rewrote national history for local, national, and international consumption as a tale of evolutionary redemption.[2] "Order and Progress," the regime's positivist motto, publicly represented their boundless enthusiasm and disciplined commitment to the nation's future. That they would insist on a modern—presumably scientific—solution to the traditional problem of crime was perhaps inevitable.[3]

Progressive to the point of faddishness, Porfirian criminology nonetheless lacked order. Inspired perhaps by their contentious European colleagues, turn-of-the-century Mexican criminologists produced works of remarkable diversity if little consistency and less scientific merit. Acceptable data ranged freely from criminal statistics to police reports to trial records to journalistic accounts to personal anecdotes. Interpretations conflated seemingly scientific analysis with traditional moralistic concerns and blatant conjecture; most reflected the class, racial, and gender prejudices of turn-of-the-century Mexican elites. Genres and narrative styles varied wildly, with criminological arguments plotted as case histories, travelogues, legal treatises, scientific treatises, or public speeches. Even the theoretical underpinnings of Porfirian criminology reflected its practitioners' eclectic approach to the causes of crime; European and North American criminologists were widely read, analyzed, and discussed, but their Mexican counterparts resolutely and self-consciously refused to commit to any one school.

This extraordinarily fluid situation closely resembles historian of science Thomas Kuhn's description of pre-paradigmatic science: the period before the ascendancy of a dominant theoretical "paradigm" that sets the parameters of subsequent research.[4] In *The Structure of Scientific Revolutions* Kuhn argues that "in the early stages of the development of any science, different men confronting the same range of phenomena, but not usually all the same particular phenomena, describe and interpret them in different ways."[5] The only missing element in Porfirian criminology is the competitiveness Kuhn sees as typical of "immature" science and that is readily apparent in its turn-of-the-century European counterpart. Mexican criminologists' status as passive onlookers probably explains their gentlemanly tolerance.

Mexican criminology also followed the developmental trajectory described by Kuhn. In Kuhn's "mature" scientific community "the members . . . see themselves and are seen by others as the men uniquely responsible for the pursuit of a set of shared goals, including the training of their successors. Within such groups communication is relatively full and professional judgment relatively unanimous."[6] Especially important to Kuhn's model is the sense of shared perception fostered by training methods that encourage future practitioners to "learn to see the same things when confronted with the same stimuli . . . by being shown examples of situations that their predecessors in the group have already learned to see like each other and as different from other sorts of situations."[7] In Mexico, which had been disrupted by revolution, reaching this "mature" stage would take nearly fifty years, but the foundations of shared perceptions, the essence of a modern Mexican criminological paradigm, were laid by Porfirian criminologists.

In one important aspect that "maturity" was superficial. Mexican criminology, like its international counterparts, never developed the unified theoretical foundation that characterizes Kuhn's paradigm.[8] Disputes over the causes of crime were subsumed into criminological science, rather than resolved. In fact, in Mexican criminology the theoretically opposed poles of hereditarian and environmental causation served not so much as a source of dispute but often as peacefully co-existing, mutually reinforcing subdisciplines within the larger field.[9] Transforming apparent weakness into strength, general practitioners typically drew on both explanations in their research, often using one theory to resolve the anomalies of the other and proposing solutions that could accommodate either or both theories.[10] Modern Mexican criminology, rooted in the Porfirian era, thus developed a strong, consensual scientific community committed to predetermined "problem-solutions" without the theoretical grounding typical of the physical sciences analyzed by Kuhn.

The source of this apparent anomaly resides in Kuhn's formulation of the scientific paradigm. Deriving his model from the less socially engaged physical sciences, Kuhn downplays the ideological role of science and scientific models in modern societies. However, during the nineteenth century in particular, science functioned discursively to naturalize social categories including criminality in ways that inevitably mirrored the preconceptions and prejudices of its educated practitioners. Scientific paradigms served not just to direct research or solve problems but also to legitimize a new, ideologically charged gestalt.[11] Social sciences like sociology and criminology were, in this sense, the step-children of paradigmatic science. Just as the adoption of a "mature," paradigm-driven approach greatly enhanced the prestige as well as the productivity of the physical sciences, the appearance of consensus and maturity served, by extension, to legitimize its not-quite kin.[12]

This legitimacy was crucial to the professional needs and aspirations of Mexican criminologists. Access to scarce public funds and the ability to influence public policy required the appearance of scientific objectivity on one hand and the implied promise of a "cure" for crime on the other. Scientific criminology, in return, helped legitimize the often criticized Mexican criminal-justice system by reassuring policymakers and a skeptical (literate) public that the system was fundamentally sound or at least capable of reform. This essentially ideological function depended heavily on the perceived kinship of the physical and social sciences. The perception of criminology's scientific maturity further reinforced that critical link.

Recognizing the ideological baggage of paradigmatic science thus allows for a broader construction of Kuhn's notion of the paradigm.[13] For Mexican criminologists, survival in a politicized world of appearances favored a paradigm based on an adaptable but consistent discourse rather than on clearly articulated theory. Under these constraints, criminological schools with their competing etiologies became subdisciplines in a discursively unified field. The wild eclecticism of Porfirian criminologists evolved into the more sedate specialization of mature Mexican criminologists. In spite of widely varied interests, mature practitioners politely acknowledged and often incorporated competing and even contradictory theories into their research. The illusion of consensus was crucial to disciplinary success. And after all, criminologists argued, criminality at its most basic level had as many causes as there were criminals. At the same time the inherent flexibility of this catholic approach to theory provided Mexican criminologists with a broad spectrum of problem-solutions that could serve both professional and ideological purposes. Given criminology's need to engage social problems, a discourse-based disciplinary paradigm was a more than satisfactory practical solution.

The history of Mexican criminology, then, reflects the gradual development of a discursively oriented "scientific" paradigm. As in Kuhn's analysis of the physical sciences, this paradigm structured perceptions and provided problem-solutions for succeeding generations of criminologists. In addition to structuring criminological research, it was also remarkable for its eclectic approach to theory, its underlying ideological orientation, and its overtly political purpose. The legitimation of criminology through its apparent affinity with "objective," paradigm-driven physical sciences thus greatly aided Mexican policymakers seeking to bolster, both ideologically and practically, an often denigrated criminal-justice system that they nonetheless recognized as crucial to national development.

More important, the gradual consolidation of the scientific criminological paradigm during the course of the nineteenth century provided the central forum for a much broader construction of criminality that helped delimit the social boundaries of modern Mexican society, to set the limits of citizenship—the "price" of admission into that society. Criminality, a perennial source of concern and discussion, became, through this process of paradigm development, a subject of focused, scientific inquiry by trained specialists.[14] These specialists helped legitimize, systematize, refine, and when necessary redefine the sometimes hazy and overly legalistic notions of criminality derived from Mexico's colonial and early national periods, bending the insights of modern science to suit the needs of national development. Social categories of class, race, and gender, invariably bound up in any discussion of criminality, were sometimes reinforced, sometimes transformed by this process. The prestige of paradigmatic science underwrote the results. Understanding the development of a scientific criminological paradigm in Mexico thus provides valuable, even crucial, insights into the forging of *la patria*.

Criminology as a recognized discipline—the systematic and purportedly scientific study of crime in Mexican society—came into its own during the Porfirian years of "order and progress" that closed out the nineteenth and began the twentieth century. Its development coincided with the growing acceptance in Europe and North America of criminology as a legitimate and even vital subdiscipline of sociology, the positivist-inspired science of human society. Mexican elites, traditionally linked to international intellectual currents, enthusiastically endorsed both positivist sociology and its new offspring as necessary corollaries to modernity. These modern technologies of knowledge (and, it was hoped, of power) seemed the ideal antidote to modern problems, especially burgeoning urban crime, and still-formidable traditional enemies like rural ignorance and church recalcitrance, that continued to signify Mexico's relative lack of development.

The integration of science into Mexican criminology was a haphazard affair at best. Positivist science prided itself on an inductive methodology that uncovered the underlying laws of biological and social organization through the careful accumulation and analysis of data. This deliberate if naïve rejection of a predetermined paradigm (either theoretical or discursive) as the basis upon which to organize rapidly accumulating data sparked a series of creative, albeit unsystematic, attempts to employ scientific insights in the ever-escalating war on crime.[15] Most practitioners agreed that science could eventually provide the key that would unlock the secrets of criminal behavior. How that would happen, however, was unclear.

### Legal Medicine and Free Will

Mexico's first "scientific" criminologist was probably Rafael de Zayas Enríquez, a francophile *jefe político* (political boss) and judge from Veracruz who published his own two-volume *Fisiología del crimen: Estudio jurídico-sociológico* in 1885–86.[16] Zayas set out expressly to clarify, in the light of modern medical science, the difficult legal question of criminal insanity. His principal complaint was judicial "indifference" to the latest advances in the study of human physiology and psychology. "For jurists," he complained, "one is either crazy or sensible; there are no nuances, no graduations, no intermediate states."[17]

According to Zayas, the principal cause of judicial indifference was the inherent conservatism of the legal profession, which was due largely to its historical ties to theology and metaphysics, "those two so-called sciences that conspire to inhibit human potential and check the progress of inductive investigation." Medical science, on the other hand, was the "most progressive of all" because it had "broken definitively with the past."[18] A typical positivist denunciation of early nineteenth-century liberalism, Zayas's critique of Mexican criminal justice replaced Enlightenment faith in inalienable human rights with a more prosaic and, in his eyes, more useful inductive science based on careful observation and research.

Although focused specifically on the issues surrounding criminal insanity, especially the execution of the criminally insane, which he opposed because it could have no possible deterrent effect, Zayas's study presaged many other important trends in later Mexican scientific criminology.[19] Geographically and culturally at one remove from mainstream European and North American criminology, Zayas adapted the moderate eclecticism of predecessors like Manuel Lardizábal and Vincente Rocafuerte. Copious citations from important and often contradictory French and Italian criminologists, including the ubiquitous Cesare Lombroso with his controversial theories of atavism and "born" criminals, comprise a considerable portion of the first volume.[20] The contradictions between hereditarian (Italian) and environmental (French) explanations for criminality he dismissed with the mild comment that "in my view both extremes are dangerous, and the truth resides somewhere in the middle."[21] This eclectic spirit, which profited from the prestige of distinguished foreign criminologists while avoiding their disciplinary squabbles, would characterize Mexican criminology into the twentieth century.[22]

So would the complex web of hidden presuppositions typical of most nineteenth-century criminology.[23] Argument by analogy—equating physiological and behavioral phenomena like muscle and mental spasms, for example—while apparently scientific, typically avoided any serious discussion or testing of the argument's actual validity. Likewise, bald assertions that "in all men especially gifted with remarkable intelligence the furrows and convolutions of the brain are deeper than in ordinary men" along with their negative corollaries (that inferior races, classes, women, and children had underdeveloped brains) were generally presented as scientifically proven in spite of scanty, questionable data even by nineteenth-century standards.[24] These scientifically validated presuppositions permitted elitist notions of the criminality of the racially mixed lower classes to move out of the realm of speculation, inference, and subtext into mainstream criminological discourse.

This was especially noticeable in Zayas's theory of criminal causation. In place of a simple dichotomy between reason and unreason he presented a typology of criminally insane behaviors that included everything from temporary insanity to compulsions (controlled and uncontrolled) to delusions and even auditory hallucinations. Rationality and self-control, the foundations of classic criminology, were still privileged as proper, "healthy" responses to criminal "impulses," but explaining the individual criminal's failure to exercise either was becoming increasingly problematic. Irrational social institutions might encourage an otherwise "normal" person to commit a crime, but the criminally insane were generally unresponsive to rational stimuli.

For Zayas the critical factor in serious criminal behavior was a defective moral sense (*yo moral* as opposed to *yo material*) that failed to check the criminal impulse at critical times, often without any obvious prior indication of criminal insanity.[25] These behavioral anomalies were sometimes difficult for nonspecialists to detect in advance and were generally physiological in nature. Both characteristics held enormous potential implications for Mexican criminal justice. The first suggested the need for a professional discipline devoted to legal medicine and charged with ferreting out society's hidden criminals for gullible or ignorant magistrates. It also implied the surrender of considerable judicial authority to scientifically trained specialists. The second characteristic warned that criminality, whether produced by heredity or environment, was likely a permanent physical condition and thus probably impossible to cure. Nor was it immediately susceptible to classic liberal social reforms geared to rationalizing the criminal-justice system.

To support his argument Zayas provided a series of international case studies of infamous, "insane" criminals. Of the notorious French criminal Alfonso Dupont, who was convicted of murdering his "young, beautiful, and virtuous" common-law wife (who was also his stepsister), Zayas noted that "the debauchery in which he lived, the laziness, the lack of resources, his immorality, his desire for gross pleasures, all indicate a profound corruption of his *moral sense* and prove that he was not a *sane* man [*un hombre que gozaba sana razón*]."[26] Dupont's moral insanity not only inspired his brutal crime but was clearly indicated by his day-to-day behavior. Traits like laziness and the enjoyment of "gross" pleasures, while not inherently class specific, nonetheless reflected typical elite critiques of lower-class lifestyles and, without further qualification, served as indicators of both class and criminality.

Zayas further implied that Dupont's physical deformity (he was a hunchback) determined his moral status, both by embittering him toward physically normal society and by signifying his flawed biological inheritance. This conflation of physicality and morality was typical. Another notorious criminal, an Italian thief and murderer, was described in similarly suggestive terms: "Beneath his broad, high forehead shine his eyes, very mobile, very black, ferocious at times, astute at others. His nose, slightly flattened at birth, rises in sharp point, like the snout of a hyena. The mouth exhibits the concupiscence of his appetites."[27] These criminals clearly exhibited what Italian criminologist Cesare Lombroso called the "stigmata" of an innate and probably inherited criminality.

In yet another unsupported analogy Zayas applied these individual characteristics to a generalized criminal class; the mental derangement of the homicidal maniac illustrated the insanity of the group. He conveniently ignored the paradox between the hidden criminal and overt physical stigmata. Apparently not all criminals were so easy to detect, especially in a crowd. These notorious criminals represented only a select, if an extreme, sampling of an entire class of criminals. "Everywhere and particularly in the large cities," he warned, "one encounters a special race, to which belong the vagrants, the people without fixed occupation, without families. Men and women live in promiscuity. Robbery is not considered immoral, drunkenness is not a vice but a habit or a necessity, and prostitution is the most natural thing in the world."[28] This special race, detectable to the untrained eye only by its obvious physical or class attributes, stood ready to rise up at the slightest provocation— to turn an honest labor dispute into a riot or a political upheaval into a revolution. Zayas's slippery but "scientific" formulation of moral insanity thus allowed him to condemn an entire class as potentially homicidal even though he employed what was, by most legal (and scientific) standards, slim and circumstantial evidence. His language also carried racist connotations that reinforced traditional elite preconceptions about the mestizo urban underclass.

Moreover, only a specially trained medical expert could hope to unravel the psychological and physiological complexities of true criminal behavior. And Zayas further reinforced the specialized nature of the new criminology by resorting to frequent biological and physiological analogies, which he couched in appropriate medical jargon. "If a disorder of nerve motor centers destroys the coordination of physical movements and gives rise to a spasmodic or convulsive muscular action," he argued, "an upheaval of the psychic centers likewise destroys mental coordination and gives rise to a spasmodic or convulsive mental action."[29] Nor was the discursive nature of the new criminological project lost on Zayas, who insisted that "the same values that cause the doctor to brave the dangers of the plague, should sustain him in his duty and force him to confront the attacks of poisoned tongues and pens."[30] The legalistic foundations of classic criminological discourse were thus challenged philosophically and discursively by the rapidly growing prestige of nineteenth-century medical science and its aspiring practitioners. These attacks would intensify as the century progressed.

Scientific jargon was not the only discursive innovation; new journalistic techniques played a significant role as well. Scientific "objectivity" aside, most analysts also saw criminality as a social construction that depended heavily on common sense, on generally accepted and broadly defined notions of normative behavior, to ensure its acceptance. The "objective" eyewitness accounts of professional journalists, then, played directly to the common sense of a growing mass readership eager, at the same time, to be titillated by the latest cause célèbre.[31]

Just as his first volume buttressed its argument with excerpts from prominent foreign criminologists, Zayas's second volume presented his readers with a broad, international spectrum of you-were-there sources including detailed personal anecdotes, newspaper accounts, and even court transcripts. In his discussion of criminal compulsions, for example, he cited a story related to a French doctor by Baron Alexander von Humboldt in which the family maid begged to be dismissed because whenever she undressed their infant son "she noticed the whiteness of his skin and felt a nearly irresistible desire to cut open his abdomen."[32] Humboldt, of course, epitomized the scientific spirit, especially for Mexican social analysts who were still citing his *Political Essay on the Kingdom of Spain* in their statistical studies.

To reinforce his journalistic credibility Zayas also took care to provide a variety of clearly identified sources whenever possible. For example, in his detailed account of the trial and execution of President Garfield's assassin, Charles Guiteau, he included the complete text of the accused's last words and a song Guiteau had composed for the occasion, along with excerpts from the trial transcripts.[33] These superfluous details testified to the journalist/author's status as "objective" witness and by extension lent credibility to his "subjective" analysis. The seemingly impersonal, inductive character of positivist science was mirrored in an inductive journalism that openly presented its evidence so that readers might draw their own conclusions.[34]

### Criminal Anthropology

Zayas intended his works to appeal to both the Mexican legal community and to a general nineteenth-century readership fascinated by gruesome murders and remorseless criminals. Designed specifically to supplement the work of European criminal anthropologists, Francisco Martínez Baca and Manuel Vergara's *Estudios de antropología criminal* was more obviously scientific and less deliberately sensationalistic.[35] Published in Puebla in 1892, in time to be presented at the International Exhibition in Chicago, it resembled a typical late-nineteenth-century scientific treatise, well illustrated by photographs, elaborate charts, and beautifully rendered drawings of scientific instruments.[36] Also, the multifaceted Martínez—"military doctor for the Mexican Army, professor of external pathology at the state [Puebla] School of Medicine and Pharmacology, teacher [profesor de Lecciones de Cosas] at the women's Normal School, doctor of the Penitentiary and head of the its Department of Anthropology"—and his assistant Vergara approached the problem of criminality as medical experts and thus evinced little concern over the legal ramifications of their research.

In spite of these stylistic and discursive differences, however, *Estudios de antropología criminal* touched on many of the same issues raised earlier by Zayas. In his prologue, for example, Veracruz lawyer Rafael Saldaña continued the positivist attack on "metaphysical" post-Enlightenment penal reforms—"the dreams of certain great and generous souls that have never and will never become reality"—that perpetuated the naïve belief that "man completely controls his own actions" [*sea dueño absoluto de sus acciones*].[37] This unrealistic belief in humanity's fundamental rationality or free will, he asserted, "ignored human psychophysics," which had proven that "the human organism is unavoidably influenced by external stimuli, and the brain is certainly no exception to this rule."[38] Thus Saldaña situated Martínez and Vergara's work firmly within a new scientific criminology that sought to distinguish itself both philosophically and discursively from its legalistic liberal predecessor.

Again, like Zayas, Martínez and Vergara declined to take sides in nationalistic European criminological disputes. Even as committed practitioners of craniology in the manner of Lombroso, they nonetheless insisted that European efforts to theorize about criminality were premature, remarking that while "the Italian and French schools dispute the genesis and etiology of crime, both schools agree on the need for observation, experience and especially reliable statistics. . . . Both are correct, resulting in an eclecticism without nationality that all would do well to accept. For now we ought to dedicate ourselves to nothing more than investigation and the acquisition of certain principles: We are too inexperienced to waste our efforts in sustaining merely speculative theories."[39] Thus environmental and social milieu was clearly an influential if not the decisive factor in the establishment of some typical criminal traits—alcoholism, lack of education, the use of cant, and tattoos; for other traits—inherited "pathological states" or underdeveloped cranial sutures—heredity likely played the decisive role. With evolutionary science still undecided about crucial issues like the inheritability of acquired characteristics, criminologists could only speculate. Environmentally acquired traits might be inherited by future generations, or inherited traits might manifest themselves environmentally. Martínez and Vergara suggested, for example, that some criminals resorted to alcoholic stimulation to compensate for an inherited physiological deficiency.[40] Regardless of their ultimate origin, however, physiological traits could be and were quantified and analyzed.

Unwilling to get caught up in foreign theoretical squabbles, Martínez and Vergara elected instead to provide specifically Mexican data to supplement international studies of criminal traits. Saldaña's prologue points out that "until now we have learned only the anthropology and anthropometry of the European criminal, which for us is practically useless, since our criminal world is clearly distinct." He noted especially "the profound differences of climate, altitude, race, education, and lifestyle that distinguish us from the Europeans."[41] Ironically, buttressed by the discoveries of nineteenth-century evolutionary science, Montesquieu's climate theory, which stressed geographically determined differences between "peoples," had reentered criminological discourse (probably via sociobiologist Ernst Haeckel) just as Enlightenment universalism went into eclipse. Late-nineteenth-century Mexican positivist advocates of so-called scientific politics took pride in its ability to adapt to local conditions, its awareness of each nation's unique social, political, and economic circumstances.[42] As representatives of one of the quintessential positivist social sciences, Mexican criminologists were no exception.

Within this nationalistic context Martínez and Vergara pushed the boundaries of criminology still further, positing a new science of the Mexican soul. "It is necessary," they argued, "that science penetrate this unfathomable abyss that is called the human soul; that it discover and analyze its component elements, its method of combination, its nature, its mode of being, the influence that milieu, climate, latitude, etc., exercise on its manifestations; and, in a word, what is its mode of execution and reexecution in the face of the infinitely varied circumstances in which it can find itself." This science would "naturally" focus on any evidence of criminality and on "the means necessary to correct its deviations."[43] Since the colonial period Mexicans had expressed considerable interest in defining their "national" characteristics (usually subdivided by race, class, and gender).[44] Positivist social science promised to bring the insights of science to bear on the identity question; Mexican criminologists like Martínez and Vergara expected to contribute their expertise to defining at least the criminal aspect of national identity.

In their quest to uncover the secrets of the Mexican criminal soul, Martínez and Vergara adapted a multifaceted approach that gave the illusion of independent verification, a touchstone for scientific methodology. They derived their data from three sources: elaborate cranial examinations and measurements of the skulls of twenty-six deceased inmates ("notable delinquents") prepared in their laboratory at the Puebla penitentiary, biographical data taken from prison records, and photographic images (mug shots) of one hundred inmates, arranged by crime. This data was then collated and compared to similar European data, both to test various theories of criminal physiology and to determine the physical characteristics of Mexican criminals. For example, recognizing signs of meningoencephalitis in eighteen of the twenty-six skulls, the authors noted that "added to the others [cranial anomalies] . . . this [finding] supports the opinion of eminent anthropologists who compare criminals with the insane."[45] Later, in support of French criminologist and forensic specialist Alexandre Lacassagne's theory of brain development, they remarked that the occipital region, "which establishes or breaks the equilibrium of the developing brain . . . is where we have encountered the most significant and largest anomalies."[46] Based primarily on the cranial measurements of twenty-six criminals, this corroborating evidence, as the authors acknowledged, was incomplete. It lacked a control group of noncriminals against which to compare the criminal skulls, and by treating criminality as an analyzable category assumed an affinity between the individual criminal skulls that was unsupported by the scanty biographical data. Much like Zayas's, their superficially careful data gathering and analysis disguised and underwrote a set of unproven, socially constructed presuppositions about an analytical category—criminality—that revealed more about elite mentality than about actual causes of crime.

On a specifically national level Martínez and Vergara argued that the physical characteristics of Mexican criminals differed significantly from those of their European counterparts. Many of the physiological anomalies that signified criminality in Europe, they noted, "lose their anomalous characteristics because they are typical and ordinary in other peoples [*pueblos*]."[47] In other words, an anomaly could be any physical characteristic that deviated from any given norm. "We deduce," they declared, "that the indicated forms [narrow-headedness, or dolichocephaly, and round-headedness, or brachycephaly] can signify degeneration when they constitute an anomaly, by being distinguishable from the common type for a given people."[48]

Thus, as Zayas suggested, any physical characteristic that deviated from the "normal" might indicate criminality. Martínez and Vergara concluded that the "ferocious and shocking aspect that most criminals exhibit, whose evil passions are reflected in their visages . . . is what distinguishes the delinquent man from the honorable man; it is the natural stigma that sets him apart from the law of selection."[49] They even distinguished between the different types of criminals exhibited in their photographic plates; the lips of rapists, for example, were "thick and arched," while the lips of robbers were "plegados" (puckered) and those of murderers, "thin."[50] In support of these conclusions they cited an old Spanish proverb from the colonial period: "Never trust a bearded Indian or a beardless Spaniard; a woman who talks like a man or a man who talks like a child."[51] Practical, positivist science, then, merely elucidated the common sense of the Mexican "folk," which not surprisingly included traditional elite anxieties about those races "sufficiently degenerated through miscegenation" and ultimately anyone whose physical or behavioral difference threatened the social order.[52]

These traditional elite concerns thus took on a new legitimacy endorsed not by colonial legal and social hierarchies but by the new "objective" language of science. This was especially true in regard to elite attitudes toward lower-class criminality. Martínez and Vergara, like their predecessor, Zayas, also paradoxically warned about Mexican society's hidden criminals, citing directly from French doctor-criminologist Emile Laurent: "How many of these men, true criminals at heart, have managed throughout their lives, thanks to the astuteness, hypocrisy, etc., typical of the delinquent man, to hide their tendencies to robbery, homicide, etc., and live among honest men!"[53]

Combined with their concerns about the criminal consequences of race mixture, these borrowed warnings especially implicated Mexico's mestizo lower classes, condemning by association a huge proportion of the urban population. Just as the mestizo lower classes often attempted to dissimulate their racial status by attempting to "pass" as Spaniards, criminal elements among these same classes sought to disguise their antisocial tendencies by pretending to be honest, hardworking proletarians. Only scientific investigation, criminal anthropology in particular, could hope to unmask this dangerous threat to the Mexican nation. Meanwhile, Mexican elites were encouraged to trust their "natural" instincts.

### The Legal Community Responds

Not all Mexican criminologists took an uncritical view of their discipline's new scientific bent. Legal practitioners, in particular, saw in the privileging of scientific knowledge a challenge to their traditional authority. In 1895 the appropriately named Agustín Verdugo defended his *licenciado*'s thesis on criminal responsibility and the modern schools of anthropology" to the Mexican Academy of Jurisprudence and Legislation. Like Martínez and Vergara, Verdugo took a nationalistic approach to criminality. "Every worthwhile people" [*pueblo del cual hay algo que esperar*], he remarked, "produces . . . a certain number of more or less moral ideas that constitute the wholesome side [*bello lado*] of national character and public morality."[54] His argument, while it acknowledged physiological and environmental causes of crime, focused principally on its social causes—on the role of a broadly defined "national character" in defining criminal behavior and thus criminality.

Unlike his provincial colleagues, Verdugo attacked French and Italian criminologists for their determinism and especially for their refusal to recognize the place of free will or individual conscience in criminal behavior. "Sociology," he complained, "overreaches the insurmountable limits imposed by human nature . . . in order to make essentially variable and multiform phenomena like crime depend on historical laws [that are] irreducible to scientific exactness."[55] Verdugo's repudiation of scientific criminology probably reflected the inherent conservatism of the Mexican legal establishment that Zayas had complained about earlier. Since lawyers and judges, in particular, stood to lose both prestige and judicial authority to specialists in criminology and legal medicine, some resistance was inevitable.

Progressive elements in the Mexico City legal community were more sympathetic to scientific criminology, and during the last decade of the Porfiriato these progressives played an increasingly influential role in national policy making.[56] In 1897 prominent *científico* and legal theorist Miguel S. Macedo gave a speech to the National College of Lawyers entitled "Criminality in Mexico: Methods for combating it."[57]

Directly concerned with national policy making and deeply committed to economic development as the key to Mexico's future, Macedo logically took a more practical, less specialized approach to the problem of crime than did other Porfirian criminologists. Not surprisingly, his science of choice was not forensic medicine but statistics.[58] Of particular concern was a perceived crime wave, "the conviction that the rising tide of crime acquires more and more force with the passing of time."[59] "This evil," he warned, "has acquired such gravity that it is imperative that society take energetic and immediate measures, without hesitation, without omitting a single sacrifice, whether of study, of work, or of monetary expense."[60] Macedo noted with disgust that the number of arrests in Mexico City over a ten-year period actually exceeded the city's population.[61] Further, according to official statistics, homicides in Mexico City were running at an annual rate of 100 per 100,000 residents, compared to Madrid, for example, with a 7.6 per 100,000 ratio. "On confronting these figures," he declared, employing a classic nineteenth-century dichotomy, "one seems to be comparing a barbarous people with a civilized people."[62]

The principal problem was image. Porfirian development was predicated on foreign investment and immigration. And investors and immigrants were notoriously leery of Mexico's past reputation for instability. To prove his point, Macedo cited an article from the North American–directed *El Financiero Mexicano* (a.k.a. The Mexican Financier) that blamed the popular press and deceptive official statistics for Mexico's poor international image: "The daily press's custom of reporting in great detail the crimes perpetuated by the lower classes [*el pueblo bajo*] and the sensationalistic style of these reports, do not fail to instill erroneous beliefs about Mexico in foreign countries. . . . Official crime statistics for the capital have found their way into reference works like the Encyclopedia Britannica, and it is likely that they have had even worse effects."[63] Whatever the material consequences of high crime rates, the bad international image they perpetuated, Macedo argued, could be even more disastrous to national development.

Furthermore, that image was unfair. According to Macedo, many residents considered Mexico City to be one of the safest cities in the world. The real issue was class. "Among the middle and upper classes," he assured his audience, "there exists a firmly rooted sense of personal security that manifests itself in an extraordinary liberty of action."[64] A typical positivist, Macedo sought to "address the peculiar conditions of our social milieu and to determine the characteristic conditions of crime, here, in our country."[65] The most noticeable of those conditions was the preponderance of violent crime among the lower classes. "Personal experience," Macedo advised, "teaches all [Mexico] city residents that homicides and violent crimes [*delitos de sangre*] in general are almost all committed by individuals of the lower class against individuals of the same class."[66]

To support his point Macedo painted a depressing picture of the casual, even trivial nature of lower-class violence reminiscent of contemporary liberal social critics like Enrique Chávarri. "The quarrels that result in the enormous number of homicides and injuries committed in Mexico," he noted, "are occasioned by insignificant motives, ordinarily accidental and momentary. . . . A casual incident, a difference of opinion over some trivial thing, a chance word and even a simple slightly provocative look frequently initiate the quarrel that deprives a man of his life. . . . It is a fact that each individual seems to boast of a savage valor, of being *manly* [*ser muy hombre*]."[67] Public drinking, the perennial bugaboo of Mexican social critics, was for Macedo, as well, the constant companion of lower-class street violence. And again the picture that emerged was of an entire lower class so submerged in hopeless poverty and chronic alcoholism that criminal behavior was inevitable and recidivism, the principal cause of inflated crime statistics, a tragic fact of life.[68]

Macedo blamed economic underdevelopment and the Mexican upper class's lack of philanthropic spirit, which created a "profound separation of the diverse classes that make up our social body," and he proposed several reforms, including adoption programs for abandoned children; moral education in public schools; state-directed campaigns against public drunkenness, vagrancy, begging, gambling, and prostitution; prison reform, including the transportation of recidivists; and a revival of the death penalty.[69] But in spite of Macedo's call "to modify our entire social structure [*estado social*]," his potpourri of suggested reforms left most structural reforms (including capitalist economic development) to state-encouraged private initiative while upholding the state's monopoly on repression.[70] Thus, while it was sympathetic to the environmental and social causes of crime, Macedo's class-based analysis of Mexican criminal behavior emphasized state repression of lower-class criminality, at least until the combination of economic development and private philanthropy had time to take effect. If the privileged would uphold their end of the social contract, he suggested, class tensions (but not classes) might disappear. Meanwhile, repression was the unsatisfactory but necessary response.

### The Sociology of Mexican Crime

The most uniquely and deliberately Mexican of all Porfirian criminologies was Julio Guerrero's 1901 *La génesis del crimen en México: Ensayo de psiquiatría social*.[71] Guerrero's work systematized the implicitly nationalistic approaches of Martínez, Vergara, Verdugo, and

Macedo. And like his predecessors (excepting Agustín Verdugo), he based his criminological analysis on a purportedly scientific, in his case Social-Darwinistic, explanation of criminality. "Modern *science* has synthesized the general concept of *life* in the formula of a struggle without respite or mercy," he noted, adding that "man is not exempt from this destiny."[72] Criminals, then, were among the failures in this struggle for life, "those unable to resist the continuous, innervating influences of the physical and social milieu . . . [who] abandon the general aspirations, desert the combat, and finally become obstacles for the other members of society." In their weakness, having lost any sense of collective action or responsibility—"altruism" in Social-Darwinist jargon—many of these victims of the struggle for life turned to crime.[73]

From this positivist foundation Guerrero argued that while criminality manifested itself in individuals—"defects, imprudences, errors in the form of the delinquent's personal antecedents"—it could only be understood in its social context, by examining "the *soul* of a society, as they used to say in the era of theology."[74] The argument echoed Verdugo's concerns about national culture; Guerrero, however, embraced rather than rejected positivist science. His sociological analysis was probably the first systematic application of scientific method to the longstanding problem of national identity. Ironically, the nature of that attempt was hardly flattering, displaying, as it inevitably did, the criminal side of Mexican character. "My study," Guerrero warned, "deals with *Psychiatry*, vices, errors, preoccupations, deficiencies and crimes; and it would be wrong to judge our society by it."[75] Previous exposés of lower-class criminality had suggested a certain degree of national pathology; Guerrero's systematic, purportedly scientific approach confirmed that depressing diagnosis and, by implicating national character, hinted that even drastic reforms could take effect only slowly.

With its curious blend of geography, science, and history, Guerrero's work bore more than passing resemblance to travelogue, a venerable genre revitalized by Prussian scientist Alexander von Humboldt during the first years of the nineteenth century. The genre was eminently suited to Guerrero's comprehensive description of the Mexican milieu. That description followed a typical positivist trajectory, beginning with the physical environment and ending with a sociological analysis of Mexico's complex class structure. The language was an odd mixture of scientific jargon and poetry. Thus Guerrero's description of Mexico City's air: "The air, continually swept by the upper currents of the planet, is pure, diaphanous, blue and luminescent; but its rarefied nature extends the pulmonary cavities . . . carrying its oxidizing particles to the most delicate branches of the pulmonary arterioles."[76] This transparent air, he argued, encouraged the use of stimulants—"coffee, chocolate, tea, pulque, beer, and wine"—to compensate for its "enervating" effects. It also produced "climate-inspired anomalies [anomalías climatéricas]" that affected "perception" and "judgment."[77] For Guerrero these factors produced in capital residents "a semi-stoic, semi-mocking philosophy that causes them to disdain life and confront death . . . over an insignificant party joke or tabloid paragraph."[78] The combined effects of decreased atmospheric pressure, he observed, helped explain the capital's extraordinarily high rate of violent crime.[79] He even argued that the traditional dominance of Mexico's central plateau had caused many of these traits to spread throughout the country. And, although Guerrero examined these traits in all classes of Mexican society, traditional elite concerns about the public drunkenness and casual violence considered characteristic of the lifestyles of the mestizo lower classes were thus revived and vindicated by positivist natural science. The upper classes might respond to the same stimuli, but that response, while often detrimental to society, was rarely criminal.

Atmospheric pressure and geography in general was only the starting point. Race mixture and demographics also played important and related roles in Mexican criminality. Guerrero particularly condemned race mixture or miscegenation, which produced "children with two heads, Siamese twins, idiots, macrocephalics, albinos, offspring with harelips, feet without toes, hands with six fingers, tuberculars, syphilitics, scrofulars, dwarves and hunchbacks."[80] Most criminologists accepted a link between physical deformities and criminality; Guerrero assumed a racial link as well.

Demographics, especially surplus labor, proved a different kind of incentive to criminality. Adding a psychological twist to Ricardian wage theory, Guerrero insisted that "competition has obliged [the Mexican worker] to continually undervalue his work and to surrender to the demands of employment all the time not needed to satisfy animal necessities. He has been condemned to learn nothing in life outside his filthy hovel [pocilga] and his workplace; his intelligence has stagnated and his inferior position has rendered him unsuited for better work." Worse yet, the generational effects of lower-class living often caused intellectual and possibly physiological degeneration.[81] Again, this pessimistic interpretation argued against any immediate change in the moral status of the Mexican lower classes even in the face of major social reforms.

Like Macedo, Guerrero saw economic development as crucial to social reform and especially to a reordering of Mexico's class structure. Guerrero's analysis, however, went much further, as he plumbed the historical record for clues not just to class formation and economic development but to national morality. Like liberal social critics, Guerrero recognized the failings of irrational colonial institutions and their role in fostering criminal behavior. But the biggest failure of all he laid at the feet of post-independence liberals. "The great accomplishment of the liberal party in Mexico," he observed, "is the separation of Church and State; but its greatest error is the secularization of public instruction without replacing Catholic morality."[82] The "passive masses," Guerrero warned, required a strict morality even if based on fear of punishment rather than respect for human rights; the abstractions of Enlightenment liberalism, on the contrary, restrained only the elite few capable of grasping its subtleties.[83] In the hands of "skeptics and immoral metaphysicians," liberal doctrine encouraged "linguistic deceptions [*deshonestidades de lenguaje*] that ultimately result in the most abject depravity of orgies and crime."[84] Predisposed by the "unnerving" air, the endemic use of stimulants, and the frustrations of "an eternal and unrewarding struggle for life," the deterioration of Mexican morals had unleashed an atavistic culture of violence. "After ten generations," Guerrero lamented, "in the bosoms of some of our compatriots, the barbarous soul of the worshipers of Huitzilopoztli beats anew."[85]

Guerrero painted a devastating portrait of national degeneration, a result of the political chaos that followed independence. "People became smaller and thinner," he observed: "horses were less robust, donkeys weaker, livestock less corpulent. A flock of sheep, a brood of chickens, a hutch of rabbits . . . produced half the nourishment of their European or North American counterparts. Even plants felt the devastating hurricane of this cursed war: the vegetables of the Valley of Mexico became less savory, the fruit less sweet, and the flowers less luxuriant and fragrant. The destructive breath that spelled death for the scattered remnants of the colony penetrated even the flower blossoms; and just as it poured out the lives of men in rivers of blood, it killed the source of vigor [*lozanía*] and idealized love [*idilios*] in the *pollen* of

flowers."[86] This exaggerated biological decline paralleled the degeneration of Mexican society—a degeneration especially noticeable, according to Guerrero, in the mestizo urban lower classes.[87]

Macedo's class analysis had been vague and based principally on un-
specified public opinion—the upper classes felt safe, the lower classes
threatened by intra-class violence. Guerrero, on the other hand, developed a more systematic class typology "based on the *private life* of individuals." The four basic categories began with "promiscuous sexual relations accompanied by sterility or the rapid extinction of the lineage"
followed by "polyandry (multiple mates) with the extinction of paternal
rights [*patria potestad*] . . . polygamy with its jealousies . . . and finally
monogamy."[88] These categories of sexual relations were directly linked
to class status. Strongly influenced by French "environmental" criminology and naturalist literary tradition, Guerrero's vivid description of
Mexico City street people was doubtless intended to inspire in his readers pity, revulsion, and even fear:

> Unhappy men and women that lack a normal, secure means of subsistence:
> they live in the streets and sleep in public dormitories; huddled in vestibules,
> in doorways, in the trash of houses under construction, in some tavern if they
> can afford three or four centavos to sleep on the floor, or put up in the house
> of some relative or friend. They are beggars, trash pickers, paper gatherers,
> grease skimmers [*seberas*], ragpickers [*hilacheras*], dishwashers [*fregonas*],
> etc. . . . They are dressed in tatters, they scratch incessantly, and their matted
> hair is covered with the dust and mud of all the barrios of the city. . . . Gener-
> ally they fail to reach old age but a precocious decrepitude, consumed by
> syphilis, misery, pulque and mescal. . . . They have lost all control of their
> lives; their language is of the tavern: they live in sexual promiscuity, they ine-
> briate themselves daily, . . . they quarrel and are the principal instigators of
> scandal; they form the traditional *lépero* class of Mexico; from their bosom
> petty thieves are recruited and they are hidden perpetrators of serious
> crimes. Insensible to moral suffering, indifferent to physical deprivation and
> pain, and little responsive to pleasure, . . . they are indifferent to other's feel-
> ings and egotistical after the fashion of animals. . . . They constitute the
> dregs of the productive classes and serve as an indicator of the vortex of vice
> into which civilization's disinherited sink.[89]

The high bourgeoisie, on the other hand, were characterized by "the
honesty of their language and private habits" and their strong family
values including respected fathers, self-sacrificing mothers ("lo que
sobre todo las carateriza es un altruísmo inagotable"), and obedient

children.[90] For Guerrero, then, the bourgeois family represented the pinnacle of "the natural evolution of civilized man and a necessary condition for true civilization," a fragile condition dangerously threatened by the propagation of degenerate lower-class sexual mores.[91] Once again the mestizo lower classes were the objects of great sympathy and greater fear. To the existing mix, evolutionary science had added concerns about their role in national degeneration.

### Studying the Criminal

In Carlos Roumagnac's 1904 *Los criminales en México* this amorphous, degenerate, mestizo lower class took on individual characteristics. Like most of his colleagues, Roumagnac saw Mexico as fertile ground for criminological study by "our jurists, doctors and psychologists." Echoing Macedo, for example, he insisted on the need for more and better crime statistics "not only by years, but by months . . . by days and even by hours."[92] Further, he advocated the careful study of "the influence of heredity, upbringing [*educación*], and environment on the individual criminal or delinquent."[93] Only by examining individual criminals, he argued, could a specially trained cadre of criminologists hope to understand and thus combat the hidden "virus that sooner or later must blossom into the bitter buds of crime."[94] Thus, as a sometime police inspector and self-described amateur criminologist, Roumagnac promoted and justified criminology's pretensions to disciplinary status as a socially necessary, distinct, and scientific profession.[95]

Within the aspiring discipline itself, his positivist methodology sought both to modify the criminological theories and typologies of foreign criminologists to suit Mexico's unique situation and to test the broad generalizations of Mexican criminologists like Macedo and Guerrero on individual delinquents.[96] Borrowing heavily from Italian criminologist Enrico Ferri, Roumagnac adopted a typology for categorizing criminals based on the underlying causes of their criminality: heredity (*influencia de raza*), environment (*influencia de medio*), or circumstance (*influencia de momento*).[97] The first group included "born" criminals who were physiologically abnormal as a result of "atavism, heredity, or congenital disease." The second comprised "habitual" criminals suffering from "lack of education, having been raised in a vicious or diseased environment, bad examples, and/or contact with other damaged beings [*seres dañados*]." The third and least dangerous group, "incidental" criminals, were those who merely responded to "the pressure of an isolated incident." Linked to each criminal type was a corrective strategy: isolation for the "born" criminals and a variety of repressive and preventive measures for the others who were "perhaps capable of regeneration."[98] This proposed typology thus provided a scientific standard for categorizing criminals that served the dual purpose of modernizing the criminal-justice system and making criminologists—who presumably understood the subtleties of typing—indispensable.

Aside from his professional interest in adapting imported criminal typologies, Roumagnac was a typical Porfirian criminologist. Thus, in spite of an obvious debt to Ferri, he favored an eclectic approach that compared and contrasted prominent foreign criminologists without regard for nationality or theoretical persuasion. "Which is the best of these classifications," he asked rhetorically at the end of his exhaustive review, "is not for me to say."[99] Roumagnac reiterated other standard themes as well: physically and morally abandoned children, corrupting prisons, debilitating poverty, and especially the link between alcohol consumption and criminality. The principal cause of crime, he warned, was "the progressive and devastating poisoning of all our classes by alcohol."[100] Not only did alcohol undermine reason and stimulate the passions, thereby encouraging criminal behavior, but it poisoned future generations who often acquired the degenerate characteristics of their alcoholic parents.[101] Alcohol abuse thus contributed both psychologically and physiologically to crime and especially to recidivism, the bête noire of a Porfirian police inspector.[102]

Roumagnac's special contribution to Porfirian criminology centered around his detailed "observations" of individual Mexican criminals. Based on police reports, trial transcripts, prison records, newspaper accounts, and extensive personal interviews conducted during incarceration, these observations attempted to describe and quantify the many different characteristics that comprised individual criminality. These characteristics ranged from careful physical measurements to fairly subjective description—"whether the face is attractive or ugly . . . the expression lively or intelligent, apathetic or brutal, sad or happy, good or bad." Also included were distinguishing marks (tattoos, scars, etc.), parentage, upbringing, medical history, current situation, personal habits, character, motives for committing the crime, criminal methods, state of mind after the crime, attitude toward incarceration, and relationships with other prisoners. The criminologist's curiosity was seemingly inexhaustible and undeniably intrusive.[103] In this context even a seemingly innocuous attribute, a tattoo or a family history of epilepsy, was often construed as an indicator of deeply ingrained criminal tendencies. And other attributes—physical descriptions, family background, personal habits—clearly reflected and implicated the observed criminal's class and race. Like his Porfirian predecessors, Roumagnac's purportedly scientific data set thus amply reinforced existing elite concerns about everything from racial degeneration to generalized lower-class criminality. Further, his observations put individual faces (including photographs) to these concerns.[104]

The unsystematic nature of Porfirian criminology makes generalization difficult. On the surface each criminologist was distinct: different issues presented, different methodologies employed, different audiences addressed, different styles adopted. Three (Zayas, Verdugo, Macedo) were lawyers, two (Zayas, Roumagnac) worked as journalists, one (Martínez) was a doctor, another (Roumagnac) a police inspector, yet another (Macedo) an influential policymaker. These multifaceted criminologists utilized various scientific fields of inquiry including forensic medicine, statistics, meteorology, psychology (social and individual), and psychiatry. Some (Zayas, Guerrero, Roumagnac) had mastered multiple literary styles including journalistic sensationalism and poetic description; others took a resolutely scientific (Martínez and Vergara) or legalistic (Verdugo) approach. Some focused on the causes of criminal behavior, some on the attributes of criminality, others on the consequences of crime.

In spite of considerable differences among its practitioners, however, modern Mexican criminology had begun to take on recognizable contours. All the Porfirian criminologists, except perhaps Zayas, were avowed nationalists concerned about Mexican crime and thus about the need for a specialized Mexican criminology. Most adopted an eclectic approach.[105] The vigorous debate in European criminology between hereditarians like the Italian Cesare Lombroso, who stressed the physiological anomalies of individual criminals, and environmentalists like French criminologist Gabriel Tarde, who saw milieu as the principal cause of crime, lost much of its acrimony in Mexico, where national pride provided no incentive for intransigence.

Science, especially evolutionary science, established a common ground for Mexican criminology. While earlier classical criminologists had been unable to reconcile the egalitarian principles of early liberalism with persisting elite anxieties about lower-class criminality, the Porfirians deployed scientific arguments that naturalized and legitimized these concerns. In these texts criminality transcended the individual criminal and became a reified attribute of mestizo lower-class culture that might manifest itself in anything from physical deformities (real or imagined) to the lack of family life. The tendency to damn the lower classes by association was nothing new; the integration of scientific discourse, however, lent credence to elite fears about lower-class violence, to developmentalist concerns about lower-class laziness, to traditional anxiety about race mixture, to Social Darwinist warnings about national degeneration. *Puro* liberalism with its universalist message and reformist pretensions had coexisted uneasily with the obvious class and racial biases, the fundamental inequalities, that underlay these assumptions. Positivist science resolved that difficulty.

No longer an unacknowledged subtext, elite visions of lower-class criminality—whether generalized as with Guerrero or personalized by Roumagnac—thus became the foundation for a demarcation of the boundaries of national citizenship. Criminality threatened order, threatened progress, threatened Mexico, and its growing presence especially in the urban lower classes clearly warranted repression.[106] For the majority who continued to endorse classic liberal reforms—secular education, modern prisons, economic development—repression might precede the right to citizenship; for those few who espoused a more deterministic position, effective repression was a permanent solution. Either way, the scientifically proven criminality of the mestizo lower classes permitted their exclusion, at least discursively, from active participation in the national project. In practical terms this meant exploitation and repression.

A decade of revolution followed by a decade of political consolidation supplied few opportunities to consolidate a criminological paradigm. By the 1930s, however, Mexican criminologists had begun to develop a coherent scientific community with standardized training at the university level, a professional organization, La Academia Mexicana de Ciencias Penales (1932), and Latin America's most prominent professional journal, *Criminalia* (1933).[107] The influx of internationally renowned Spanish criminologists fleeing the Franco regime after 1939 further solidified Mexican criminology, strengthening its ties to the larger international community and increasing the prestige of its training programs. By the 1940s, then, Mexican criminology seemed a mature scientifically grounded discipline fostered by a thriving community of well-trained, committed criminologists.

In spite of its idiosyncrasies, Porfirian criminology had provided the foundation for a mature Mexican criminological paradigm. Later professional practitioners, criminologists by training rather than just by predilection or self-identification, absorbed and adapted its distinct styles, different scientific orientations, and various methodologies to the requirements of a recognized "scientific" discipline of criminology. Some criminologists still measured skulls, while others investigated the culture of crime. Some still took a popular, journalistic approach, while others protected their professional space with an obfuscating scientific discourse. Criminological studies still intersected with a wide range of other sciences: medicine, statistics, psychology, psychiatry, even meteorology. Post-revolutionary Mexican criminologists, many of whom had received their training in Europe (generally Spain), eagerly adopted new methodologies like biotyping or new theories like Freudian psychology. But the application of these new methods to Mexican "reality" relied on an existing tradition of social analysis that guaranteed a considerable degree of perceptual continuity.

The persistence of nineteenth-century constructions of lower-class criminality made this continuity particularly evident. Modern Mexican criminologists generally respected the social boundaries delimited by their pre-revolutionary predecessors. In spite of an acknowledged revolutionary commitment to social justice, criminality continued to represent an important analytical category, and presuppositions about the lower classes' criminality persisted as well. Although the overt racism of Martínez, Vergara, and Guerrero had disappeared, racist assumptions lingered covertly in criminological discourse. Elite anxieties about the lower classes, however, which had been further legitimized by a professionalized Mexican criminology, continued undisturbed; so did the exclusion of the lower class from active participation in Mexican society. In spite of revolutionary rhetoric, paternalistic, top-down reform of the socially dysfunctional lower classes was still the only conceivable solution.

# ULAR CRIMINOLOGY

The Female Offender

La mujer es una pera
Que en el árbol está dura
Cuando se cae de madura
La coge el que no la espera
Y goza de su hermosura – Mexican Popular Song

The criminality of a people [*pueblo*] is not only in the great crimes that touch an entire society: it is all those small and repeated antisocial acts that, at times, can suppose more perversity and certainly more regularity and thus greater danger. – Carlos Roumagnac, *La estadística criminal en México*

In mid-September 1897, at the height of the Porfiriato, a Federal District court convicted Mexico City prostitute María Villa of murdering her professional colleague and rival in love, Esperanza Gutiérrez.[1] In her prison diary María lamented the harshness of her twenty-year sentence, the maximum penalty for premeditated homicide by a woman. "My God! My God!" she wrote, "What will become of me? . . . It's true that I'm a criminal but, as God is my witness, I don't merit this punishment. I didn't really mean to do it; I never planned to take Esperanza's life. Why do they punish me so cruelly and hurl at me all the rigor of the law?"

María had grounds for complaint. Legal authorities typically treated men and women convicted of crimes of passion leniently, regarding them as temporarily deranged lovers or spouses who represented little danger to society.[2] Unusually harsh, María's punishment testified to a growing concern about female criminality among Porfirian elites, whose optimistic dreams of progress were haunted by the specter of national degeneration.[3] That the Mexico City press had made her case something of a cause célèbre in the six months preceding her sentencing demonstrates the depth of this concern.

Interest in María's case persisted. Five years after her conviction prominent Mexican criminologist, police inspector, and journalist Carlos Roumagnac interviewed María in prison, incorporating her story, along with the stories of fifteen other women, into his discussion of Mexican criminals, *Los criminales en México*. Intended to attract a general readership to the new science of criminology, these stories of female delinquents offer a revealing glimpse of the ideologically charged foundations of turn-of-the-century elite discourse about the criminality of women.

Latin American elite concerns about female criminality have recently become the focus of considerable scholarly attention.[4] Studies on the topic, however, have concentrated almost exclusively on the innovative content of elite discourse (when they have addressed elite discourse at all), often marginalizing its more traditional elements and generally ignoring its formal characteristics.[5] Although the need to synthesize numerous texts makes this approach unavoidable, it nevertheless runs the risk of being too selective. This selectivity results in two related problems. First, the focus on innovative aspects of elite discourse often creates a compelling periodization (i.e., positivism supplants liberalism) that misses or downplays fundamental discursive continuities—continuities crucial to the acceptance of new ideas.[6] Second, juxtaposing quotations from diverse texts overlooks the narrative techniques that bind together these disparate discursive strands, even though it is this very binding process that produces the essential illusion of coherence that allows discourse to function as ideology. The much-used technique of winnowing relevant quotations without regard for their narrative context thus limits, distorts, or even misrepresents the discursive field.

Effective representation of a complex, ideologically charged discourse like criminology requires a reasonably accurate portrayal of all its constituent elements. This level of analysis can only come from the close reading of a single text. That reading must take into account not only the complementary and contradictory discursive strands that comprise criminology but also the role of form in binding these strands together into a coherent narrative. The following analysis of Carlos Roumagnac's *Los criminales en México* seeks then to broaden standard interpretations of late-nineteenth-century elite discourse on crime by demonstrating the dialectical interplay between form and content in

Porfirian criminology—the methodology behind a "new" vision of female criminality.

Modernity in Mexico (as elsewhere) was a heavily gendered project. Social reformers were principally concerned with men, who—once they were cured of corporate loyalties and chronic alcoholism—would become the patriotic citizens and disciplined workers of the new Mexican nation-state. Nevertheless, women, as the supportive wives, mothers, and daughters of male citizens, played a crucial role in this projected social transformation. Supportive women, reformers hypothesized, would provide a spiritual and moral (but not political or economic) center for the "modern" Mexican family, engendering in their menfolks new loyalties that would complement the demands of national citizenship and wean them from unpatriotic corporate and clientist ties. Reformers also argued that exposure to the civilizing influence of women within the nurturing bosom of the family would supplant the disruptive influence of the public tavern, thus reducing male violence and alcoholism.[7] Female criminality subverted this idealistic vision, as delinquent women by definition shirked their duties to family and nation.

The accelerated modernization efforts of the Díaz regime intensified elite anxieties about female criminality. Like their predecessors, Porfirian elites saw modern families anchored by morally irreproachable mothers, wives, and daughters as a crucial support system for productive male workers and citizens. They also readily acknowledged the fact that delinquent women undermined national progress. The Social Darwinian subtext of the regime's dominant positivist discourse exacerbated these concerns. Women, especially mothers, symbolized national fertility. And, as women performed vital reproductive and civilizing functions in Porfirian social engineering, their transgressions threatened Mexico's biological and moral survival in the international "struggle for life."[8] Not surprisingly, then, Porfirian attempts at social reconstruction prompted a retracing of the social boundaries of acceptable female behavior—boundaries semiotically inscribed on the bodies and souls of Roumagnac's sixteen female offenders.

### The "Compleat" Criminologist

Roumagnac began *Los criminales en México* modestly enough, with the caveat that "I harbor no pretensions about presenting [the public] a scientific work," and identified himself as a mere "aficionado" of criminology.[9] The exhaustive scholarly review of contemporary European criminology that followed this disclaimer, however, testified to his disingenuousness. In fact, this casual, self-deprecating renunciation of his own readily apparent expertise disguised an ulterior motive: attracting a general audience. Despite the Porfirian obsession with crime and criminality, the pedantic treatises of late nineteenth-century Mexican criminologists with their endless statistics, anatomical jargon, and elaborate measurements had done little to disseminate new ideas about crime and criminals. The stage was set for a popularizer, for someone who could convey basic criminological concepts along with their attendant ideological baggage to an uninitiated if eager reading public.

Roumagnac was admirably suited to the task. As a specialized intellectual working in the new field of criminology, he reflected and articulated the concerns of Mexican elites about disciplining a complex, heterogeneous society in the throes of modernity.[10] Desperate to overcome a post-independence legacy of political chaos and economic stagnation, Mexican policymakers had eagerly sought out new technologies of power and social control. These included institutional improvements like modern police techniques and penitentiaries as well as discursive strategies like penology and criminology. Such discursive strategies helped elite policymakers construct (or reconstruct) notions of punishment and criminality that would delimit the social boundaries of a future, more cohesive Mexican nation-state. Efforts to import these modern technologies had accelerated with the accession of Porfirio Díaz in 1876.[11] As a Mexico City police inspector and criminologist, Roumagnac figured prominently in the theorization and implementation of Porfirian social engineering.

It was his other attributes, however, that especially qualified him to proselytize the new gospel of crime and citizenship. Translator of French literature (the plays of Maeterlinck), coauthor of the *Diccionario de geografía, historia y biografía mexicana* (he wrote the articles on geography), and prominent member of the prestigious Sociedad Mexicana de Geografía y Estadística, Roumagnac moved in the highest circles of the Porfirian científico elite.[12] Not surprisingly, *Los criminales en México* carried a dedication to his patron and fellow científico, Vice President Ramón Corral. Extensive experience as a professional journalist who reported on everything from high culture to low crime nicely complemented his status as a scientifically inclined intellectual. And, it was this mastery of the symbolic languages of science, moral reform, literature, and sensationalist journalism that made his work a particularly effective vehicle for the transmission of new ideas about female criminality.[13]

But Roumagnac offered far more than a popular application of scientific principles to the old problem of female criminality. He used his technical mastery of various symbolic languages to weave scientific criminology into a fabric of existing concerns, many dating back to the colonial period, about women's place in Mexican society. In fact, the strength of his synthesis lay primarily in his literary abilities and in his willingness to tell a good story. These abilities facilitated the successful integration of traditional discourses and new "scientific" notions of criminality that reassured uninitiated, possibly skeptical readers, thereby enhancing the ideological potential of the text. As his introductory disclaimer implies, Roumagnac's contribution to Porfirian criminology resided in his narrative skills rather than in his science.

### Narrative Structure

Roumagnac's successful integration of new and traditional concerns was the product of a complex, if not entirely self-conscious, narrative technique. This methodology enabled him to unify diverse structural, symbolic, and linguistic elements under the general theme of female delinquency. These different elements worked together to produce his particular (re)construction of female criminality.

The individual "observations" of each subject formed the basic narrative unit. Structural divisions within these observations highlighted different aspects of each woman's criminality. In each of the sixteen observations Roumagnac employed a simple three-part structure. Each section supplied a different data set—administrative, historical, scientific—and each served a different narrative function. These sections also made it easy for the reader to distinguish between women and to compare their stories. More important, each section also contributed descriptive subtexts regarding race, class, and sexuality that, taken collectively, identified a "typical" female delinquent.

Each observation began with a standard administrative section designed to locate the subject within both the criminal-justice system and Mexican society. Much like census data, this administrative description included the subject's age, birthplace, current residence, marital status, occupation, level of education, and crime. For example, Roumagnac informed readers that convicted murderer María V. was a twenty-eight-year-old unmarried Mexico City prostitute born in San Pedro, Jalisco, who had "received some instruction and good examples" during her five years in a Guadalajara orphanage.[14] Aside from the notoriety of her crime, María was typical of Roumagnac's sixteen subjects. Most were unmarried lower-class women between twenty and forty years old, with little or no schooling. The only exception was a relatively well-educated, legally married sales clerk who emphatically and atypically denied committing the homicide for which she had been incarcerated. Half the women had migrated to Mexico City, usually from neighboring provincial capitals. All had worked for wages in the public sphere as prostitutes, domestics, laundresses, seamstresses, clerks, or *tortilleras*.[15] Matter-of-fact and neutral in tone, these administrative descriptions instantly revealed the subject's class standing in Mexican society and alerted readers to the criminal potential of lower-class women.

Having socially located his subject, Roumagnac provided an extensive historical description, using the crime that had resulted in incarceration as the central narrative focus. This historical section comprised five subsections: family history, personal history, history of the crime, prison history, and future plans. Each subsection provided a piece of the larger puzzle, producing a seemingly thorough account of each woman's descent into criminality that served to illuminate both particular circumstance and general process.

The family histories explored the class status, medical history, and moral state of each woman's immediate family. For example, María's father was a "self-employed worker" [*empleado particular*] who died of pneumonia at age seventy-five and who "was always healthy and led a well-ordered life." Her mother died of tuberculosis at age twenty-nine, leaving behind nine-year-old María and two healthy older children. María's maternal grandmother had also died of tuberculosis. Most of the other women were considerably less fortunate, with family histories of epilepsy and abusive, chronically alcoholic parents. These genealogies supplemented the administrative descriptions, providing additional, specifically historical indicators of class and background. They also exposed typically positivistic concerns about lower-class degeneration, the physical and moral weaknesses of lower-class parents seeming to condemn their daughters to a life of crime.

Personal histories reinforced these conclusions. As the most "notorious" of Roumagnac's subjects, María had a personal history more detailed than those of the others, although without fundamental differences. Again, Roumagnac provided his readers a brief medical history.

He noted that María had smallpox at age six or seven, yellow fever two years later. She had a history of migraines, wet the bed until she was eleven, and at the time of her observation suffered from a spastic upper colon that often required hospitalization. He also paid considerable attention to the formation of her character: her education in a Guadalajara orphanage; her sexual initiation at age thirteen by her patron's twenty-two-year-old son, her introduction to prostitution at age fifteen by a Mexico City madam on a recruiting trip, her three years as the mistress of a German, which ended when he surprised her in the arms of another man, her introduction to morphine, her experiments with homosexual activities (safismo). As in the family histories, Roumagnac conflated biological and moral degeneration, implying a deliberately ambiguous and mutually reinforcing causal nexus that harbored a number of interpretive possibilities. But regardless of whether readers saw these histories as evidence of physiological, environmental, or moral pollution, they could hardly fail to grasp the underlying message about the degenerative nature of lower-class life. Coupled with the family genealogical data, the evidence seemed irrefutable in its science and overwhelming in its sheer volume.

As the denouement to these histories, events leading up to and including the crime itself occupied the central place in each observation. These defining events, retold in classic you-were-there journalese, supplied both narrative focus and dramatic interest. In addition to the specifics of the crime, Roumagnac included snippets of dialogue, personal observations, and a plethora of seemingly insignificant details all designed to lend ambiance and credibility to his account. His recounting of the moment after Esperanza's murder, for example, adroitly placed his reader simultaneously at the scene of the crime, at María's trial, and at her interview with Roumagnac: "Esperanza G. collapsed mortally wounded and [María] V. adds that on seeing her fall she felt truly horrible, that she lost consciousness, that she could not even move, that she lost track of [Esperanza] and even failed to recall—a detail that she was unaware of until later at the trial—that the maid had reproached her, shouting: 'Wicked women, you have killed my mistress.'"[16] Thus Roumagnac the journalist titillated his readers with the sensational aspects of the murder, Roumagnac the policeman recounted the facts of the case, Roumagnac the criminologist noted possible indicators of criminality, and Roumagnac the moralist demonstrated with regret the wages of sin. The overall effect provided his readers entertainment, instruction, and numerous specific examples of degenerate lower-class behavior. This dramatic climax thus buttressed the underlying messages of the other, less exciting historical subsections by supplying the journalistic "hook" necessary to attract the casual reader.

The two final subsections, while anticlimatic, further refined these criminal portraits, focusing on the dangers of criminal dissimulation that sought to disguise the dangers of lower-class degeneracy. Roumagnac followed the reconstructed crime with a brief history of the subjects' prison experience. This section included a broad variety of information about each woman's medical problems, sexual practices, prison status, and general comportment. He recounted, for example, that prison officials had dismissed María from her job in the prison tobacco shop for "bad conduct," that she admitted to having "purely Platonic" relations with two male prisoners, and that prison doctors were attempting unsuccessfully to treat her morphine addiction. He also showed great interest in possible homosexual activities among incarcerated women. He commented that María "did not wish to confess—notwithstanding that all reports suggest the contrary—that she engaged in homosexual acts [practica el safismo] with her fellow prisoners or that she had ever seen it done, although she was aware that this vice was prevalent because of fights she had witnessed between the other women."[17] Another woman had observed fellow inmates "kissing, embracing and nibbling" each other and informed her inquisitor that women who parted their hair on the right side were "men."[18] Yet another subject had been accused of kidnapping and seducing a fifteen-year-old girl, a charge she vigorously denied.[19] In fact Roumagnac systematically questioned each of his subjects about "safismo," evoking nearly identical responses. He reacted to these denials with cynicism, implying a hidden affinity between criminality and homosexual activity that his subjects recognized but deliberately sought to conceal.[20] That prostitutes like María had doubtless developed considerable skill at feigning sexual pleasure corroborated these fears of deception. Roumagnac thus conflated social and sexual "deviance," which he then linked to a conspiratorial criminal mentality that cleverly dissimulated efforts to undermine Mexican social development by blurring social boundaries even as elites attempted to clarify them. And, on a more obvious level, these inquiries joined sensationalism and scientific investigation in a manner that enlivened the narrative and titillated the reader while disguising, to a certain extent, its pornographic attractions.

Roumagnac concluded his histories with a brief comment on future plans that supplemented his image of dissimulating women. This is the least-developed section of his narratives and was often omitted. In María's case, he noted only that "her intentions are to completely rehabilitate herself [*regenerarse*], lead an ordered life and if God permits her to leave prison alive, to give up vice and dedicate herself to work."[21] The concerns of the criminologist (rehabilitation), policeman (ordered life), moralist (if God . . . give up vice), and social reformer (dedicate herself to work) were all deliberately addressed in this brief statement. After a few years in the Mexican criminal-justice system María had clearly mastered, if not internalized, the new criminological discourse. In Roumagnac's jaded estimation, however, these promises were either duplicitous or naïve, and he often juxtaposed them with footnotes documenting subsequent arrests. As before, this duplicity signaled a strong affinity between criminality and dissimulation.

The image of female criminality that emerged from these histories reinforced class stereotypes implicit in the earlier administrative descriptions. These historical descriptions also served as genealogies of individual criminality, tracing the roots of each woman's criminal behavior while simultaneously identifying the biological and moral dangers of female delinquency in general. Supplementing this causal chain was a cautionary subtext that hinted at an unacknowledged conspiracy on the part of female delinquents to disguise the extent of their deviance and thus the seriousness of their threat to Mexican society. Roumagnac further implied that, because of their exposure to similar biological and environmental conditions, all urban lower-class women were potentially dangerous and probably untrustworthy.

Anxieties about race and especially race mixture or *mestizaje* surfaced in an appended third section, a scientific description of each subject based on the internationally recognized Bertillon system. Derived from the recommendations of Parisian police clerk Alphonse Bertillon, the system comprised a complex series of observations and measurements designed to provide foolproof identification of criminals (before fingerprints) so that repeat offenders (recidivists) could no longer avoid detection by merely adopting aliases or changing their fields of operation.[22] As with criminological narrative in general, the Bertillon system conflated "subjective" observation and "objective" measurement, although both data sets were ostensibly constructed to ensure uniform standards. Thus Roumagnac described María as having black hair, brown eyes, lightly pigmented skin, moles, scars from smallpox and gunshot wounds inflicted by her jealous German ex-lover, and no tattoos. At the same time he recorded that she was 1.506 meters tall, that her head was 0.172 meters long and 0.149 meters wide, and that her left middle finger measured 0.097 meters. Data also included measurements typical of criminal anthropology such as María's right ear and lobe, nose, forehead, and stature. Much of this data carried an interpretive subtext derived from physiological indicators of criminality or "stigmata" often unacknowledged by practitioners like Roumagnac. That many of these stigmata also carried racial implications likewise went unremarked, although even casual readers would have recognized broad noses, broad cheekbones, and inclined foreheads as typically "Indian" or associated tattooing with primitive "Africans." As a good Porfirian liberal, Roumagnac resisted the overt racism of criminal anthropologists. The Indian heritage of liberal hero Benito Juárez, and Porfirio Díaz's acknowledged *mestizaje*, probably encouraged circumspection. Bertillon measurements, however, conveniently buried vulgar racism under an avalanche of objective but nonetheless suggestive statistics. They also disclosed, at least theoretically, evidence of race mixture, a still-potent source of elite anxiety about blurred social boundaries with deep roots in the Mexican historical experience.[23] Racial ambivalence thus took its place alongside concerns about lower-class degeneracy and dissimulation in Roumagnac's histories.

Photographic images accompanied each of Roumagnac's observations, supplementing and reinforcing the written text. These images illustrated each section differently. The photograph as "mug shot" supported the administrative description by facilitating the subject's identification as a prisoner and potential recidivist. At the same time the photograph enriched the historical description by giving the subject a personal and social identity that included any obvious racial characteristics or class indicators. For example, María appears well groomed in a fancy ruffled dress and earrings, and she is gazing confidently at the camera. Another of Roumagnac's subjects, the young Inés T., who had been convicted of infanticide, appears disheveled. She has a matronly shawl draped around her shoulders, and her eyes are carefully diverted. Both women are clearly mestizas. María's attire reinforces her image as a prostitute, while Inés's shawl is typical of lower-class women of the time. In this historical context the photographic image seems to capture the subject's persona, reinforcing the author's personal description while tacitly illuminating his classist and racist subtexts.

Paired with the scientific description, however, the photograph intensifies the gaze of the observer/reader and depersonalizes the subject. The image becomes an x-ray, going beyond superficial appearances to uncover, along with the Bertillon measurements, the hidden physical stigmata of criminality. The photograph is thus transformed from identifying image to social locator to an intrusive technology of power that strips away the subject's personal and social identities, turning her into an object of scientific study and analysis.[24] That photographic images made explicit the racial as well as the criminal implications of measured stigmata greatly enhanced the credibility of both.

Taken collectively, Roumagnac's tripartite observations, reinforced by photographic images, facilitated a complex reconstruction of female criminality. This reconstruction logically reflected Porfirian anxieties about race, class, sexuality, and gender. It sought to dispel the shadows surrounding lower-class degeneracy by illuminating the historical roots, physiological stigmata, and moral dissimulations of female criminals. It also told a good story, filled with dramatic climaxes and pseudo-pornographic innuendos. As with all effective ideologies, form and content, entertainment and propaganda operated hand in hand.

## Symbolic Languages

Woven into the formal narrative are the complementary and sometimes contradictory symbolic languages of criminal science, moral reform, and journalistic sensationalism. Complementing the formal narrative, these symbolic languages reinforce the ideological impact of the text by legitimizing elite anxieties with imported science, providing the reader multiple points of entry into the narrative, and accommodating a variety of interpretive agendas. Traditional concerns buttressed new science; new science validated traditional concerns. As with the narrative structure, the different elements (symbolic languages, in this case) functioned dialectically to bind new and traditional discourses in an ideologically potent rearticulation of elite concerns about lower-class female criminality.

Not surprisingly in an avowedly criminological work, the symbolic language of science occupied the most prominent place. In spite of his introductory disavowal, Roumagnac's subtitle, "an essay in criminal psychology," betrayed the serious side of his study. And, in an extensive introduction, he guided the lay reader through a reasonably thorough review of contemporary European criminology. He even acknowledged disagreements within the field, especially between Italian criminal anthropologists like Cesare Lombroso and French environmental criminologists like Gabriel Tarde.

Roumagnac refused to commit to either school, electing instead to provide data for both. Lombrosian criminal anthropologists were informed of congenital diseases like epilepsy or María's chronic migraines, which comprised the behavioral stigmata of born criminals, and were provided with the Bertillon data (reinforced by photographic images), which provided empirical evidence of anomalies like small skulls, sloping foreheads, broad noses, and jutting jaws, which they invariably associated with atavism, or biological regression to a less evolved racial type. At the same time Roumagnac supplied the Tardian environmentalists with evidence of a polluted milieu that included chronic alcoholism, drug use, and debilitating diseases like María's tuberculosis. That the two schools of criminology often used the same data to buttress their competing etiologies facilitated Roumagnac's pragmatic approach.

While the symbolic language of science reflected criminologists' specialized concerns and validated elite concerns about criminality, the symbolic language of moral reform supplied the normative values that defined proper female behavior. This older moral-reform discourse complemented many aspects of positivist criminology (especially Tardian environmentalism) in spite of its traditional commitment to individual "free will" as the principal cause of crime. Long before the advent of scientific criminology, moral reformers had decried the debilitating effects of alcoholism, especially on the Mexican lower classes, linking it directly to increased crime rates. In their colonial guise, concerns about alcoholism and crime revolved around the religious notion of sin, while later liberal reformers linked these concerns to a new set of normative values centered on post-Enlightenment notions of citizenship and social responsibility.[25] By the end of the colonial period women figured prominently in moral reform discourse as nurturers and educators of male citizens whose familial and civic obligations were incompatible with the moral and physical debilitation associated with alcoholism.

This nineteenth-century moral reform discourse permeated Roumagnac's observations. For example, increased alcohol consumption exacerbated by morphine addiction played a major role in María's personal descent into criminality. In other observations, Roumagnac presented alcoholism as a family trait, passed on from alcoholic parents, especially mothers, to their criminally inclined children. By failing to fulfill their familial obligations, he suggested, alcoholic women, like female delinquents, undermined Mexican society. Characteristically, Roumagnac left unresolved the question of whether environmental or biological factors ultimately determined familial alcoholism. He also failed to resolve the controversial issue of personal responsibility that was fundamental to earlier religious and liberal constructions of criminality. This deliberate ambiguity permitted the reader to see alcoholic lower-class women as inherently degenerate, which might justify their continued exploitation and isolation in prisons or as candidates for serious and usually coercive rehabilitation that would transform them into responsible wives and mothers. Either way, their unsuitability for citizenship was clear.

This moralistic agenda also prompted Roumagnac to inquire into his subjects' religious feelings. He quizzed some women extensively about their possible repentance, noting that most had little real grasp of religious concepts. Of María, who was educated by nuns in a Guadalajara orphanage, he noted that "she told me that she was a Catholic and that before becoming a prostitute she was practically a fanatic. She conceives of God as all powerful and believes that if he failed to stop her crime, it was because at that moment 'the devil won out.' . . . She is very superstitious. She believes that a broken mirror or spilled salt predicts a grave calamity."[26] Hardly surprising coming from a liberal científico was the implication that the Catholic Church had failed in its fundamental mission to oversee the spiritual and moral well-being of Mexican women. Encouraged by a self-serving church, Roumagnac suggested, women's fanaticism often fueled future criminal behavior.

This exposé of the Catholic Church was closely tied to traditional liberal concerns about lower-class education. Since the mid-eighteenth century liberal reformers had insisted that only widespread access to secular, popular education could properly inculcate modern values of citizenship and work discipline. And, as mothers and teachers of male citizens, women played an important, albeit circumscribed, role in education reform. Under the Díaz regime reformers like education minister Justo Sierra had undertaken serious if limited efforts to reform Mexican education.[27]

Not surprisingly, Sierra's fellow científico, Roumagnac, shared his concern, citing lack of education as instrumental in the failure of many of his subjects to resist criminality. As before, he sought to have it both ways, denouncing Mexico's inadequate educational infrastructure while at the same time noting that many subjects had actively resisted educational opportunities first as children and later as prisoners. And again, this deliberate ambiguity, which implicated both individual criminals and society, allowed interpretative latitude that could serve to absolve those who favored exploitation, isolation, or coercive reform. It also stigmatized uneducated women as unpatriotic and potentially criminal, thus justifying negative social sanctions ranging from regulation to incarceration that might complement the positive efforts of education reformers like Sierra.

In tacit recognition of the essentially ideological purpose of the moral reform discourse, Roumagnac attempted to gauge his subjects' socialization by soliciting their views on the fairness of the criminal-justice system. Acknowledgment of the system's legitimacy by its transgressors would indicate its success in garnering the consent of the governed and in inculcating the duties of citizenship. Given the circumstances of the interview and the status of the interviewer it is hardly surprising that most women nominally accepted the legitimacy of their punishment, even when they considered it harsh. That Roumagnac would ask the question shows his awareness of the underlying ideological nature of both liberal and Porfirian moral reform.

To bind together the symbolic languages of science and morality Roumagnac proposed a physiological link between moral training and criminal biology. In his introductory review of modern European criminology he quoted an 1898 French study of the criminal "soul," which noted that a healthy brain, stimulated by moral training, transmitted from "neuron to neuron" restraining images that discouraged criminal behavior, while a dissipated brain (cerebro agotado), "whose neurons have lost flexibility of movement through habitual inertia" was unfit to take advantage of "the healthful notions deposited by education" and resist the criminal impulse.[28] Thus improper moral training stunted proper brain development, which unbalanced the central nervous system, which in turn failed to discourage the criminal impulses that a healthy brain resisted.[29] The model effectively linked scientific and moralistic agendas, providing science with a moral purpose and morality (retroactively) with a scientific foundation. It also subsumed the contra-

dictory notion of "free will" within an essentially deterministic explanation. Individuals were free to resist criminal impulses if they were exposed to appropriate environmental influences.

The concerns of earlier moral reformers thus figure prominently
throughout Roumagnac's narrative, reinforcing the leitmotif of inherent lower-class degeneracy and the compelling need for reform, and re-
capitulating late-nineteenth-century normative values. Science merely
confirmed a diagnosis reformers had known all along. At the same time,
with its ongoing promise that it would bring Mexico out of its "feudal"
past and ameliorate dislocations caused by that profound social transformation, the reformist agenda served its traditional function of legitimation. The symbolic languages of science and moral reform embedded in Roumagnac's text thus reinforced each other. Science revitalized
a moral reform agenda undermined by a century of failures, while the
promise of reform served to mitigate any dislocations caused by scientific modernization.

To spice up this rather bland mixture of science and moralism, Roumagnac borrowed heavily from the symbolic language of sensationalist
journalism. The gritty naturalism of late-nineteenth-century European
novelists like Emile Zola and Fyodor Dostoyevsky had found an echo in
the works of their Mexican counterparts.[30] Novels such as Federico
Gamboa's *Santa* appealed to a reading public fascinated by the perceived violence and illicit sexuality of the Mexico City underworld.[31] In
Zola and Gamboa the deceptive allure of secretly diseased prostitutes
admonished readers about the dangers of transgression. Roumagnac
targeted that same audience, even including graphic photographs of
hermaphrodites' genitalia in a gratuitous appendix. His subsequent
publication of a work dedicated specifically to sexual crimes and crimes
of passions further testified to his deliberate manipulation and exploitation of a reading public fascinated by criminal perversions.[32]

Like Roumagnac's repeated inquiries into homosexual activities, this
recurrent conflation of sexuality and criminality demonstrated deep-
seated elite anxiety about all activities that violated social norms. The
aberrant and ambiguous physiology of the hermaphrodite—or the
prostitute for that matter—thus functioned as a metaphor for the shifting social boundaries of Porfirian Mexico. By extension, subjecting
these aberrant bodies to scientific examination and the unblinking gaze
of the photographic image acknowledged the Porfirian commitment to
locating those boundaries—at least in a metaphorical sense—on the

bodies of the socially disenfranchised. Moreover, these powerful images of degeneration, couched in the pseudo-pornographic idiom of sensationalist journalism that simultaneously titillated and bludgeoned the reader, stressed the sexually deviant nature of criminals. This conflation thus categorized criminals, including women, as essentially different from "normal" citizens—as a morally and biologically distinct criminal class.

Roumagnac also recognized the need to establish his credentials as a journalist. To this end, as proof of his expertise, he proffered an extensive glossary of "*lunfardo*," the slang of the Mexican underworld.[33] Providing the aliases of notorious criminals like María "la Chiquita" and her victim Esperanza "la Malagueña" reinforced this impression. And, within the observations, he enhanced the reader's sense of immediacy with snippets of dialogue between protagonists (i.e., María and Esperanza) or between interviewer and interviewee (i.e., María and Roumagnac). He also gave personal impressions of his subjects, describing them to his audience in a decidedly journalistic fashion. Of María, he noted that:

> She told me her history in a tranquil voice, without violent outbursts, demonstrating emotion only in the climactic passages. Nevertheless, I noted in her something the French call . . . *pose*; and, a detail that shows the inexorable presence of feminine coquetry: in our first interview, [María] presented herself to me as she doubtlessly was in her cell, unkempt and without decoration; while in subsequent [interviews] she dressed as best she could, putting a red ribbon in her hair, and on her hands and ears, the few and humble jewels that she still possessed.[34]

These bits of dialogue and personal impressions supplemented by photographs (and in María's case by fragments of her diary) reinforced the author's credibility as both criminologist and journalist. This credibility, in turn, encouraged the reader to accept other, less believable or familiar aspects of the text.

As part of this literary treatment Roumagnac routinely structured his observations around classic themes of betrayal and exploitation of unprotected women by trusted men, usually lovers or fathers. María, for example, was betrayed first at age thirteen by the son of her patron and later by her "handsome and adored" X. Other women suffered at the hands of alcoholic and abusive fathers. Each betrayal led these women farther from the protection of the patriarchal family and out into the "street," which since the colonial period had symbolized a woman's fall from grace into perdition and criminality.[35]

These moralistic tales, with their stress on individual circumstance, seemingly contradicted the scientific tone and deterministic explanations of criminology. In the face of this incongruity Roumagnac provided a linkage of sorts, arguing that modern novelists were universally recognized as acute observers and interpreters of the human condition and were thus unconscious masters of basic criminological techniques. Like Roumagnac himself, novelists recorded as discrete events the manifestations of a greater social malaise, the insights of artistic genius penetrating beneath superficial appearances to reveal the soft underbelly of nineteenth-century progress. The implied association with the great nineteenth- century novelists also added a touch of much-needed class to an often dull and occasionally sordid profession.

Ironically, while Mexican criminologists devoted considerable energy to carefully delimiting the social boundaries between citizenship and criminality, practitioners like Roumagnac consciously blurred the edges of their own discourse. In spite of a positivist criminology that ostensibly rejected liberal individualism in favor of environmental or biological explanations for crime, Roumagnac felt no compunction about resorting to melodramatic tales of heartless men and fallen women driven to crime by unlucky fate, uncontrollable lust, and unrequited love. Despite their unscientific character these narrative devices played to the expectations of the general reader of nineteenth-century romantic melodrama. That these stories also illuminated the sordidness of Mexican lower-class lifestyles further reinforced one of the text's principal themes.

The themes of the novelist, the journalist, the moralist, and the criminologist thus merged in Roumagnac's observations in spite of his warning that most "people of good will . . . know the delinquent only under the frightful and repugnant aspect conveyed by the novel and sensationalist reporting."[36] While careful to preserve a scientific veneer, Roumagnac hardly eschewed the sensationalism associated with criminality in the popular mind. In so doing he attracted a new, impressionable audience of general readers unwilling to wade through the ponderous criminologies of his more elitist or scrupulous colleagues. Once attracted, these general readers were reassured by a venerable moral reform tradition that reaffirmed existing normative values, and bedazzled by the validating brilliance of imported science. Roumagnac's successful manipulation of these different symbolic languages then vastly increased his potential audience and thus the ideological possibilities of his text.

### The Illusion of Coherence

To weave together the different sections and various symbolic languages that comprised an "observation," Roumagnac employed two distinct strategies, one architectural and the other linguistic.[37] These strategies facilitated the dialectical interplay between form and content, filling awkward spaces in the formal narrative and creating important linkages between the often-contradictory images and meanings embedded in different symbolic languages. These strategic sleights of hand represented the essential act of conjuring—the illusion of coherence—that realized the ideological potential of *Los criminales en México*.

First, Roumagnac employed three consecutive, overarching themes—the crime, the interview, the criminal—to unify the different sections and subsections that comprised each observation. The criminal, as the focal point of positivist criminology, generally served as the principal unifying theme: the administrative description of each subject blended almost imperceptibly into the historical descriptions of her family background, her life before prison, her crime, her life in prison, her future plans, while the Bertillon measurements and photographic images reaffirmed her administrative identity, meanwhile penetrating beneath the superficial impressions of even the most acute observer to reveal the quantifiable criminal within. These distinct narrative components became for the reader complementary images. Each portrait displayed a different facet of a single female subject.

Other unifying themes played a supporting role. The crime provided a dramatic climax to each observation, the moment when each woman's historical and biological development intersected with her defining criminal act. Roumagnac's genealogical approach to the criminal act justified the inclusion of any relevant data, including statistics that might illuminate its cause. The interview also served to integrate the narrative. For example, Roumagnac often highlighted the interview process by including the subject's verbatim responses to his questions and his personal impressions of the subject. These constant reminders not only provided the human interest (in both Roumagnac and his subject) essential to effective journalism but also made the mug shots and Bertillon measurements seem less extraneous to the narrative and more a part of the general prison experience, which included the interview itself. These overarching themes then drew together the disparate sections and subsections of each observation, imbuing them with a necessary coherence.

Second, Roumagnac integrated distinct symbolic languages, blurring distinctions between "subjective" observation (analysis) and "objective" facts (data). This blurring occurred at a number of levels. The previously mentioned juxtaposition of Bertillon measurements with melodramatic historical narrative represented perhaps the most egregious example. Roumagnac's description of the beginning stages of María's morphine addiction was considerably more subtle: "She quit injecting morphine for some time, but after she began her relationship with X. who was to play an unforgettable role in her existence, and when she began to quarrel with him, one of her companions insisted that she continue using morphine and she herself applied the injections, raising the dosage to two centigrams. The first night that she injected this quantity, she says that she felt very ill."[38] In this quotation, specific objective information—raising the dosage to two centigrams, for example—lent credence to this brief episode in Roumagnac's constructed narrative about María's descent into criminality. The objective data reinforced the work's scientific pretensions and added an element of gritty realism, while the dramatic narrative helped sell the importance and glamour of scientific police techniques within the context of a cautionary anecdote about the dangers of drug abuse.

Often the confusion of data and analysis depended on context rather than on direct juxtaposition. For example, the meaning of a stereotypical female characteristic like "sensitivity" often varied considerably. Roumagnac "objectively" classified María as one "of those criminals, that with Ferri we would have to call *passionnel*, and with Laurent, degenerate."[39] And, as proof of her excessive, degenerate passion, he included as data excerpts from her prison diary. In one entry, for example, she lamented that "I have had not one notice of X. My God! What could have happened to him? Doesn't he understand that now is when I need him most? Doesn't he understand that even one letter from him removes one of my poor heart's many spines? What will become of me? My God! I have no other consolation than to pray to God, the only one who can send me if not tranquility at least the resignation that I need, because I suffer greatly, greatly, my suffering has no limits."[40] For criminologists like Roumagnac, María's religiosity and capacity for love would have been typically feminine had she been a mother instead of a prostitute and the object of her affections a child rather than a unfaithful lover.[41] As it stood, however, her extreme passion exposed her criminality. Roumagnac's judgment was scientific in its typologies and presentation of raw data but moralistic in its condemnation of María's excessive passion; the boundary between the two interpretations, however, is far from clear. That he also implied a causal relation between her menstrual cycle and her crime is another indicator of this ambiguous duality.[42] According to this formulation María was an extreme example of the inherent instability of women, and her criminality was an extension (and perversion) of her femininity. Women were to feel, even to feel deeply, but without excessive passion.

Under such circumstances the context in which Roumagnac presented the subject's voice, María's diary, or the snippets of dialogue effectively subsumed its message. Rather than presenting their own versions of events, women in Roumagnac's narrative damned themselves in their own words, their melodramatic style constituting further evidence of their unstable natures.[43] In this conflation of data and analysis, their voices, reduced to little more than scientific data or journalistic ambiance by the literary machinations of their recorder, lost resonance. This reduction by conflation did, however, effectively link the symbolic languages of science, moralism, and yellow journalism. The meaning(s) of female sensitivity or María's diary extracts were deeply embedded in each of these languages. In these examples data and analysis became practically indistinguishable.

This blurring of objective data and subjective analysis also occurred simultaneously, with single words or images taking on multiple meanings. The case of Bertillon measurements, according to which even numbers carried considerable interpretive baggage, including a racist subtext, has already been noted. Medical terms also took on different meanings in different symbolic languages. For example, in addition to their medical significance, epilepsy, venereal diseases, and even tuberculosis might simultaneously signify biological inferiority, moral degradation, and the sexual danger (to men) of lower-class women.[44] These shifting images of disease also warned all women of the physical degeneration that invariably accompanied moral decline.

As with the other linguistic strategies, these multitextured images fostered a conscious ambiguity that allowed the reader considerable interpretive latitude. And the work's ideological potential was strengthened rather than diminished by this apparent flexibility that seemingly resolved potential objections by being all things to all readers. Thus Roumagnac, for example, never bothered to annotate or analyze his Bertillon data, which therefore signify the modernization of police techniques, the objectivity of science, or the racial degeneracy of lower-class Mexican women, depending on the reader or reading. That these multiple readings might be mutually exclusive—some meanings being biologically deterministic, others being dependent on environmental causation or even individual free will—bothered Roumagnac not at all. As scientific criminology, *Los criminales en México* might have had deep epistemological flaws, but its virtues were ideological rather than philosophical; its principal contribution was to Porfirian social engineering rather than to social science.

Aside from its admirable concision and technical mastery, Roumagnac's cleverly constructed criminology was fairly representative of late-nineteenth-century Porfirian police narratives. Criminal anthropologists often interrupted their seemingly endless litany of technical descriptions and anatomical measurements to deliver diatribes on the debilitating effects of alcohol on the morals and bodies of the Mexican lower classes. By the same token, environmentalists regularly cited elaborate physiological evidence, from medical terminology to statistics on atmospheric pressure, in support of their theories (see chapter 2). Both criminological schools shamelessly conflated scientific, moral, and sensationalistic agendas, just as Roumagnac had. Even secretariat of justice dossiers on convicted criminals employed a similar structure, which included administrative and historical descriptions taken from police reports (although they were generally without family background or medical histories) and, in some cases, elaborate Bertillon forms printed on expensive paper and complete with high-quality photographs. These raw materials awaited only the artist-criminologist's hand to bring them to life.

Precisely because *Los criminales en México* is typical, an understanding of Roumagnac's narrative techniques provides valuable insights into the foundation of elite male discourse about social boundaries in turn-of-the-century Mexico. Construed narrowly, the fundamental purpose of an ideologically charged discourse like criminology is to reinforce the legitimacy of a political regime, in this case the authoritarian regime of Porfirio Díaz. In a broader sense it legitimizes and even proselytizes the normative values of its generally elite practitioners. Success for either purpose, however, depends on persuasion rather than on authority. The prestige of a new science or a new political system exists not in a vacuum but within a social context, where it is often resisted. Criminology's roots in European science probably explain its attraction for Mexican intellectuals like Roumagnac, but its conversion into an effective ideology was hardly automatic. In this context an analysis of Roumagnac's methodology, the form and content of his criminological narrative, helps explain its attractions, at least for literate Mexicans.

For the historian of nineteenth-century Mexican elite culture the discursive continuities in Roumagnac's text are particularly intriguing. Rather than an "objective," scientific examination of female criminality, *Los criminales en México* is a culturally constructed text that uses the prestige of science to relegitimize and revitalize existing concerns about race mixture, "dangerous classes," deviant sexuality, and "fallen" women. According to Roumagnac's "observations," received notions of race, class, gender, and sexuality intersected with European criminological science to map out a new social landscape for Mexican women that often resembled more traditional topographies.

Roumagnac's text comprised a deliberately eclectic blend of modern criminologies, liberal-Porfirian social engineering, traditional religious imagery, and journalistic sensationalism. The "new" science of criminology was inextricably embedded in a rearticulation of traditional discourses about social control, which compromised any attempts at stylistic or epistemological clarity.[45] This eclecticism did permit, however, a broad variety of possible readings that could easily be adapted to different interpretive agendas, including traditional constructions of criminality familiar to a general reader. This flexibility, combined with Roumagnac's salacious journalistic style, attracted a broad audience to a difficult and often dull subject, facilitating acceptance of his reconstruction of the delinquent Mexican woman.

A variety of literary techniques provided this hodgepodge of complementary and sometimes conflicting explanations for female criminality with much-needed coherence and a pretense to objectivity.[46] By embedding elite anxieties about race, class, sexuality, and gender in different sections of his formal narrative; by conflating the symbolic languages of science, moral reform, and sensationalist journalism; by employing unifying themes like the criminal or the crime; by using ambiguous imagery; by simply telling a good story; Roumagnac managed the illusion of coherence. That illusion was crucial to his project. The manner in which he constructed his narrative reinforced his vision of female criminality and strengthened the ideological impact of his text.

Roumagnac's (re)construction of female criminality was a warning to Mexican men about personal and social dangers that lurked beneath the gilded veneer of Porfirian progress. It reinforced their anxieties about degenerate Mexican lower-class lifestyles, specifically those of lower-class, mestiza women and dissimulating female delinquents. Even as Porfirian modernization opened new possibilities for Mexican women, the texts of male elites reminded them of their new responsibilities, their new "place" in Mexican society.[47]

# 4. Revolutionary Reform

Capitalist Development,
Prison Reform, and
Executive Power

Todo cambiará en el futuro. – PLM program, 1906

On Christmas afternoon 1916 José Natividad Macías, still angry over the bitter credentials fight of three weeks earlier, addressed the Constitutional Convention at Querétaro for the first time. A prominent lawyer, national deputy under the three previous presidents, and coauthor of President Carranza's proposed constitution, Macías had declined for twenty-two long December afternoons to participate in a convention dominated by radical young "Jacobins" who had vehemently denounced him as a "neo-Porfirian" and a "huertista."[1]

When the Committee on the Constitution presented its revision of proposed article 18 on prison reform, however, his stoic detachment quickly evaporated.[2] The committee's mutilation of the original article, Macías insisted, betrayed an appalling ignorance of recent advances in modern penology and threatened to undo sixty years of progress by Mexican penal reformers. As the self-appointed spokesman for this distinguished tradition, he demanded that the new constitution demonstrate a firm commitment to the nation's moral advancement. A comprehensive national prison system, he declared, was crucial to a modern, "civilized" Mexico and thus merited a constitutional mandate.[3]

The Mexican Revolution was ultimately a struggle to control political discourse—a process that culminated in the 1916–17 constitutional convention debates.[4] Having achieved nominal political control, Venustiano Carranza's constitutionalist regime faced the unavoidable and difficult task of establishing its legitimacy in the face of a militant, mobilized populace led by actual or potential adversaries purporting to represent different but seldom clearly defined political agendas. Under these circumstances, control of political discourse was a matter of survival. But, in order to control the Revolution, constitutionalists had first to define it—to produce a revolutionary agenda that coopted, defused, or discredited that of their opponents.[5] Carranza responded by calling a constitutional convention.

Defining the terms and formulating the parameters of "legitimate" discourse, even within the constitutionalist coalition, was far from easy. The nature of revolutionary reform, the issue that prompted Macías's outburst, occupied the central place in these debates. The presence of two distinct reform traditions complicated matters considerably. Delegates to the Mexican constitutional convention sought both to reclaim a nineteenth-century liberal reform agenda that included education, prison reform, and temperance and to introduce new social reforms like workers' rights and agrarian reform.[6] Both reform agendas served to ensure the legitimacy and thus the political authority of the revolutionary regime by publicizing its concern for the "people" and excusing its many transgressions. Only the promise of social reform could justify the tremendous sacrifices of the Revolution, and only a broad spectrum of reforms could hold together a heterogeneous revolutionary coalition.[7]

In spite of this link between nineteenth- and twentieth-century reform agendas, constitutional scholars have ignored the debate over prison reform, focusing instead on innovative constitutional commitments to agrarian reform and workers' rights. In *La ideología de la Revolución Mexicana*, Arnaldo Córdova argues that, by insisting on a strong executive to carry out the constitution's more radical provisions, convention delegates effectively undermined the traditional reform agenda of liberal precursors. The Mexican presidency, he concludes, was stronger after the Revolution than before. And revolutionary regimes were just as committed to capitalist development as were either Díaz or Madero, regardless of their radical constitutional mandate.[8] Given subsequent political and economic developments in Mexico, Córdova's conclusions seem self-evident.

The prison reform debate, however, sheds new light on the 1917 constitution and especially on the revolutionary vision of executive power. Revisionists, like Córdova, have long noted continuities, especially in the developmentalist agenda of Mexican elites.[9] Closely linked to nineteenth-century liberal economic development, the prison reform discourse logically reflects these continuities. Along with their positive counterpart, modern schools, reformed prisons were to inculcate liberal values like hard work and respect for authority and to provide an institutional model for the reform of Mexican society. They would also preserve social order by punishing and isolating dangerous criminals. Further, as an essential component of liberal ideology, prison reform would help mitigate and legitimize the dislocations caused by liberal social engineering. Although specific goals shifted occasionally, reflecting the incidental concerns of individuals or generations of reformers, most reformers continued to accept the fundamental tenets of liberal prison reform.

In spite of these continuities, pre-revolutionary prison reformers never resolved the crucial issue of jurisdiction. Most accepted the government's role in prison reform. But, while some reformers favored local or state control, others insisted that only a national prison system guaranteed comprehensive reform. Porfirian prison reformers, in particular, favored centralized administration as a necessary corrective to an overly heterogeneous society that undermined the development of a Mexican national identity. Abuses perpetuated by the Díaz regime, however, revived concerns about control of the prison system. This debate carried over into the constitutional convention. Thus convention delegates hotly contested jurisdictional aspects of prison reform even while reaching a general consensus on its underlying assumptions.

Explaining these continuities and contestations in the prison reform discourse is essential to an understanding of Mexican liberalism and its contribution to Mexico's discursive revolution.[10] While the 1917 Constitution created a political system that favored a strong executive, it also retained many of the checks and balances of traditional liberalism, including a decentralized prison system. Convention delegates contested prison reform not because they disputed its underlying principles but because they disagreed about who should administer it. The convention's rejection of a centrally controlled prison system, the issue that so angered Macías, suggests that most delegates recognized the inherent dangers of a strong executive and sought to restrict its access to the means of repression. And they realized their goal in traditional liberal fashion by decentralizing and thus diffusing the locus of power.

### Liberal Prison Reform

In Mexico the nineteenth-century prison reform discourse was closely associated with liberalism—Mexican and European—and the progressive ideas of European and North American penologists, especially those of English legal philosopher Jeremy Bentham. Bentham's utilitarian doctrine, with its emphasis on efficient management systems, appealed to a broad spectrum of elite liberal reformers who sought to replace "feudal" colonial institutions with "rational" modern ones. This included the prison system, which, along with modern schools, served as a paradigm for the reform of Mexican society. Secular public schools would teach the requirements of citizenship, and modern penitentiaries would isolate and rehabilitate the transgressors.

The first Enlightenment-inspired prison reform proposals surfaced in the late eighteenth century under the reform-minded Bourbon monarchs. In his 1782 *Discurso sobre las penas*, Mexican-born penologist Manuel de Lardizábal y Uribe remarked that the punishments typically inflicted on late-eighteenth-century criminals—confinement to presidios, shipyards (*arsenales*), and jails—by refusing to discriminate between incidental and hardened criminals corrupted the relatively innocuous victim of unfortunate circumstance without reforming the dangerous habitual offender. He thus advised the crown of the "indispensable necessity of creating correctional facilities [*casas de correción*] in which work and punishment were proportional to the crime and the criminal."[11] The emphasis on work as a corrective to "the continual and forced idleness" of jail inmates coincided nicely with Bourbon developmentalists' concerns about the productivity of the colonial workforce.[12]

Their post-independence Creole counterparts shared these concerns. Drawing on extensive personal observation of modern prisons in the United States, Britain, and France, Vincente Rocafuerte, Ecuadorian diplomat and advisor to the Anastasio Bustamante government, formulated specific proposals for the reform of Mexico's notorious prisons. In his "Nuevo sistema de cárceles," he argued that inmates had "the right to be treated humanely and encouraged in the exercise of their physical and moral faculties . . . because their correction is the object of the punishment imposed upon them." To facilitate rehabilitation his modernized prisons would reflect concern about "the conservation of [the inmate's] health, the purity of the air that he breathes, the cleanliness of his room, productive work, religious instruction, silence, reflection, and order in everything he does."[13] To this end he recommended the adoption of the internationally renowned "Philadelphia" system, which isolated inmates to prevent them from corrupting each other and to provide them a quiet cell in which to contemplate their mistakes. And as early as 1824 he had offered Mexico City officials the use of a "treading mill" acquired during his tour of the United States, which was designed to accustom inmates to regular—and meaningless—work.[14]

In the 1840s Rocafuerte's recommendations received further endorsement from Mariano Otero, who at that time was interior minister, and official foreign correspondent José María Luis Mora. Otero condemned the Federal District's three penal facilities—La Diputación, La Acordada, and the old convent of Santiago Tlalteloco—as "dens of iniquity [*sentinas de corrupción*], where the innocent man encounters a school of crime."[15] These colonial institutions, by encouraging rather than discouraging crime, represented yet another obstacle to liberal modernization efforts. He proposed instead the adaptation of a modern "penitentiary system" based on "solitude that forces reflection, work that dominates evil tendencies, isolation that protects, instruction that elevates, religion that moralizes, and repentance that regenerates."[16]

Mora, in his report on English prisons, generally concurred, but with the caveat that the "silent" Philadelphia system favored by Rocafuerte and Otero, although effective, was too expensive and unnecessarily oppressive. He recommended instead a "system of individual isolation" that allowed inmates contact with moralizing influences, especially with the prison chaplain.[17] Not surprisingly, given their concerns about corrupting prisons and their underlying faith in uncorrupted human potential, both Mora and Otero also stressed the need for separate facilities and even distinct punishments for juvenile offenders, who as fledgling criminals stood the best chance of rehabilitation.[18]

According to these Mexican utilitarians, rationally ordered penal institutions would ultimately rid society of crime. Specifically, utilitarian prison reforms stressed the regenerative power of supervised work in a suitable environment, the penitentiary. The salutary effect of enforced productivity and a wholesome environment would remove the criminal from evil influences, inculcate respect for authority, and teach the value of remunerated work. Isolation of delinquents also protected society from their disruptive influence.[19] These two principal themes of isolation and rehabilitation, directly linked to the larger developmentalist agenda of modernizing elites, dominated nineteenth-century Mexican prison reform efforts.[20]

In keeping with liberalism's egalitarian pretensions, Mexican prison reformers generally ignored issues of race, gender, and age. This ignorance was both selective and self-serving. Reformers recognized that

Native Americans would react differently than mestizos and whites to certain prison regimens, especially solitary confinement, which penologists believed punished only gregarious mestizos and whites.[21] But since Mexican prison reformers sought to discipline a largely mestizo urban workforce they expressed little interest in recognizing or accommodating racial differences.[22] And, prominent liberal presidents of Native American ancestry like Benito Juárez and Porfirio Díaz doubtless discouraged an overtly racist discourse.[23]

Prison reformers also paid scant attention to the needs of female inmates, in part because female criminality also posed little threat to the liberal disciplinary project. They noted that male criminals far outnumbered their female counterparts and represented a much greater danger to society, therefore warranting more attention. The same rationale justified the neglect of juvenile offenders. Thus although prison reformers occasionally discussed the special needs of Native Americans and women, they made no serious efforts to reform penal facilities for either group.[24]

Although concern about prison conditions in Mexico had surfaced even before independence, the prison-reform movement's first noteworthy act was to establish workshops in Mexico City's Cárcel Nacional in 1833. These workshops served two practical purposes, forcing indigent inmates to work to cover expenses while permitting those with resources to earn extra money during incarceration, presumably to help support their families. Typically the workshops had a moralistic purpose as well, keeping the inmates from "excessive leisure," an acknowledged cause of crime, especially among the marginal classes.[25]

Concern, especially over the inmates' moral state, continued to grow. In 1840 Mexico City passed a prison-reform law that sought to separate convicted criminals and simple detainees previously endangered by exposure to hardened criminals.[26] Early prison reform efforts culminated in October 1848 when the national congress passed a law obliging the government to develop a penitentiary system. The newly established Junta Directiva, which included Mariano Otero, submitted plans for a Federal District penitentiary with over five hundred cells and suggested adaptation of the Philadelphia system, with its strict segregation of inmates.[27] Political turmoil and a perennial lack of funds, however, undermined these early efforts. Article 23 of the 1857 Constitution again enjoined the central government to establish a penitentiary system "as soon as possible."[28]

Frustrated during the Second Empire, liberal prison reformers redoubled their efforts with the coming of the new Republic.[29] In 1868 the Juárez administration approved plans for a Federal District penitentiary to house fourteen hundred inmates. In deference to recent advances in penology, Antonio Martínez de Castro proposed a mixed regimen that isolated prisoners from each other but permitted contact with prison personnel and "persons capable of providing moral guidance." A new penal code, written by Martínez de Castro, went into effect in 1871, and that same year the interior minister allocated two hundred thousand pesos to construct the penitentiary.[30] The prologue to the 1871 Penal Code eloquently expressed the pride and optimism of Mexican penal reformers during the first years of the Republic, noting that "today, with scientific spirit and resolute will, immeasurable distances have been suddenly crossed and monuments of science and culture have emerged unexpectedly from chaos."[31] After years of debilitating civil war Mexico had suddenly emerged as a "civilized" nation with an innovative new penal code and plans for a modern penitentiary that symbolized its commitment to the future.

As part of this commitment Juárez appointed prominent American penal reformer Enoch C. Wines to represent Mexico at the First International Penitentiary Congress held in London in 1872.[32] These international congresses, held regularly during the late nineteenth and early twentieth centuries, provided a forum for the discussion and dissemination of the latest advances in penology. They also demonstrated, according to Wines, "the comparative condition of nations as regards intellectual and social development."[33]

For self-conscious Mexican prison reformers the lack of modern penal institutions reflected badly on Mexico, and they continued to lobby vigorously for a penitentiary. Wines's critical "Report on Penitentiary Systems presented to the Supreme Government of the Mexican Republic," published in 1873 and followed two years later by Francisco Javier Peña's damning expose of Mexican prison conditions, reinforced their demands.[34] Peña noted that most Mexican prisons "benefited from changes imposed by civilization, yet still exhibited the traces of barbarism."[35]

Unfortunately for prison reformers, political unrest continued and hard-pressed national governments again postponed action on the proposed penitentiary. Wines reported that "though all Mexican statesmen and philanthropists have of late become aware of the importance and utility to the public of the establishment of a penitentiary system, the financial difficulties, the instability of the Governments, and the constant necessity in which the State has been placed to defend its existence . . . have until now prevented the realization of this great social reform."[36] Mexican prison reformers realized that without an extended period of political stability, significant prison reform would remain a frustrating chimera.

### Porfirian Prison Reform

The ascension of Porfirio Díaz in 1876 marked a watershed in Mexican prison reform. During the next thirty-five years the prison reform discourse underwent various changes as supporters and opponents of the regime manipulated it to suit their respective ends. The Porfiriato also saw the construction of the long-awaited Federal District penitentiary and a new penal colony off the Pacific Coast—the culmination of a fifty-year struggle to bring modern penal institutions to Mexico. These discursive and institutional changes, in turn, laid the foundation for the 1917 Constitutional Convention debate and the resulting dispute over prison reform.

The most significant change in the Mexican prison reform discourse came with the widespread dissemination of European positivism among liberal intellectuals during the Reforma. Although most positivists accepted liberal critiques of colonial institutions as inefficient and irrational, they took issue with earlier liberals' reliance on abstract, ideal solutions that ignored reality.[37] Institutions, they insisted, should reflect scientifically determined needs, not metaphysically constructed ideals. Rationality still figured prominently in the positivist prison-reform discourse, but its meaning had shifted considerably.

The positivist emphasis on practical, scientific solutions found an especially sympathetic audience among Porfirian científico intellectuals eager to create the effective disciplinary system necessary to economic and social development. Traditional liberalism had failed, they declared, precisely because it ignored Mexican reality, attempting to impose inappropriate institutions and thereby encouraging disorder. Justo Sierra, a prominent científico, noted in an 1889 essay that "the moral and social state of human societies depends on their economic state."[38] For Mexico to achieve "liberty" and "individual rights" the country must first advance economically. Economic development, científicos agreed, was impossible without long-term political stability. In a reveal-

ing twist on French positivist Auguste Comte's original motto "love, order, and progress," the Díaz administration chose to replace "love"
with the less ambitious "peace."[39] Enforced peace ensured social stability, which encouraged economic growth, the only practical solution,
científicos insisted, to Mexican "backwardness."

This increased focus on social order reflected not only the fear of continued political chaos but also growing concern about a perceived crime
wave, especially in the capital. In his 1901 study *La génesis del crímen en
México*, Julio Guerrero, a respected Mexican lawyer, thoroughly examined all possible causes of crime in Mexico, including geography, climate, class structure, and social development, but singled out overpop-
ulation ("Ley de Malthus") as especially pernicious.[40] The urban poor,
he warned, were alcoholic, promiscuous, uneducated, and potentially
criminal. Only positivist education, industrial development (which fostered "the morality of the workshop"), and Porfirio Díaz ("with his ex-
emplary behavior") had kept Mexico from "degenerating" into chaos.[41]
In a scientific study of Mexican criminals published three years later,
criminologist Carlos Roumagnac noted three principal "social causes"
for the rise in crime: "abandoned children, begging, and drunkenness."[42] These perceived problems, generally associated with rapid
urbanization, reinforced efforts to promote social order.

Some observers considered inadequate, overcrowded prisons among
the principal causes of crime. Justo Sierra, in an 1875 article in *El Federalista*, denounced conditions in Belén, the national jail. He remarked
sardonically that "the State prison system actually encourages crime,
providing the criminal with everything he needs to complete his education [in crime]."[43] That same year Francisco Peña published the following vivid description of Belén's notorious "galleries": "The principal
dormitories are high-ceilinged, badly ventilated with an open latrine in
one corner, and furnished with sleeping mats for approximately six
hundred inmates. Here they pass the time lying around, smoking mari-
juana and tobacco."[44] Under these circumstances minor offenders
quickly became experienced criminals. According to an 1882 account,
even the establishment of workshops had failed to "dislodge idleness,
that inexhaustible source of vice and prostitution exacerbated by the
presence of so many individuals advanced in crime."[45] Miguel S. Macedo, the Porfiriato's leading penologist, remarked that first-time,
minor offenders "are not properly criminals but draftees in the army of
crime, who, without proper direction will . . . become teachers and vet-

erans."[46] For these observers, existing penal institutions not only failed to rehabilitate inmates but actually served as schools for criminal behavior and thereby contributed directly to rising crime.

A penitentiary, reformers insisted, was an indispensable weapon in a modern society's war on crime. The 1882 report on conditions in Belén observed that "a penitentiary system is one of our society's greatest needs."[47] Macedo concurred, noting somewhat pedantically that "the punitive function of the State, which can do so much for social morality when directed with knowledge, conscience, and rectitude and which causes so many and such profound evils when badly or immorally administered . . . is surely one of the principal elements of social order."[48] With General Díaz guaranteeing peace, prison reformers said, the time had come to restore order to Mexican society.

Spurred by growing public concern, in 1881 Federal District governor Ramón Fernández appointed a blue-ribbon commission, which included Miguel Macedo and future finance minister José Limantour, to formulate plans for a penitentiary. The following year the commission presented an elaborate proposal that boasted an innovative French-inspired radial design, an up-to-date internal regimen, and corresponding modifications of the 1871 Penal Code. Construction began in the plains of San Lázaro, northeast of Mexico City, three years later in 1885. Delayed by unstable soil and forced to await the completion of the "Great Drainage Canal" in 1897, the new penitentiary finally opened on September 29, 1900.[49]

Attended by the crème of the Porfirian elite, including General Díaz himself, the inaugural ceremonies were both social event and celebration of Mexico's long-awaited arrival as a civilized nation. In his opening remarks Macedo paid homage to his predecessors. He noted that the penitentiary "was not just a building but a social institution, crowning the efforts of more than half a century and many generations."[50] It was also, Macedo continued, a symbol of successful government, "of the already fecund fields of our efforts and ingenuity, whose fruits . . . mark a new era in the annals of national progress."[51] Delegates to future international penitentiary congresses could point with pride to Mexico's model penal facility.

For the Porfirian elite, however, the penitentiary represented more than just progress. Along with related efforts to reorganize federal prisons, professionalize Mexico City police, and control the notorious rurales, the new facility symbolized the Díaz administration's commitment to maintaining order and rationalizing national institutions. In his inaugural speech Federal District governor Rafael Rebollar noted portentously that the opening of the penitentiary heralded "a new era in the evolution of repressive systems in Mexico."[52] These symbols of order served a less obvious function as well, demonstrating the administration's vigor and control to political opponents and anxious investors in Mexico's expanding economy.[53]

The penitentiary's avowed purpose, however, was rehabilitation and social defense—in the words of Carlos Roumagnac, "to correct those capable of correction and isolate those who, incapable of correction, endanger others through their pernicious contact."[54] Rebollar agreed, noting pessimistically that "even if it proves worthless as a means of rehabilitation, the [penitentiary] will still segregate criminals from the medium in which they have exercised their abnormal and pernicious activity."[55] Macedo, equally gloomy, observed that "experience, coldly and serenely analyzed, demonstrates the impotence as well as the necessity of penal institutions." Nevertheless, he added, "this Penitentiary, even if it fails to return virtuous men to the bosom of society, shall never be a source of moral corruption . . . nor a chamber of pain, misery, infamy and horror."[56]

In spite of their reservations, commission members recommended an elaborate internal regimen based on the innovative Irish or Crofton system, which had received the endorsement of recent international penitentiary congresses.[57] This regimen comprised an intricate system of rewards and punishments designed to modify and direct an inmate's behavior, firmly but without violence. Every facet of prison life played a role, including access to food, clothing, furnishings, exercise, remunerated work, education, fellow prisoners, and medical care.[58] The regimen allowed inmates to accumulate "points" for good behavior, work, and school attendance that decreased the severity of their internment and led, in some cases, to early release on "parole."[59] Conversely, inmates who failed to cooperate were increasingly isolated to prevent them from contaminating their more cooperative fellows. The commission report noted contentedly that "a system based on these principles forces the delinquent to choose between pleasure and pain, inspiring both terror and hope . . . and it is hardly surprising that they are controlled like docile sheep."[60] Macedo announced proudly that "here for the first time, a complete regimen has been established, directed toward moral correction and encompassing all facets of an inmate's life."[61] In the new penitentiary, so it seemed, Bentham's panoptic vision had finally been realized.

Like its liberal predecessor, the Porfirian penitentiary regimen became a paradigm for the reformation of Mexican society. The system worked, supporters observed, because, unlike earlier "unnatural" systems, it utilized existing social mechanisms like reward and punishment, which provided inmates with incentives for self-improvement. The commission report noted the penitentiary's resemblance to an idealized version of society, remarking that this similarity "should teach the prisoner that . . . the means of obtaining health and happiness is honesty and that vice always leads to pain and ends in misfortune."[62] The lesson for Mexico City proletarians was clear.

As good Porfirians, commission members also emphasized the role of the director. Without the proper director, they concluded, "the penitentiary will be completely useless."[63] In this sense, too, the new facility and its internal regimen reflected an idealized Mexican society and symbolized Porfirian intentions. A benevolent but authoritarian administrator and his resident technocrats presided over both penitentiary and country. In científico social engineering, reform invariably came from above.

The Islas Marías penal colony off the coast of Tepic represented a further refinement of the Porfirian prison-reform discourse. Acquired by the national government in 1905 and opened three years later, the penal colony, like the penitentiary, resulted from more than sixty years of lobbying by determined prison reformers.[64] As they had been for the penitentiary, great pains were taken to define its function and determine the proper internal regimen.

Islas Marías was destined to play a distinct role in the new federal penal system. Querido Moheno—a prominent political journalist and Porfirian national deputy who would later serve under Madero and Huerta—wrote the initial proposal and enabling legislation.[65] His instructions from Interior Minister and Vice President Ramón Corral were to "find a practical method, both scientific and legitimate to end delinquency . . . in our cultured capital."[66] Moheno noted that while the penitentiary isolated serious offenders, the overcrowded jails continued to breed petty criminals: habitual alcoholics, vagrants, pimps, prostitutes, beggars, thieves. Repeat offenders or recidivists were a particular problem. The Islas Marías penal colony, Moheno declared, would "free us of the habitual criminals . . . who comprise the daily clientele of our jails."[67] Appealing astutely to the Díaz administration's obsession with national image, he insisted that removing recidivists would relieve overcrowded jails, remove a potent source of social contamination, improve police efficiency, and ultimately reduce crime in "our cultured capital." It would also reduce criminality among the working classes, thus promoting economic development.

Moheno's regimen, like that of the penitentiary, sought to reproduce a controlled version of Mexican society within which the inmates could learn to function normally. To promote the inmates' social instincts, Moheno even suggested that the government transport their families to the penal colony at state expense. "It is to be hoped," he noted, that "penal colonies will one day be organized along accepted social lines, and the most effective way of achieving this is through the colonist's family."[68] Moheno's system also provided considerable "executive" latitude, allowing the president or his proxy to double an incorrigible inmate's sentence at his own discretion.[69] Thus, although designed to serve different functions within the federal penal system, both model Porfirian penal institutions exhibited two essential characteristics: strong executive control, and scientific management techniques that relied heavily on behavior modification.

### The Political Opposition and Prison Reform

Drawing on the same liberal reform tradition, Díaz's political opponents generally supported both the científicos' social diagnosis and their proposed solutions.[70] Like their científico opponents, the editors of the liberal journal *El Monitor Republicano* attributed Mexico City's crime wave to alcoholism, gambling, prostitution, "habitual idleness," lack of respect for the police, and "bloody spectacles" like bull fighting that incited the lower classes to violence.[71] Enrique Chávarri, writing as "Juvenal," lobbied persistently for a larger, better-trained police force to protect the capital.[72] His editorial counterpart, Enrique M. de los Ríos, went still further, calling for enforcement of penal-code regulations against the sale of alcohol and gambling as well as for a prohibition of "bloody spectacles."[73] Both editors also insisted that the penitentiary needed to be completed. In a series of articles exposing unsanitary, overcrowded conditions at Belén, Chávarri noted that "it is evident that these conditions will never improve until the establishment of the penitentiary."[74] An "adequate penal system," he insisted, was a fundamental corrective to rising crime.[75]

Although the Porfiriato's liberal opponents participated unreservedly in the prison reform discourse, they nevertheless vigorously protested the Díaz administration's misuse of its penal institutions. In 1885, angry over the exposure of a crony, Díaz imprisoned a number of opposition journalists, including Chávarri and De los Ríos.[76] This group, the Club de Periodistas Encarcelados, bitterly attacked the administration for its hypocritical approach to prison reform. De los Ríos, commenting on Díaz's 1889 presidential address, noted an inherent contradiction in his advocacy of "rehabilitation that transforms the delinquent into a useful member of society." The president's theory was unassailable, de los Ríos sarcastically conceded, adding that "it is regrettable that journalists are to be made the exception."[77]

A product of his time, De los Ríos never questioned Díaz's right to imprison his opposition, insisting only on separate facilities. In his influential *State of Prisons and of Child-Saving Institutions*, North American penologist Enoch Wines, who had earlier advised the Juarez administration, had observed that: "As to political offenders, it has been taken into account that, if in some cases they proceed from unruly passions, they may in others be the result of errors of opinion, yet of good intentions. For this reason the offenders of this class are not placed on the same level as ordinary criminals but are simply confined in a special prison used for this object alone."[78]

De los Ríos concurred, noting the importance of "avoiding the mixing of prisoners that is so repugnant to those incarcerated only for political reasons."[79] In fact, the Penitentiary Commission's reforms of the penal code recognized the special status of political prisoners by allowing them to keep all prison wages and permitting them relative freedom within the institution.[80]

Their experience as political prisoners strongly affected the attitude of other Díaz opponents toward prison reform as well. Some years later Mexican Liberal Party (PLM) leader Ricardo Flores Magón offered a dramatic description of an early experience in Díaz's prisons: "The jail lacked a proper floor . . . and the walls oozed a thick fluid that prevented the spittle of countless, careless occupants from ever drying. Huge webs hung from the ceiling, covered with enormous, black horrible spiders. . . . My pallet was wet, as were my clothes, and from time to time I heard the sound of spiders falling on the pallet or floor, or in early morning on my body."[81] Fellow PLM conspirator Juan Sarabia's experience in the notorious military prison of San Juan de Ulua was equally horrific. "They took away our clothes," he complained in a 1907 letter to Ricardo's brother Jesús, "and gave us gray striped clothes, the prisoner's uniform, old, ragged, dirty, and straw hats. We are in filthy [*infectas*], damp galleries in which there is neither light nor air. The mess [*rancho*] is infernal. The meat is nauseating and frequently has to be thrown out. . . . The work is brutal. The beatings and whippings are frequent. The circumstances to which we have been reduced is a shocking outrage."[82] Not surprisingly, the revised draft of the 1906 PLM program included an article on prison reform.[83] The program's manifesto noted that "existing prisons serve only to punish men, not to better them."[84] As a solution, article 44 of the program itself recommended "the establishment, whenever possible, of penal colonies based on regeneration in place of the jails and penitentiaries in which delinquents currently suffer punishment."[85]

Like the liberal editors of *El Monitor Republicano*, PLM leaders endorsed prison reform while denouncing Díaz's abuse of the penal system. A 1903 article in *El Hijo del Ahuizote* remarked that Díaz "treated the jails like his personal property that he used to remove his opposition when he could not justify having them killed."[86] This systematic abuse of public institutions indicated, according to opposition leaders, the larger criminality of the Díaz government itself.

As opposition to Díaz intensified, increasingly radical PLM leaders refined their position on prison reform. They identified structural inequalities within the capitalist economic system rather than the moral failings of the marginal classes as the true cause of crime. A 1911 PLM manifesto observed that systematic exploitation of the laboring classes generated "antisocial behavior, crime, prostitution, and disloyalty . . . the natural fruits of an old and hated system."[87] That same year, Ricardo Flores Magón noted optimistically that "with the disappearance of the greed and falsity necessary to survival under existing circumstances, there will be no reason for crime."[88] Implicit in this new explanation for delinquency was the need to restructure Mexican society. Prison reform, while a necessary corrective within an exploitive system, would prove unnecessary in a truly equitable society. This radical position was, however, the exception that proved the rule.

### Revolutionary Prison Reform

After Díaz's fall, less radical revolutionaries like Carranza took up the call for social justice. In his 1913 Hermosillo speech, Carranza scorned the Porfiriato as a time of "hopeless calm . . . without material or social progress in which the people found themselves for thirty years without schools, hygiene, food, and worst of all, liberty." Two years later, in San Luis Potosí, Carranza identified the Revolution with a "general systemic transformation" that would bring real progress to Mexico.[89] From prohibitionist governor of Coahuila under Madero, Carranza had become, at least rhetorically, a social reformer.

On December 1, 1916, President Carranza convened the constitutional convention at Querétaro to "reform" the 1857 Constitution. In his inaugural speech he proudly noted that his proposed constitution, drafted by lawyers José Natividad Macías and Luis Manuel Rojas, reflected "all the political reforms that years of experience and careful observation have suggested to me are indispensable."[90] Félix Palavicini, a Carranza delegate, observed that Macías and Rojas "following the President's inspiration, have given the revolution the program that would make it a true Social Revolution."[91]

That Christmas Macías made similar claims for the proposed prison reform article. The president, he noted, "after pondering prison organization in the United States, England, and Germany, realized the need for far-reaching reform in Mexico."[92] Recent advances in penology rendered existing legislation obsolete. For Macías the "classical penal system" which had inspired the 1857 constitutional article on prison reform was based on abstractions that punished the crime but ignored the intent and background of the criminal.[93] He proposed instead a modern penal system, based on penal colonies controlled by the national government, that would not just punish crime but that would also address the moral, biological, and environmental factors affecting each criminal's behavior. According to Macías this new system would "provide all Mexican criminals, the majority delinquent because of poverty, heredity, training, and the lack of available education, the means to satisfy the demands of life."[94]

Delegates generally agreed with Macías on the multiple causes of crime. Prohibitionists, including nominal opponents like Macías and General Francisco Múgica, linked the adverse effects of alcohol, drug abuse, gambling, and bullfighting to lower-class criminality and recommended severe sanctions. Dr. José María Rodríguez, head of Mexico City's Superior Council of Public Health, attributed 80 percent of Mexico City's violent crimes to drinking, estimating that nine-tenths of the lower classes were alcoholics.[95] Other delegates noted structural causes for crime, especially "lack of education and general ignorance."[96]

Nor was there debate on the need for prison reform. Macías observed that "many delegates present today were imprisoned with me in the penitentiary." One of those delegates, Félix Palavicini, incarcerated by Huerta along with Macías and Rojas, recalled his month in solitary confinement as "the only time I ever contemplated suicide." He confessed that "from that moment I saw prison in a new light."[97] Many convention delegates shared Palavicini's reaction to Porfirian prisons and his desire for reform.

Macías attacked the Díaz administration's blatant misuse of existing penal facilities on practical grounds as well. He noted that the penitentiary, designed to hold only fifteen hundred inmates, now contained more than four thousand.[98] He condemned the Porfiriato's model penal institution as "fatal, infernal, detestable," adding that it "warrants destruction even at the loss of millions spent on its construction."[99] Under such conditions rehabilitation of inmates was clearly impossible.

Although delegates frequently cited Italian "positive" criminologists Lombroso, Ferri, and Garofalo to support their respective cases, they sometimes differed in their analyses of the penal system's fundamental purpose. Querétaro lawyer José María Truchuelo credited positive criminologists with developing a modern penal system "based on the theory of the correctability of man," and insisted that workshops and schools be integrated into future penal facilities.[100] Enrique Colunga, speaking for the Committee on the Constitution, took a less humanitarian approach. "The Committee," Colunga declared "does not believe that the penal system should be based on public vendetta, but neither does it believe in readaptation. For Committee members, the penal system is based on the principle of social defense."[101] But these were differences of focus rather than of substance, representing the extremes of prison reformers' concern for both rehabilitation and isolation.

In fact the influence of the liberal-Porfirian prison reform discourse on convention delegates was profound. Delegates agreed that Díaz had grossly abused the penal system, but most never questioned the fundamental tenets of Porfirian prison reform: rehabilitation, social defense, and top-down reform. And in spite of some concern about the structural causes of crime, many delegates continued, in the Porfirian tradition, to focus on the moral state of the lower classes.

The controversy centered not on prison reform itself but on the issue of national government control—what Luis Manuel Rojas called the "old and much debated question of 'federalism' and 'centralism.'"[102]

The Committee on the Constitution refused to consider Carranza's proposed article 18, principally because it called for national government control of the proposed penal colonies. Committee president General Múgica noted that "the one thing the Committee could not accept was that [penal colonies] be established exclusively by the Federal Government."[103] Rebutting Macías's argument that centralized control meant better prisons, the committee insisted on each state's right to punish its own criminals. Enrique Colunga, the committee's secretary, warned that the penal colonies "would become a terrible political weapon . . . should a ferocious, cruel man occupy the presidency." He added that "if we accept this penal system, tomorrow we will have in Islas Marías and Quintana Roo, a sinister reflection of the deportations to Siberia."[104]

Given the recent experience of many of the delegates, Colunga's argument seemed quite sensible. Although Macías promised that future penal colonies would be run by doctors and professors rather than by the executive, pragmatic General Heriberto Jara expressed serious reservations. Representing Vera Cruz with its notorious military prison of San Juan de Ulúa, Jara insisted that penal colonies, because of their isolation and resultant lack of proper supervision, "lent themselves only to abuses." The Díaz administration's recent misuse of Islas Marías and Quintana Roo, he observed, was typical.[105]

Pragmatists objected to penal colonies for other reasons. One delegate cited the obvious expense and construction time involved. Another, responding to Macías's argument that isolation from contaminating environments was crucial to rehabilitation, retorted that isolating prisoners in penal colonies cut "civilizing" family ties and discriminated against the "poorer classes" who could not afford transportation.[106]

These practical arguments won the day for states' rights advocates. Although the supporters of national penal colonies insisted that poorer states lacked funds to build proper penal facilities, most delegates agreed that the potential for abuse and the considerable expense involved represented too great a risk. Logistical problems and the need to curb the national government's power far outweighed the less-tangible benefits of nationally directed penal reform.

After its initial rejection on a technicality, the convention finally approved article 18 on January 3, 1917, by a vote of 155 to 37. The article's first paragraph required separate facilities for detainees and convicted criminals. The second instructed the state and national governments "to organize their respective penal systems—colonies, penitentiaries, or military prisons—on the basis of work as the means of regeneration."[107]

For Macías, the approved article, "instead of advancing our humanitarian and republican institutions, drags us back to . . . 1857."[108] The delegates' misunderstanding of modern advances in penal reform, and their oversensitivity to past abuses, he implied, had set Mexican prison reform back sixty years. Lack of centralized administration, he argued, precluded national standards and thus the effective administration of Mexican prisons, especially in the poorer states.

The discursive struggle over prison reform, however, had little actual impact on Mexican prisons, national or otherwise. The national government showed little interest in building any new model penal institutions, and the penitentiary and Islas Marías continued to function as inefficiently as before. Typically, General Múgica, who had so adamantly opposed federal penal colonies during convention debates, became director of the penal colony on Islas Marías in 1928. Having reclaimed the prison-reform discourse of the liberal and Porfirian eras, financially strapped revolutionary governments failed to follow through with expensive reforms until the relatively flush 1960s.[109]

Aside from addressing the issue of jurisdiction, the constitutional convention debate had little effect on the prison reform discourse. In 1922 an article in the *Boletín de la Sociedad Mexicana de Geografía y Estadística* lamented the ongoing Mexico City crime wave in typically liberal-Porfirian terms. The study cited alcoholism, abandoned children, consensual relations outside marriage, and lax enforcement of existing laws as the principal causes of rising crime.[110] Penal solutions likewise followed Porfirian guidelines, stressing scientific management by trained administrators. Significantly, Miguel Macedo, the Porfiriato's leading penologist and godfather of the penitentiary, continued to influence Mexican penology, first as professor of penal law at the Escuela Nacional de Jurisprudencia from 1883 to 1904 and later at the Escuela Libre de Derecho from 1912 to 1920. Mexico's leading post-revolutionary penologists, including the editors of *Criminalia*, the professional journal for Mexican criminologists and penologists, proudly admitted his ongoing influence on Mexican penology.[111]

In *Judas at the Jockey Club* William Beezley explores Porfirian efforts to replace public spectacles like Judas burnings, which excited the "dangerous classes," with more controlled bicycle parades in the latest European fashion.[112] Perceived danger from a growing urban underclass and obsession with international image also affected prison reform. In fact prison reform came of age during the Porfiriato, as modernizing elites like Miguel Macedo oversaw the construction of model penal facilities and the consolidation of a liberal-positivist prison reform discourse. Prison reform thus served as an essential element in Porfirian plans to develop a disciplinary Mexican carceral system that included everything from public education to bicycle races.[113]

The revolutionary prison reform discourse, as demonstrated by the 1917 Constitutional Convention debate, was in many ways an extension of its predecessors. Most convention delegates recognized an established prison-reform tradition closely linked to nineteenth-century liberal efforts to modernize Mexico. Institutional reform, including prisons and schools, played a key role in the liberal project. Liberal prison reformers advocated a prison system that would isolate criminals, provide for their rehabilitation, and permit their eventual reintegration as productive members of society. But, caught between contradictory ideological commitments to individual freedom and a rationally ordered society, liberal reformers never resolved the vital questions of agency and jurisdiction.

Porfirian científicos saw centralized control as the solution to this liberal dilemma. Drawing on the insights of European positivists, the científicos insisted that only specifically Mexican solutions could solve Mexico's problems. Since social disorder and economic underdevelopment precluded private initiative, a strong centralized administration seemed the logical answer. Porfirian prison reformers thus favored disciplinary prison regimens based on behavior modification that inculcated liberal values like hard work, honesty, and respect for authority under the administration of a powerful director and his team of scientifically trained experts, who supervised reform and guaranteed order. They also insisted that, given Mexico's heterogenous nature, only centralized control by the national government could guarantee comprehensive prison reform. Accepting the basic tenets of liberal prison reform, científicos sought to devise effective means for their realization.

At the constitutional convention debates delegates acknowledged the científicos' contribution to penal reform but insisted that abuses perpetuated by the Porfirian prison system far outweighed its accomplishments. Many spoke from firsthand experiences in Díaz's prisons. But, in spite of this consensus on the accomplishments and failures of Porfirian prison reform, delegates hotly contested the nature of the constitutional mandate, focusing especially on the issue of state versus national control. Taking their cue from científico social engineering, Carrancista delegates like Macías argued that only a network of nationally controlled penal colonies could ensure effective administration and reform of all Mexican prisons. The majority disagreed, noting the tremendous potential for abuse inherent in a nationally controlled system and contesting Macías's assertion that centralized administration was necessarily more efficient or humane.

The resulting constitutional article represented a defeat for Macías's centrally administered prison system. While the accepted article acknowledged the need for different kinds of penal institutions and their general reformative purpose, it rejected national government control as too risky. For most delegates a decentralized prison system limited a strong president's ability to dominate the Mexican penal system, as Díaz had attempted to do. The greater means available to post-revolutionary presidents made checks and balances that much more critical. Thus, although the 1917 Constitution created a strong president capable of imposing broad social reforms, it also sought to check potential abuse of executive power in traditional liberal fashion, by decentralizing the means of repression.

# 5. LOOKING FORWARD, LOOKING BACK

Judicial Discretion and
the Legitimation
of the Mexican State

Esta fué la razon por que fué fecha la ley, que la maldad de los omnes
fuese refrenada, por miedo della, é que los buenos viquiesen segura-
mente entre los malos; é que los malos fuesen penados por la ley, é dex-
asen de fazer mal por el miedo de la pena. [This is the reason that the
law was made, that the evil of men should be restrained for fear of it
and the good should live secure among the evil, and that the evil
should be punished by the law, and that they should leave off evildoing
for fear of punishment.] – *Fuero Juzgo*

If we ignore our ancestors, how they thought, felt and acted, we will
find ourselves overcome in our own land [*patria*] and we will perish in
the deeply tangled roots that impede our resisting the assaults of more
united peoples [*pueblos*], with more homogeneous aspirations and
conscious of their history. – Miguel Macedo

On the surface, Mexican criminal law has closely followed the progressive trajectory depicted in legal historiography.[1] For most scholars the
new and reformed penal codes that followed independence from Spain
represented a series of necessary if halting steps toward a modern legal
infrastructure.[2] For legal reformers, modern criminal laws were a harbinger of modern social relations that presented, like the nation's various constitutions, an ideal to which the progressing nation might as-
pire. (This is, of course, the classic apologia for failing to realize the
more radical provisions of the 1917 Constitution—"obedezco pero no
cumplo," as colonial officials typically replied to unenforceable royal
decrees.) This interpretation has much to recommend it: Mexican penologists understood and acted upon the latest international (primarily
European) advances in criminal law. Moreover, their legacy persists:
Mexico's criminal laws were (and are) as modern as any in the world.

Sold in inexpensive paperback editions by street vendors outside most courthouses and police stations, Mexican criminal laws and procedures are also among the most accessible.

This progressive vision is somewhat deceptive. Just as modernizing discourses like criminology re-articulated traditional concerns about class, race, and gender, penology also exhibited strong ties to Mexico's past. In the tumultuous post-independence decades, most liberal penologists—and penologists were by and large liberal—stuck resolutely to revolutionary principles of universal human rights and absolute equality under the law. But with the consolidation of liberal power in the late nineteenth century, mainstream policymakers began to construct an elitist "scientific politics" that represented—under the guise of Mexicanizing the "metaphysical" Jacobin agenda of midcentury liberals—a return to colonial-style paternalism, albeit with a technocratic slant.[3] And despite significant changes in public policy after Mexico's great social revolution (1910–20), paternalism—this time under the auspices of the post-revolutionary *estado papá*—remained the preferred mode for social and legal reform efforts.

Both visions of Mexican criminal law—one looking forward, the other back—were part of ongoing elite efforts to re-legitimize political control in the shifting discursive terrain that announced (or so they hoped) the onset of modernity. These re-legitimation efforts that began with the "enlightened" reforms of late-eighteenth-century Bourbon monarchs (c. 1760s–1810) took a Jacobin turn after independence as liberals wrested control of the central government from their conservative rivals (by 1867), acquired a technocratic gloss under Porfirio Díaz's autocratic gaze (1876–1911), and culminated in the post-revolutionary paternalistic populism of Lázaro Cárdenas (1934–40). In practice, legal modernization often produced contention and disorder—witness the nineteenth-century liberal "reform" laws attacking corporate privilege that raised the considerable ire of the Catholic Church, the army, and incorporated Indian communities. But not all legal reform threatened social order. Mexican penologists argued that criminal law, with its far-reaching punitive power, especially over the recently "empowered" lower classes, represented a particularly potent source of political legitimacy. And, as the sovereign "people" came to play an ever larger role in the elite political imaginary (if not in actual politics), popular acceptance of legal authority emerged as an area of special concern.[4]

This bifurcated focus on the sometimes-contradictory goals of legal modernization and popular acceptance considerably complicated efforts to reform Mexican criminal law and thereby activate its legitimizing potential. Among other things, the broad spectrum of interest groups operating within Mexico's heterogeneous class structure held sometimes related, sometimes contradictory views of legal legitimacy. The criminal-justice professionals who controlled the initial stages of the lawmaking process were publicly committed to legal modernization after the latest European fashion, but it was a commitment often moderated by practical experience and professional aspirations. Politicians, while generally supportive of legal modernization, also insisted that the criminal-justice system help preserve political order by balancing the usually contrary means of repression or cooptation. Penal reformers demanded an end to corruption and inept policemen, judges, and jailers while at the same time warning of the degenerate and dangerous lower classes against which society had to defend itself. What the "people" might have wanted was as various as the people themselves. The literate upper and middle classes generally favored repression of lower-class crime. The loosely defined lower classes, although concerned about crime (the lower classes provided the bulk of victims as well as the bulk of perpetrators), also desired a sympathetic ear in court. Thus legal legitimacy for one group might easily alienate another, and individuals were by no means confined to a single interest group. This contested vision of the proper role of criminal law in Mexican society hindered and ultimately helped shape legal reform efforts.

In this ideologically charged context the somewhat arcane legal issue of judicial discretion—the individual magistrate's ability to tailor punishment to suit the crime—became an important site of contestation, among elite policymakers at least, over the nature of the liberal state. The end result, the 1931 Federal Penal Code, was a step forward, reflecting the latest international advances in penology; it was also a step back, returning judicial discretionary powers that had been eroded by a century of liberal attacks on "arbitrary" colonial criminal justice. On the surface, increased judicial discretion promised and in some cases doubtless delivered a more responsive criminal-justice system that buttressed the state's legitimacy, much as earlier Bourbon reforms had done in the decades preceding independence.[5] Moreover, popular pressure—which arose perhaps in response to a political system bound together by patron-client relations—encouraged and supported the shift.[6] At the same time increased discretion reinforced a paternalistic approach to

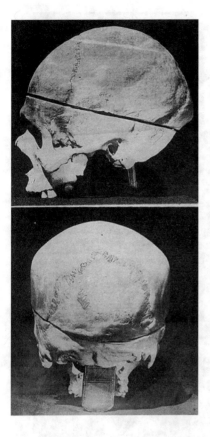

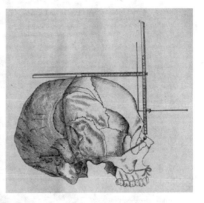

Two views of the skull of an indigenous criminal from Francisco Martínez Baca and Manuel Vergara's *Estudios de antropología criminal* (see chapter 2).

A special instument designed by Martínez and Vergara for measuring skulls, from their *Estudios de antropología criminal* (see chapter 2).

Photographs of different criminal types from Martínez and Vergara's *Estudios de antropología criminal*. Criminologists typically used photos like these to derive common characteristics for different kinds of criminals. Photos 1–5 are assailants (*lesión* implies a wound), 6–17 are rapists, and 18–20 are thieves (see chapter 2).

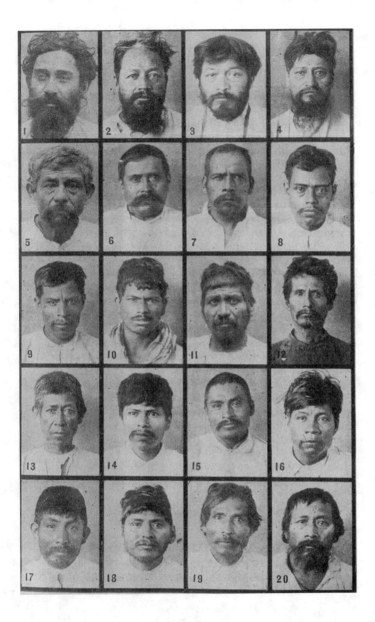

Murderers from Martínez and Vergara's *Estudios de antropología crimi-nal*. The class and, to a certain extent, race of criminals in this figure and figure 3 are self-evident (see chapter 2).

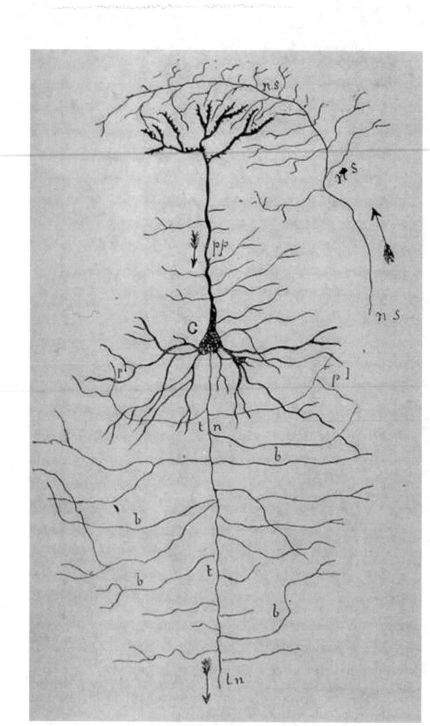

(*Opposite*) This sketch from Carlos Roumagnac's *Los criminales en México* demonstrates "scientifically" how outside stimuli (shown as arrows) affect the human nervous system, sometimes producing criminal behavior (see chapter 2).

(*Above*) Two mug shots from Roumagnac's *Los criminales en México*. The bottom photo is María Villa, the female subject of one of his "observations" (see chapter 3). The top photo is one of the young boys who allegedly engaged in "homosexual" activities in prison (see chapter 6).

A broadside illustrated by José Guadalupe Posada titled "Ballad of the Penitentiary of Mexico." The last verse reads: "There everyone is separate / it's everyone in their cell / there no one visits you / and there's no one to give you a cigarette" (see chapter 4). Courtesy of the Taylor Museum for Southwest Studies of the Colorado Springs Fine Arts Center.

A broadside illustrated by Posada titled "Very Sad Lamentations of an Exile Sent to Islas Marías." The last verse reads: "Now there's nothing to be done / bad times have come at last / for being a no-good bum / the law will now transport me" (see chapter 4). Courtesy of the Taylor Museum for Southwest Studies of the Colorado Springs Fine Arts Center.

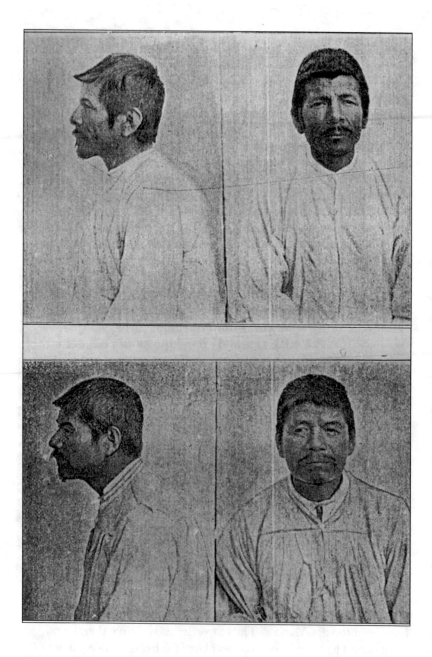

Photographs of two "male indigenous types from the valley of Teotihuacán" from Manuel Gamio's *La población del valle de Teotihuacán* (see chapter 7).

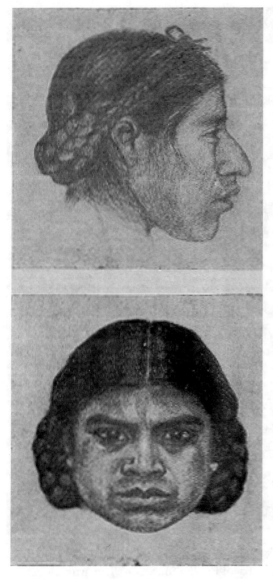

Drawings by prominent Zacatecan artist Francisco Goitia (here credited as "Goytia") of two "indigenous types from Xochimilco." Goitia's sketches illustrate an article by Lucio Mendieta y Núñez titled "Influence of the Physical Environment on Primitive Peoples" in *Ethnos*, a "journal dedicated to the study and betterment of the indigenous population of Mexico" (see chapter 7).

Title page from *Ethnos*'s "third epoch" in which Gamio cedes control of the journal to the Ministry of Public Education's Department of Anthropology. The caption under Calles's picture reads, "General Plutarco Elías Calles, constitutional president of the United States of Mexico, in whose governmental program figures, as a point of capital importance, the scientific study of the indigenous populations, with the object of obtaining their economic and moral education" (see chapter 7).

state-citizen relations that would come to fruition with *tata* Cárdenas's consolidation of the *estado papá* in the late 1930s.

Social theorist Jürgen Habermas has argued that "refeudalization" is an inevitable by-product of the transformation of the liberal constitutional state into a social-welfare state where "publicity imitates the kind of aura proper to personal prestige and supernatural representation" typical of pre-Enlightenment European monarchies.[7] This was certainly the case in Mexico. Mexican policymakers saw increased judicial discretion—which manifested "the aura proper to personal prestige" of judges—as a form of "publicity" that *publicly* represented the populist aspirations of the post-revolutionary nation-state. Not coincidentally, the decisive shift occurred at the precise moment (1929) when a newly constituted official party—precursor to the Partido Revolucionario Institucional (PRI), which still controls the presidency—was poised to abandon traditional modes of democratic representation in favor of a "modern," corporatist, one-party state.

The combination of modernity, nationalism, and paternalism has proven potent if not quite hegemonic. The 1931 Penal Code, although much revised, is still in place. So too, at least for the time being, is the paternalistic political system that produced it. This remarkable durability, especially in a region not known for stability, has been much noted but never adequately explained. And while a definitive explanation for the Mexican "exception" is far beyond the scope of this chapter (its mysteries may well elude scholars for years to come), this brief history of judicial discretion seeks to provide a crucial piece to that larger puzzle by exploring the way elite policymakers used legal reform to forge a truly paternal fatherland. (Seen in this light, the deep historical roots of president Ernesto Zedillo's efforts to diffuse criticism of his troubled regime with a highly publicized reform of the criminal justice system are very apparent.)

### Rejecting the Colonial Legacy

Colonial criminal law institutionalized social inequalities by punishing convicted criminals according to their legally defined social, racial, or corporate status. The shift after independence to an Enlightenment-inspired, "liberal" legal system under which all citizens were theoretically equal thus marked a watershed in Mexican penal law.

It was a watershed that would last fifty years. Drawing on French, Spanish, and North American constitutional commitments to the "rights of man and citizen," the liberal 1824 Constitution guaranteed legal equality for all Mexican citizens, thus technically ending institutionalized discrimination and bolstering the legitimacy of secession.[8] Ironically, the political instability that followed independence forced practitioners to fall back on Spanish colonial criminal (and civil) law and procedures, especially the medieval *Siete partidas* (1265) and the *Novísima recopilación* (1805). Supplemented by reactive, stopgap criminal legislation intended principally to restore public order, this confusing situation persisted until the liberal Juárez regime promulgated a penal code in 1871.[9]

But despite post-independence political disputes between liberals and conservatives that blocked attempts to develop a Mexican penal code, the reform and codification of criminal laws was a widely acknowledged desideratum. Even before the break with Spain, staunchly royalist, Mexican-born jurist Manuel de Lardizábal y Uribe had insisted that "nothing is more important to a nation than having good criminal laws because they ensure civil liberty and, in large part, the well-being and security of the State." He warned, however, that "there is no enterprise more difficult than the perfection of criminal legislation."[10]

Such was the case in independent Mexico. In his 1839 *Pandectas hispano megicanas*, Juan N. Rodríguez de San Miguel summarized the practical problems that emerged from the colonial legal legacy: "Our [legislation] after nearly thirty years of revolution, not only of arms, but of customs, government, and estate, suffers more than anything from the complication, diversity, and uncertainty of the laws . . . [that] retard the administration of justice, hinder the response and ability of the authorities, and impede the investigation of cases."[11] Apart from its unwieldiness, this convoluted legacy, in the biased eyes of liberal reformers, threatened the legitimacy of a new order that promised legal equality to all citizens. Liberal theorist José María Luis Mora even reprinted a Bourbon-era critique of colonial criminal justice that warned of the dangers of legal discrimination: "What affection," it inquired, "what benevolence can [castas and indios] feel toward the ministers of the law that only exercise authority in order to send them to jail, the gibbet [*picota*], the presidio, or the gallows? What bonds can link these classes to a government whose protection they are incapable of comprehending?"[12] In an era of political violence that exacerbated elite fears of popular mobilization, such warnings seemed prescient, and the need to reform criminal law painfully obvious. "Criminal legislation," Mora's liberal colleague Manuel Otero advised, "is at the same time the foundation and proof of social institutions." While recognizing the inevitability of crime, he argued that the conscientious legislator "needs to demonstrate his genius by conquering bad inclinations, setting men on the path of duty . . . governing society, pushing it toward the good, guiding it to perfection."[13] For Otero good criminal laws would not only repress the criminal but would also instruct the potential citizen, thereby ensuring their popular acceptance—a necessary prerequisite to social progress in a modern democratic Republic.

One proposed solution was the adoption of the jury system. Mora even advocated popular juries in an 1827 "dissertation" for his law degree, noting that jurors were less susceptible to corruption than judges were, and were more in tune with the criminal-justice system's typically lower-class clientele. "The knowledge of persons," he pointed out, "their habits and customs, their vices and virtues, and their individual character, are beyond the reach of a judge who knows little about them and before whom they necessarily dissemble, as do most of their fellow citizens with whom they [the accused, witnesses, etc.] contract the relations that allows them [their fellow citizens on the jury] to know and evaluate the degree of probability or certitude that ought to be given to testimony and motives."[14] For Mora, then, only an English or North American–style jury of peers could transcend the profound class divisions in Mexican society and provide the understanding and insight necessary to a fair trial.

Concern about popular justice carried over to the liberal 1857 Constitutional Congress, where commission members revived Mora's arguments in favor of popular juries. They noted in their initial proposal that "the sovereignty of the people, the foundation of republican principles, point of departure for all its applications, secure gauge for the solution of all its problems, is incomprehensible, is inconceivable, without the institution of the jury."[15] In what was to become a classic riposte, opponents countered that juries were inappropriate for "our population and territory," because to be effective they required an educated, moral citizenry which "is disgracefully not characteristic of most of our population."[16] Not surprisingly, in 1869, when legislators amended criminal procedures to include juries for some cases, they compromised; literacy and income requirements effectively excluded lower-class participation.[17]

But in spite of disputes over the extent of popular empowerment, legal reformers clearly recognized the pressing need to reform criminal laws and procedures. They also stressed the importance of popular acceptance of, if not always active participation in, the criminal-justice system. In fact, attempts to reconcile (at least discursively) the potentially conflicted requirements of appropriate institutions and popular acceptance became the hallmark of future Mexican criminal jurisprudence. By the mid-nineteenth century the terms of the debate had been chosen; the exact meaning of those terms, however, was far from clear.

### Codifying Criminal Law: The 1871 Penal Code

The promulgation of the liberal 1857 Constitution, which included Mexico's first real bill of rights—"De los derechos del hombre" (Of the rights of man)—marked the crucial first step toward the codification of Mexican criminal law. The constitution officially ended many of the more onerous aspects of colonial criminal law: not only legal discrimination, but also most special tribunals, unauthorized arrest, lengthy detention, torture, unlawful seizure of property, and transcendental punishment.[18] Procedure was reformed as well. The constitution eliminated court fees, making the judicial system economically accessible to all Mexicans. Article 20 guaranteed the accused the following rights:

I. That they be informed of the motive for the proceeding and the name of the accuser, if one existed.

II. That their preliminary statement be taken within forty-eight hours. . . .

III. That they be allowed to confront the witnesses against them.

IV. That they have easy access to the facts needed to prepare their defense.

V. That they and persons they trusted be allowed to testify on their behalf. And, if they had no one to defend them, that they be given a list of public defenders from which to choose.[19]

Drafters of the 1857 Constitution intended these rights, typical of most nineteenth-century liberal constitutions, to correct the most egregious failures of colonial criminal justice, to facilitate popular acceptance of the liberal regime, and to set the parameters of subsequent criminal law.

These lofty goals were not easily realized. By incorporating controversial "reform" laws that sought to undermine the considerable power of corporate entities like the Catholic Church and the army, the 1857 Constitution sparked a bloody three-year civil war. With the legal assault on corporations tearing Mexico apart, the liberal push to reform criminal law, a generally well-regarded and noncontroversial project, became even more acute. In 1862, with the liberals temporarily victorious, Benito Juárez's minister of justice Jesús Terán appointed a commission to formulate a penal code for the Federal District and Territory of Baja California. The successful French invasion in May of the following year, and puppet emperor Maximilian's subsequent three-year reign, delayed liberal reform efforts. But following liberal victory in 1867 Juárez reformed his cabinet, appointing penal-code commission member Antonio Martínez de Castro as his minister of justice and public instruction.

Martínez de Castro moved quickly: just a year later the penal code commission was up and running again.[20] In his 1868 message to congress he reminded deputies of the legitimizing potential of reformed criminal laws. "The punishments applied today are truly arbitrary," he admonished, "and ought to be replaced by others better suited to the nature of the crimes, and which will not deprive prisoners of their modesty, their shame, nor the hope of rehabilitating themselves in the public eye." With characteristic utilitarian faith in the value of public instruction he added that "in publishing a good penal code that even the poorest can acquire at little cost, so that they might learn their duties, know the deformity of crime, and advise themselves of the punishments they might incur, one will doubtless see a rapid decline in the number of delinquents."[21]

Appropriately enough, as minister of justice and public instruction, Martínez de Castro was charged not only with drafting a penal code but also with educating the populace so that they could read it. These were the halcyon days of public education in Mexico, although the most notable achievement, Gabino Barreda's founding of the Escuela Nacional Preparatoria with its "scientific" positivist education, benefited mostly elite males. Unfortunately the immense task of educating the lower classes and of thus realizing Martínez de Castro's dream of a didactic penal code would quickly prove beyond the means (and possibly the intentions) of the fledgling liberal state. Nevertheless, the desire to win popular acceptance for the criminal-justice system, and thereby legitimacy for the liberal regime, persisted, and with some success.

The promulgation of the Federal District penal code on April 1, 1871, ended the long gestation of Mexican criminal law. (The State of Vera Cruz, generally at the forefront of Mexican criminology and penology, promulgated the nation's first penal code on May 5, 1869, but it lacked the prestige and influence of the 1871 Federal District code.) As Martínez de Castro had promised, the penal code aspired to be both modern and popular. And, although it had been modeled on the 1848 and 1870 Spanish Penal Codes, even to the point of copying their grammatical errors, the Mexican code made a deliberate appeal to nationalist sentiment.[22] In his "Exposition of Motives" Martínez de Castro cited Montesquieu's classic comments on appropriate legislation, a favorite of Mexican jurists, and added his own specific if typically restrained critique of Spanish colonial criminal law. "Formed in large part centuries ago by absolutist governments," he observed, "in times of ignorance and for a different kind of people with different customs and education, [Spanish criminal laws] have no place in independent, republican, and democratic Mexico where equality is dogma, where one enjoys liberties and rights unknown in the times of Alonso el Sabio."[23] This penal code was, for its principal author, both conceptually up to date and eminently suited to Mexico's unique historical and geographical situation, two crucial criteria, at least for elite acceptance.

The code was also designed to attract the popular support deemed critical to domestic tranquillity. After the fifty years of post-independence turmoil, Martínez de Castro concluded, "the authorities have not been able to count on public cooperation, and because of this they have been unable to guarantee the public security that is essential to the prosperity of the arts, industry, and commerce."[24] A well-ordered, easily accessible penal code that promised speedy, impartial, moderate justice, that reformed prisons and ended presidio confinements and forced labor, seemed just the remedy for Mexico's ills. The 1871 Penal Code thus attacked the perceived essence of the colonial criminal-justice system: inhumane punishment and excessive judicial discretion, which encouraged arbitrary justice.

To ensure impartiality and moderation the code provided an elaborately calibrated system of punishments that left little room for the capricious exercise of judicial discretion by an individual magistrate. A product of classic criminology via English legal theorist Jeremy Bentham, this punitive calculus reflects Martínez de Castro's profound faith in human rationality.[25] Article 4 states plainly that "Crime is: the *voluntary* infraction of a penal law, doing that which it prohibits or neglecting to do that which it demands."[26] Further, those without the ability to reason—young children, the insane, the senile, deaf mutes, and even loyal servants acting under orders—lacked the requisite "criminal responsibility" or "imputability" and could not be convicted of a crime.[27]

Assuming a rational, "responsible" criminal meant that punishments could be rationalized as well. And, to ensure that judicial rationality was exercised in the national interest rather than in the personal or class interests of an individual magistrate, this system was deliberately formulaic. For example, the penal code recognized four levels of criminal acts—planned, intended, frustrated, consummated—each punished with increasing severity.[28] It also recognized four classes of attenuating and aggravating circumstances, with each circumstance augmenting or diminishing punishment by a set proportion according to its class. Attenuating circumstances could be simply "good prior customs" or anything that indicated an unintentionally diminished capacity to reason, such as involuntary drunkenness or gross "ignorance." Conversely, aggravating circumstances might include the use of violence or disguises, taking advantage of a riot, abuse of confidence, or simply having had enough education to know better.[29] Recidivism, always a source of grave concern, was a special aggravating circumstance and could drastically increase punishment, especially if the repeat offense was more serious than its predecessor.[30] Both lists of circumstances were long and fairly explicit, leaving little apparent room for arbitrary judicial maneuvers. (In practice, evaluating an attenuating circumstance like "good prior customs" inevitably reflected the prejudices of the presiding magistrate.) Using these predetermined formulas, then, a judge need only establish guilt and determine circumstances in order to calculate the proper punishment. In this classic liberal formulation of "rule of law," rationality was a systemic rather than an individual trait; predetermined punishments, equally applied, ensured impartiality to a presumably skeptical people accustomed to capricious colonial justice. The extensive section of the penal code devoted exclusively to the crimes of public functionaries and legal representatives served a similar redemptive purpose.[31]

Judicial discretion, although severely limited, was not without its place in this rationalized system. A judge could grant a "preparatory liberty" (*libertad preparatoria*) under police supervision to inmates who exhibited "good behavior" in prison and who had the means to support themselves once released. In keeping with its rationalist premises, the penal code defined good behavior as "positive acts" on the part of the inmate, "habits of order, work, and morality, and especially having dominated the passion or inclination that led to crime."[32] Preparatory liberty thus rewarded normative behavior and complemented the rehabilitation process begun in prison. But the penal code limited even this grant of judicial discretion to a simple decision for or against the inmate.[33] Although it clearly recognized the need to individualize punishment, the manifesto of later positivist-inspired penology, the 1871 Penal Code, tightly controlled judicial discretion. Liberal "memories" of arbitrary colonial justice were still too fresh.

### Preserving the Status Quo: The Porfirian Revisions

This reluctance diminished as the century waned. Firmly in power after the defeat and execution of Maximilian in 1867, fin-de-siècle liberal presidents Benito Juárez, Sebastián Lerdo de Tejada, Porfirio Díaz, and Manuel González encouraged a more authoritarian brand of liberalism that they hoped would undermine the power of regional strongmen (*caciques*) and accelerate national economic development. The growing influence of positivist ideas in Mexico—an eclectic mixture of Comtean scientism and Spencerian Social Darwinism—especially during the second half of the Porfiriato, provided ideological justification for oligarchical rule (although in a nominally liberal context) and encouraged the development of a "scientific politics" appropriately administered by elite científicos.

In spite of its enormous prestige, however, positivism had little immediate effect on Mexican criminal law. Although very much aware of the latest advances in European criminology and deeply committed to "scientific politics," científico reformers preferred a gradualist approach to penal reform that respected the integrity of the 1871 code in spite of its presumably metaphysical views on crime and punishment. Headed by prominent penologist Miguel S. Macedo, the commission established in 1903 to revise the penal code even refused to correct grammatical or stylistic errors in the text unless these errors obscured or distorted its meaning. The commission saw fit only to modify vague language; revise laws that had proved either too harsh, too lenient, or unworkable in the courtroom; and update the laws related to modern technologies, like electricity and telephones. For example, the commission simplified procedures and encouraged fines rather than incarceration for those convicted of public drunkenness, while at the same time expanding the penalties and requirements for recidivism and illegal public disturbances.[34] In general, however, commission members saw little reason to do more than "respect the general principles of the 1871 Code, conserve the nucleus of its system and limit [themselves] to incorporating only the new precepts or new institutions whose usefulness had been proven and whose inclusion is demanded by the present social state of the nation."[35] The only significant addition, a North American–style parole system (*condena condicional*), did further judicial discretion and the individualization of punishment, to a certain extent. Even this "innovation," however, retained the rationalist premise that rewarding nondangerous criminals for good behavior would help reverse their descent into criminality.

In the conservative estimation of penologists like Macedo, practical positivist concerns about the appropriate response to social realities outweighed the theoretical concerns of positivist criminology, which argued that proper social defense included basing the punishment of criminals solely on their "dangerousness" to society. Thus the Porfirian penal code revisions, finally completed in June 1912 during Francisco Madero's troubled presidency, modified rather than revised Martínez's liberal code.[36]

In his chapter on Mexico's "judicial evolution" in the ambitious Porfirian positivist history, *México: Su evolución social* (Mexico: Its social evolution), Jorge Vera Estañol explained this legal conservatism in Social Darwinistic terms. "An abyss," he observed, "divides societies whose progress is intrinsic from those that have managed it thanks to the irresistible contagion of foreign institutions." He added pessimistically that "only time is capable of serving as a gigantic bridge to a vigorous race."[37] For Porfirian penologists, the liberal legal revolution that overthrew the colonial legal system represented a premature, ill-considered (although, as most agreed, necessary and inevitable) attempt to alter Mexican society radically. Conversely, this time around an appropriate response would respect social realities, including the need to modernize (socially and politically, if not economically) in a gradual, controlled fashion. Legal evolution would occur in Mexico, but slowly, so as not to disturb newly won "order and progress." The argument was positivistic but reflected a profoundly conservative positivism that defined social change in nearly glacial terms. Paradoxically, by the early years of the twentieth century, the post-independence liberal legal revolution had become a permanent fixture of the social landscape, an institution to be carefully nurtured and perhaps judiciously modified but never unduly shocked or uprooted. The Mexican Revolution would change all that.

### Punishing the Criminal: The Revolution and Positivist Penology

Disorganized and unsystematic, Porfirian criminology had been ill equipped to challenge the legal establishment. A criminologist of sorts himself, Macedo had publicly criticized liberal penology and lauded the "ever broadening horizons" opened by "the study of crime as a natural phenomenon."[38] Positivist criminology, however, had more of an impact on his discourse than it did on his penal-code reforms. A traditionalist at heart, he continued to use classical legal texts in his law classes.[39] Nevertheless, the professionalization of criminology and the consolidation of the scientific criminological paradigm in the years following the Revolution had made the positivist criminological agenda more difficult to ignore.[40]

In the eyes of most knowledgeable observers, positivist critiques called into question the continued legitimacy and, by extension, the legitimizing potential of Mexican criminal law. Coming on the heels of a massive social revolution that promised social justice for all Mexicans, the push for legal reform to complement political change became yet more intense. Even Macedo's conservative colleague, law professor Antonio Ramos Pedrueza, began his revolutionary-era course in penal law with a detailed discussion of the relative merits of classic and positivist criminology that attacked the underlying premises of Mexican criminal law.[41] Taking inspiration from Italian criminologist Enrico Ferri, Ramos concluded that the rational criminal, the foundation of classic criminology, had never existed. "Observed reality in prisons and asylums affirms that delinquents are abnormal," he noted, "admitting nevertheless that they are very different and that the passage from hardened criminal type to normal human type is not a brusque transition but a series of gradations, just as in animal species." After positivist criminologists' discovery of the criminal's inherent abnormality (typically signified by irrational behavior), Ramos argued that subsequent legislation and judicial practice should seek to judge not the "criminal *and* the crime" but the "criminal *in* the crime."[42]

The positivists' insistence on individualizing punishment in order to better rehabilitate the criminal but especially to "defend" society by keeping dangerous criminals off the streets (regardless of the severity of their actual crime) was beginning to make serious inroads into mainstream Mexican legal theory as well. José Angel Ceniceros, acting as adjunct professor in a 1926 course in penal law directed by his mentor, Miguel Macedo, noted that "crime, more than an act, is a state [of mind]."[43] The translation of positivist theory into practice lacked only opportunity.

That opportunity came in 1925 when President Plutarco Elías Calles created revisory commissions to bring Mexico's various legal codes into line with the 1917 Constitution and with post-revolutionary expectations. A year later the fateful addition of committed positivist José Almaraz to the penal code commission (which included Ramos Pedrueza) marked the beginning of a frontal assault on classical criminology and the 1871 Penal Code. In Almaraz's eyes, Mexico's latest perceived crime wave testified to the ineffectualness of the existing penal code and thus to its theoretical poverty. "The classical school," Almaraz recalled, "had become completely bankrupt and could no longer serve as the foundation for penal legislation."[44] With this blunt assessment the revisory commission set out to bring Mexican criminal laws into line with modern positivist penal theory.

What the commission attempted was nothing less than a theoretical revolution in Mexican criminal law. As positivists they insisted on contextualizing crime. The classical school, Almaraz observed with some exaggeration, "forgets the criminal and concerns itself only with the crime committed." Attempting "absolute mathematical equality between crime and punishment," he insisted, often resulted in inappropriate punishments. This formulaic system inevitably released unreformed dangerous criminals back into society, while at the same time it condemned relatively harmless incidental criminals to the corrupting influence of prison confinement. Under the classical legal regimen, Almaraz declared, "the toxic current of crime grows day by day."[45] As an antidote to this misguided rationalism the commission argued for a fundamental redefinition of the criminal act as "a natural product, born not of free will but of physical, anthropological, and social factors."[46] The theoretical inspiration was probably French sociologist Emile Durkheim, whose influential 1893 *Rules of the Sociological Method* had insisted that crime was a normal "social fact" in all human societies. Moreover, with a purportedly revolutionary regime in power, lingering social inequalities—exacerbated by the sins of the Porfiriato—also provided an easy scapegoat for Mexico's latest crime wave and helped legitimize the new political order bent on their eventual elimination.

Having determined the causes of crime, the commission then sought to redefine criminal responsibility. For classical penology, establishing the rationality of the individual criminal was a prerequisite to punishment; to positivists like Almaraz this seemed absurd. "Given that in-fractors reveal hereditary or acquired, permanent or temporary bio-psychic anomalies," Almaraz argued, "the foundations of a fight against delinquency based on moral responsibility disappear and the entire classical edifice comes crashing to the ground." He concluded that healthy, "rational" societies, in a Social Darwinistic spirit of self-preservation, protected themselves from all threats, regardless of these threats' motivation. In fact, this conflation of social health and social ra-tionality effectively denied rationality to any individual "organism" that threatened society's collective well-being. Recognizing this funda-mental discursive shift, Almaraz proposed that "social responsibility" replace moral responsibility and that "sanctions" substitute for punish-ments in a more workable, nonmoralistic system of "social defense."[47]

This discursive shift carried two important corollaries. First, by privi-leging an abstraction, criminality, over the more narrow category of lawbreaker, it encompassed many more people. "An individual can be dangerous to society," Almaraz advised, "even before committing a crime [lesionar un derecho]," and he especially singled out alcoholics, drug addicts, vagrants, beggars, and even paranoids.[48] Mexican elites had traditionally persecuted most of these groups. Nevertheless the le-gal "sanctioning" of potentially (but not always technically) criminal categories—punishing states of mind rather than pre-defined criminal acts—was one inevitable and potentially portentous consequence of using social defense as the principal criteria for criminal law. "All law is essentially doctrine," Almaraz reminded his readers, "politically per-sonalized doctrine."[49]

The second corollary, typical of positivist endeavors, was a consider-able expansion in the prestige and scope of scientifically trained experts. Any serious attempt to transcend a relatively simple determination of guilt and to evaluate the dangerousness (estado peligroso) of an individ-ual criminal required considerable expertise. Almaraz warned that "the prior and indispensable study of the delinquent's integral personality demands functionaries and judges trained in the modern doctrines of criminal psychology" among which he included everything from endo-crinology to the interpretation of tattoos.[50] This new requirement was clearly self-serving and designed to insinuate criminology into the jus-tice system by creating professional spaces for trained criminologists. It also ensured their domination of legal discourse. To this end the 1929 Penal Code established a Supreme Council of Social Defense and Prevention to oversee the entire federal prison and detention system, supervise the "individualization of punishment," and ensure that criminal-justice personnel upheld the basic tenets of social defense.[51]

Other innovative features appeared as provisions of the new penal code. For example, in an effort to individualize punishment—to make the punishment suit the criminal rather than the crime—the revisory commission greatly expanded the alternatives to incarceration by broadening the *condena condicional* and substituting fines for short sentences. To support these changes the commission revived the time-honored complaint about corrupting prisons. "It is necessary to oppose short incarcerations," it advised, "which in their current form fail to correct, intimidate, or inoculate; but which oblige the first-time offender to transform himself into a professional [criminal]."[52] Therapeutic solutions, especially for juveniles and the insane, were favored over simple incarceration and, in keeping with the principles of social defense, sanctions against the dangerous criminally insane could be extended indefinitely. Not surprisingly, this broadening of "sanctions" required not only more professional training but also greater judicial discretion in sentencing, albeit under the watchful eye of the supreme council and its ever-vigilant president, José Almaraz.

Liberal human rights provisions of the 1917 Constitution, however, thwarted efforts to formulate a truly positivist penal code. Punishing everyone judged dangerous to society clearly violated basic constitutional guarantees. "Since the Constitution prevents the realization of all the logical consequences that can be derived from the adoption of the principle of social defense," Almaraz noted with regret, "the Revisory Commission had to forego many important innovations."[53] This gave the new penal code a "transitory" character, at least in the eyes of its principal architect. These gaps between theory and practice also provided future opponents of the code an easy avenue of attack—one that they quickly exploited.

### Pragmatism over Positivism: The Legal Establishment Responds

Legal establishment attacks on the 1929 penal code were swift and devastating. Critics complained that the new code, for all its theoretical innovations, was inconsistent, unnecessarily radical, and unacceptably impractical. Future professor of criminal law Juan José González Bustamante, a young lawyer at the time and a former Macedo student, recalled Almaraz's discursive revolution as "simply a conceit [*snobismo*], an irresponsible word play, because Penal Law is fundamentally a protector of society and punishment is essentially retributive and is imposed as a necessary evil in order to procure the conservation of social order. . . . If the means employed, whether it is called punishment or sanction, produces even a little suffering on the part of its recipient we must conclude that it is indeed a punishment."[54]

Other critics lauded Almaraz's efforts to supplant outdated classical precepts but argued that the new code failed to live up to its promise. One observer noted that "the code suffered from redundancies, occasional duplicity of concepts, contradictions, and difficulties of application."[55] These obvious defects encouraged an overdetermined criticism that attacked the code's internal contradictions, theoretical foundations, and constitutionality. Another critic, for example, observed that although the code was purportedly based on theories of social defense and dangerousness, in fact it retained the "objective criteria" of classical penology, in particular the formulaic system of aggravating and attenuating circumstances of the 1871 Penal Code. Also, its expanded system of sanctions included a confusing table of indemnizations and an elaborate system of fines based on income, which made administration time-consuming and difficult.[56] González added that condemning "delinquents, the insane, idiots, imbeciles or those who suffer any other debility, illness or mental anomaly" to indefinite internment was "a wise security measure but contrary to dictates of the Constitution."[57] Most critics agreed on the need to bring the penal code into line with modern criminological theory. Many, however, insisted that the 1929 code had missed the point, promising a theoretical innovation that it failed to deliver and that was furthermore unsuited to Mexico's social and constitutional realities. Not coincidentally, these defects also undermined its ideological potential.

In the face of this barrage of criticism, interim president Emilio Portes Gil quickly established a new revisory commission. To avoid future dissension and resistance, the five voting members of the commission represented the heart of the capital's legal establishment: the interior ministry, the attorney general of the Republic, the attorney general of the Federal District and territories, the Federal District superior court, and the penal courts. Representatives of the Supreme Council of Social Defense and Prevention and the previous revisory commission were in attendance, but only as nonvoting advisors.[58] The two most prominent voting members, José Angel Ceniceros and Luis Garrido, were Macedo acolytes and vocal critics of the 1929 code.

Given the practical orientation and the relative conservatism of the new revisory commission, the repudiation of Almaraz's dogmatic positivism was inevitable. Garrido noted that "most of us had been brought up on the Comtism of the old National Preparatory School and viewed with great sympathy the survival of positivism in the modern schools of penology, without finding feasible the construction of a code based exclusively on positivist principles."[59] The stated principles of the 1931 Penal Code then included not only the standard admonition to simplicity and clarity but a promise to modernize only "up to the point permitted by our constitutional framework, our judicial traditions, and our social and economic conditions."[60] Commission spokesman Alfonso Teja Zabre argued that "no school, doctrine, or penal system can serve as the integral foundation of a Penal Code. It is possible only to follow an eclectic and pragmatic tendency, which is to say practical and realizable."[61] Thus, instead of concentrating on positivist dogma, commission members focused on "pragmatic" means. Specific goals included a simplification of procedures, the effective reparation of damages, the individualization of punishment, a decreased reliance on abstract ethical standards (casuismo), and an increase in judicial discretion within constitutional limits.[62] The first two of these five goals addressed the practical failings of the 1929 code; the next two restated positivist critiques of classical penology. The last goal—increased judicial discretion—represented the new penal code's principal innovation.

Articles 51 and 52 codified this increase in judicial discretion. Article 51 advised judges "inside legally fixed limits" to take under consideration both "external circumstances" and "the peculiarities of the delinquent." Article 52 suggested that along with the traditional mitigating circumstances judges also consider "the special conditions in which [the delinquent] found himself at the moment the crime was committed and other personal antecedents and conditions . . . that demonstrate his greater or lesser dangerousness [temibilidad]."[63] Ceniceros and Garrido even suggested that the positivist motto, "There are no crimes, only criminals" should be modified to "There are no criminals, only men."[64] This mixture of traditional and modern, liberal and positivist, concerns typified the self-consciously pragmatic nature of the new code.

Like each of their predecessors, the supporters of the 1931 code argued that it was the first penal code to reflect national realities. One observer noted that the 1931 code "modestly but firmly develops its desiderata in accordance with naked Mexican reality . . . recognizing, organizing, and balancing reality itself."[65] Another remarked that "the division of classes and castes by economic and racial differences in Mexico, causes grave difficulties in the application of penal laws, especially for unassimilated indigenous groups. . . . The only recourse is to simplify norms and procedures, prescribing broad and generic regulations that effectively permit the individualization of sanctions."[66] The argument that culturally and racially heterogenous Mexico required greater judicial latitude accorded with post-revolutionary concerns about addressing the needs of the now-mobilized popular sectors. While the 1929 code had attempted a retheorization of criminal law that appealed primarily to elite modernizers, the drafters of the 1931 Penal Code sought a broader audience. By individualizing punishment they not only protected society from dangerous criminals but also protected relatively harmless offenders from an arbitrary, mechanistic justice that even their positivist predecessors had been unable to supplant. To this end the new code broadened the range of punishments and abandoned the elaborate calculus of aggravating and attenuating circumstances that had characterized the two previous codes.

The expanded discretionary powers of the judge permitted a flexibility that was impossible under the previous penal codes. The ideological benefits of a more responsive justice system were obvious. Previously marginalized groups could now hope for clemency from a sympathetic if paternalistic judge: a throwback to the colonial tradition of royal mercy preserved perhaps in more informal justice systems, and for both reasons eminently suited to perceived Mexican social realities.[67] The international vogue for state socialism and the desire to institutionalize (and thus control) popular justice doubtless encouraged paternalistic solutions as well.

In this case at least, modernity and tradition were not necessarily mutually exclusive. Garrido's three criteria for the penal code included consideration of "the Mexican juridical tradition . . . the doctrines and sentiments of the people . . . [and] the conditions of Mexico's collective life." He added that "the work thus realized sought to establish itself in human terms . . . in a dynamic relation between penal norms and social reality [*realidad del ambiente*]."[68] In fact these apparently contradictory sources enhanced the 1931 code's ideological possibilities. Because it could appeal to both modernizers and traditionalists, paternalistic discretionary justice seemed the ideal solution to the admittedly complex and contradictory legitimation problems generated by a wildly heterogenous society. Theoretically at least, individual judges could tailor the law to the social, cultural, and even racial circumstances of their clientele.

Some observers recognized potential dangers. Reviving traditional liberal concerns, one commentator warned that "judicial discretion requires a broad understanding on the part of those charged with applying the law, in order that it not turn into arbitrariness."[69] The possible dangers of paternalism, however, seemed a small price to pay for the popular acceptance that would presumably result from a more flexible criminal-justice system. "A fundamentally humane justice," Garrido advised, "will take into account the sensibilities of the transgressor." He added that "punishing a man of exquisite sensibilities is not the same as punishing a calloused and crude man."[70] The argument could have come from Lardizábal himself. By the third decade of the twentieth century colonial legal institutions had receded far enough into the historical past to be viewed with a certain dispassionate nostalgia, the dangers of arbitrary justice having been mitigated to a certain extent by the assumed benefits of a paternal state.

The paternalism implicit in individualizing punishment was nothing new. Almaraz's code, for example, had fostered the paternalistic pretensions of positive criminology and by extension the place of positive criminologists in the criminal-justice system. The Supreme Council of Social Defense and Prevention's central role in ensuring ideological correctness, however, had rankled the legal establishment. Almaraz's opponents, most of them judges trained in criminology, had resisted this oversight for both practical and professional reasons; it created administrative problems, and it usurped their authority. Increased judicial discretion, on the other hand, transferred that authority from the supreme council (which subsequently dropped "supreme" from its name) to the judges themselves. This represented a Pyrrhic victory for positive criminology; while it did permit judges greater latitude to individualize punishment, the insistence on observing constitutional forms and thus metaphysical liberal notions of human rights precluded any legal justification for a comprehensive program of social defense.[71] Consequently, after 1931 criminology became the handmaiden rather than the ultimate arbiter of the modern Mexican criminal-justice system. And again, theoretical inconsistencies—the mishmash of liberalism, state socialism, and neopaternalism masquerading as "pragmatism" (or even Hegelian synthesis)—probably enhanced the 1931 Penal Code's ideological potential by appealing to a broad social spectrum for a wide variety of reasons.

Evaluating the practical impact of legal reforms on the Mexican criminal-justice system is considerably more difficult than is determining its ideological contribution. Mexican criminal justice, like criminal justice in general, retains an important measure of its legitimacy through an inherent conservatism that respects the traditional expectations of its practitioners and clients. This conservative tendency must be acknowledged. When change occurs it occurs most often at the ideological rather than the practical level; traditional forms take on new content without seriously affecting longstanding legal ritual.

Modern trial records for Mexico City courts are hard to access, and they are scattered among various archives. The uncatalogued Secretariat of Justice files at the National Archive contain several boxes of judicial decisions and sentences, mostly from the Porfiriato. The judicial archives of the Reclusorio del Sur and the Reclusorio Oriente have some court records and police reports from the post-revolutionary period. However, the very randomness of the records consulted suggests that they were probably typical. Based on this narrow and very random sample of trial records from the 1870s through the 1930s, the continuities in the practice of Mexican criminal law seem remarkable. A simple juxtaposition suffices: An 1803 recommendation for sentencing advised that a convicted thief be excused from public punishment because, "being a minor, already sentenced to five months in prison, and especially not having repeated the offense and it being his first offense, suggests that he is not incorrigible and is capable of correction. For which reason and so that he not lose his sense of honor in the company of the idle and vile rabble, being Spanish and of good family as is well known, it would behoove your honor to commute his punishment of six months in public works."[72] A 1908 judicial decision remarked simply that "the accused has been previously of good habits [buenas costumbres] and is so ignorant and crude [rudo] that while committing the crime he lacked the discernment necessary to understand its illicitness."[73] A 1935 judicial decision reflected similar considerations, but with greater precision. It noted that the accused "is Catholic, earns one peso a day as a street vendor, has never attended school, is not in the habit of using alcoholic beverages or narcotics, has never suffered from infectious or contagious diseases. . . . This the first time he has been detained, he has no aliases and no worldly possessions."[74] Underlying all these documents is a fundamental concern about mitigating circumstances and proper punishment.[75] Apparently the broader discretion accorded colonial and post-1931 magistrates encouraged greater precision, even though changing penal philosophies might justify their decisions in very different ways. Nevertheless, in spite of obvious philosophical and stylistic changes, judicial criteria had undergone surprisingly little change since the colonial period.

Reflected in the increased precision of later trial records, the greater latitude allowed under the 1931 Penal Code partially restored discretionary powers judges had enjoyed before the 1871 Penal Code came into effect. Nineteenth-century liberals had transferred these powers to an impartial code that was theoretically immune from corruption and arbitrary rulings. To later legal reformers, however, mechanistic justice seemed arbitrary as well. Furthermore, it seemed incapable of responding effectively to the diverse circumstances engendered by a heterogeneous Mexican people; a people that post-revolutionary governments in particular hoped to accommodate at least rhetorically.

Whatever the practical consequences of the 1931 Penal Code, its drafters, most of them judges themselves, returned limited discretionary powers to presiding magistrates so that they might better exercise a presumably flexible and benevolent judicial paternalism: an ideological harbinger of, perhaps even a rehearsal for, the advent of the *estado papá*. Moreover, just as late-nineteenth-century scientific criminology had "naturalized" the covert exclusions of liberal constitutionalism, increased judicial discretion further enhanced the nation-state's power to define and police normative—rather than just unlawful—behavior. The post-revolutionary Mexican state prided itself on its responsiveness to its most marginalized clients. But even actively solicited clientage was (and still is) a far cry from real citizenship.

# 6. Los Jotos

Contested Visions
of Homosexuality

For late-nineteenth- and early-twentieth-century Mexican criminologists, sexual deviance of any kind was unnatural, antisocial, and linked to innate criminality; criminals constituted an identifiable class with distinct traits that included atavistic homosexual tendencies. Thus, in the criminological imagination, sexual deviance indicated criminality, which in turn threatened national, political, economic, and social development. Homosexuality in particular undermined a nation's very existence by fostering unfruitful sexual unions in an era obsessed with national reproduction and the international "struggle for life."[1] Either way, the perceived need to study the problem was urgent.

The Mexican inmate subjects of criminological study had a much different vision of homosexuality than did their professional observers. Prison inmates did indeed engage fairly often, by most accounts, in what criminologists defined as homosexual activities. Many inmates, like their criminologist counterparts, stigmatized the participants. Upon closer examination, however, the correspondence breaks down. Some sexual acts—those in which men took the passive role with other men—were denigrated by criminologists and inmates alike, although for very different reasons. Other behaviors—men taking the active role with other men—deeply concerned criminologists but bothered inmates hardly at all. The link between sexual and criminal deviance thus proved more complex and more socially (as opposed to scientifically) constructed than criminologists had supposed. Why this was so and what it means are the subjects of this chapter.[2]

The most exhaustive criminological investigation into sexual deviance was conducted at the turn of the century by Porfirian criminologist, journalist, and littérateur Carlos Roumagnac.[3] In the spirit of the era he begins with a dire warning about national degeneration conveyed through the ubiquitous medical metaphor: "What epidemic [is] more dangerous than that for which we know . . . no hygienic measures with which to combat it and for which quarantines are useless because we carry it inside ourselves, infiltrated in our blood for years and years, and which we transmit to our descendants, passing on to them without thought but not without guilt, the virus that sooner or later will flower into the bitter blossoms of crime and transgression?"[4] The mixture of melodrama and medical science was not only typical of the period; it also presumed the criminologist/physician's right—as an agent of "social defense" against the contagion of crime—to gaze frankly and intimately into the bodies and lives of his (and early Mexican criminologists were all male) inmate/patients. That sexual behavior, especially deviant sexual behavior, would appear as a leitmotiv or recurring theme in his study is thus hardly surprising. Sex was after all the unspoken obsession of the Victorian age.[5]

Roumagnac's "scientific" method involved extensive case histories of his inmate subjects compiled in large part from personal interviews conducted inside Mexico City's principal jail, Belén, and the newly built Federal Penitentiary. Inmates were photographed, measured, inspected, and questioned about everything from their extended family's health history to their post-prison plans. And at every opportunity they were quizzed on their sexual habits. Not surprisingly, given his expectations, Roumagnac's "observations" of individual inmates established a positive correlation between the criminal and sexual deviance of all his subjects: boys, women, and men.

Since youth figuratively and literally represented Mexico's future, the boys' case was particularly revealing. Although Roumagnac acknowledged—as the previous quotation indicates—a powerful link between inherited traits and potential criminality, he also expressed great interest in the environmental (as opposed to genetic) factors that either caused or sparked criminal behavior. These factors, he insisted, played a potent role in transforming Mexico City's legions of "morally" and physically abandoned children into hardened criminals. One of his many case studies, for example, included a thirteen-year-old boy, brought in for assisting a blind beggar, who "didn't know his father and knew of his mother only that she got sick a lot, suffered from rheumatism, and drank and got drunk frequently." "I don't doubt," Roumagnac pessimistically concluded, "that someday he will reappear as a beggar in his own right and blind as well."[6] Alcoholism and sexual promiscuity were problems too. In Roumagnac's professional estimation, these environmental factors—abandonment, alcoholism, promiscuity—thwarted the development of proper moral restraints in children: criminal and sexual deviance was the inevitable and deplorable result.

Roumagnac included five case histories in a chapter on "juvenile criminals," and in each interview he asked his young subjects about sexual practices outside and inside the prison. Most admitted to encounters with female prostitutes before incarceration but vigorously denied engaging in homosexual encounters in prison. "I'm sure," he observed of a fourteen-year-old convicted murderer, "that if I had asked him the question somewhere else, he would have hit me." Nevertheless, Roumagnac persisted, ultimately uncovering the "inevitable" evidence of homosexual behavior: an ongoing relationship between two boys in which the older boy took the active (and often aggressive) role of the *mayate* (dung beetle) while his sometimes unwilling partner acted as the passive *caballo* (horse).[7]

Roumagnac's "objective," style, whereby he presented his data without formal analysis, obscured his reading of this encounter. The general drift, however, was clear. While he stigmatized both parties as "sexual degenerates," Roumagnac, if anything, sympathized more with the younger boy, relating his attempts at resistance (after confession) and attributing "vicious appetites" to his partner. This bias was hardly surprising. For a guardian of public order, passivity and a willingness to reform were positive attributes, while aggressive immorality directly challenged proper political and moral authority. Nevertheless, the shame felt by the passive partner—"I'm more of a man than you are," the younger boy shouts at his partner/rapist in Roumagnac's account—indicated that inmates interpreted the situation quite differently (as we shall see).[8]

Roumagnac's investigation of adult male homosexuality suggests that it followed a pattern similar to homosexuality among youths, with one significant difference: overt homosexual behavior was accepted practice (within certain bounds), especially within the poorly supervised confines of Belén. When one director attempted to isolate "all known pederasts" in a separate area to put an end to the "bloody squabbles" of jealous men, targeted inmates responded by "parading in front of other inmates, without bashfulness or shame, making, on the contrary, an ostentatious display of feminine voices and mannerisms."[9] Unlike the young boy forced to "play horse" for his older partner, adult male sexual inverts (as turn-of-the-century observers described effemi-

nate men) flamboyantly asserted their difference, often taking suggestive, feminized nicknames like "la Golondrina" (the swallow) and "la
Bicicleta" (the bicycle).[10] For Roumagnac they were dangerous sexual
degenerates. And in his view the problem penetrated far deeper into the
inmate population.[11]

Like the boys, adult male inmate-subjects were quizzed about their
sexuality at every opportunity. Like the boys, most had been sexually
promiscuous before incarceration. Like the boys, most emphatically denied any involvement in homosexual activity even while acknowledging
its presence in the prison. And, like the boys, they maintained their "innocence," even in the face of contrary evidence. One inmate, accused by
many others of "pederasty," suggested that his principal accuser was
seeking revenge for his refusal to "grant [sexual] favors."[12] Roumagnac,
noncommittal as usual, later cited the man's accuser's allegation that
another inmate who "acted as his [the accused's] woman" was contem-
plating murder in order to stay in prison with his lover.[13] To further
complicate matters, the accuser's own brother accused him (the accuser) of seducing him (the brother) as a child and of being a "horse" or
passive partner to other inmates.[14] Even without interpretation, these
intricate webs of accusations and counteraccusations—as they do in
the previously cited case of the young boys—demonstrated the fundamental deceitfulness of criminals and thus reinforced Roumagnac's
efforts to link criminal and sexual deviance. They also, not coincidentally, signaled the need for trained observers to expose these elaborate
dissimulations.

One sensational case—a man convicted of murdering a five-year-old
boy he had just raped—further cemented this link. Roumagnac identified this as a clear case of "moral insanity." He noted that the subject
had begun by watching his sisters undress and observing copulating
dogs and had then progressed to pornography and group sex. Coupled
with a family history of mental illness and the subject's own alcoholic
tendencies, the rape and murder of a child seemed inevitable, according
to Roumagnac's narrative. And his juxtaposition of this case with other,
less dramatic tales of moral decline created a guilt by inference in which
all deviants share the blame for the most atrocious of their collective
crimes. In this context even the subject's seeming disinterest in homosexual activities in prison paradoxically suggests that these activities
were not isolated sexual phenomena but were part of a generalized deviancy that manifested itself in different ways at different times and in dif-

ferent situations: the appearance of any deviant behavior thus signified the hidden presence of its other possible manifestations.[15]

Nor were Roumagnac's observations about deviancy confined to males. Women too felt the probing gaze of the professional criminologist. And their responses were remarkably similar to, if less ostentatious than, those of their male counterparts. Some women, for example, openly acknowledged their sexual relations with other women: according to Roumagnac's informants "manly" women parted their hair on the right side, while their "feminine" partners parted it on the left. At the same time, however, most of Roumagnac's subjects denied participating in homosexual activities even while they accused their fellow inmates of *safismo* (female homosexual relations). As is noted in chapter 3, one particularly vociferous inmate condemned the frequent fights between jealous women and their habit of "kissing, embracing, and nibbling" each other in public.[16] As he did of boys' and men's refusal to acknowledge their own participation in homosexual acts, Roumagnac implied that most of these denials were disingenuous and cited various contradictions and ambiguities in the different accounts. Again, the overall impression was of dissimulating inmates attempting to cover up the rampant homosexual activity that signified their deviance.

As it did in the case of the men and boys, this deviance had a history. The most prominent of Roumagnac's morality tales, for example, chronicled the fall of a young girl seduced and abandoned by her patron's son, who turned to prostitution, morphine, and *safismo* (which she "learned" from two Spanish colleagues) before committing the murder—she killed another prostitute in a dispute over a man—that landed her in jail.[17] This tale and his other narratives of women's "descent into crime" resembled those of the men, with one significant difference. For the women, moral lassitude, rather than leading directly to criminal acts, increased their vulnerability to unsavory, outside influences—dishonest young men, procuresses, madams, drug dealers, pimps, and Spanish sapphists—who turned them to crime. The assumption that deviant women failed to control their own destinies gave female homosexuality a slightly different spin, especially for the general inmate population that—as we will see—interpreted male homosexual behavior very differently.[18] For Roumagnac, this difference signified much less, because female criminality hardly threatened public order; forging the theoretical link between sexual and criminal deviance in both men and women was a far more important undertaking.[19]

By the 1930s the pioneering efforts of men like Roumagnac had borne their expected fruit. Early criminologists had struggled to find the proper words—sexual inverts (for both sexes), pederasts (for men), sapphists (for women)—to describe what was after all a rather complex set of deviant behaviors. Later generations confidently lumped these variegated phenomena into a new conceptual category they called "homosexuality."

Typically, this new category was closely tied to criminality. In a 1934 article on the "Antisocial character of homosexuals" written for *Criminalia,* the newly inaugurated professional journal for Mexican criminologists, Dr. Alfonso Millán buttressed Lombroso's old argument about atavistic homosexuals with up-to-date references to Freudian psychology and recent discoveries in endocrinology (the study of hormones). Extrapolating from these prestigious "scientific" sources, he concluded that male homosexuals took on the negative traits of both sexes: "from the man [*macho*] he has a somewhat aggressive, hostile, and vain spirit, while from the woman, the gossipy scheming, the subtle intrigue of the eighteenth-century salon, and traitorous coquetry." These traits resulted in a "psychology . . . that seems more prejudicial than the physical practices themselves." And, while he distinguished between passive and active homosexual types, he added—as Roumagnac had already implied—that active partners were "as or more dangerous" than their passive counterparts because they were more aggressive and difficult to identify.[20] A 1935 article on "Homosexuality and the dangerous state [*estado peligroso*]" written for the same journal by his Peruvian colleague, Dr. Susana Solano, expanded on Millán's themes. She noted that "other peculiarities like being lazy, indolent, and egotistical augment [the homosexual's] dangerousness." More to the point, she added confidently that "a certain pathological sexual affinity between the insane, criminals, and homosexuals is proven."[21] For these later criminologists (both of whom were medical doctors as well), Roumagnac's inferences had become criminological doctrine. By 1935 the links between criminal and sexual deviance had been "proven."

Some criminologists went a step further. Since the Revolution most Mexican social scientists had stressed the social and environmental causes of criminality. This environmentalist bent shifted some of the blame from the criminal to society and committed the national government (at least rhetorically) to improving living conditions for all Mexicans as well as to rehabilitating the criminals produced by these social inequities. The rhetorical commitment to social justice for the previously criminalized lower classes also affected criminological discourse.

In this context sexual deviance and especially homosexuality—which criminologists still considered primarily biological problems—threatened to contaminate "normal" criminals. In his book on criminal methods in Mexico, police reporter José Raúl Aguilar related an anecdote about a macho convicted murderer transported to the penal colony at Islas Marías whose voice became increasingly "high pitched and effeminate" after he was forced (literally kicking and screaming) to travel with a group of obviously homosexual convicts.[22] Aguilar's preoccupation with the contamination of a murderer suggests that some criminologists were restructuring the hierarchy of deviance.

In response to the perceived threat of homosexual contamination, Mexican criminologists like Raúl González Enríquez pioneered the "conjugal visit"—which allowed prisoners sexual access to their "spouses"—specifically to alleviate the problem of homosexuality in the all-male world of the prison. In his prize-winning book, *El problema sexual del hombre en la penitenciaría* (The sexual problem of men in the penitentiary), he warned that in some inmates "the taste for fairies [*los jotos*] . . . becomes so ingrained that afterwards they need to mix in illicit acts [*coitos bastardos*] to satisfy their wayward instinct." Like Roumagnac, he recognized fundamental differences between passive "sexual inverts" and aggressive "sexual perverts," while pointing out the specific dangers posed by each group. Inverts he criticized for introducing young inmates to "unsuspected pleasures." Perverts he especially condemned for their "violent passions . . . , [which] are the source of many acts that could be classified as criminal." To support his point he cited frequent fights between jealous men and particularly graphic examples of younger inmates raped at knifepoint. As it does in Roumagnac's work, the affinity between criminal and sexual deviance appears obvious. But, according to González, homosexuality was even more dangerous than criminality because it could permanently corrupt the moral character of a potentially redeemable criminal.[23]

This restructuring of deviance by post-revolutionary Mexican criminologists underscores the political, even ideological, agenda that formed the foundation of criminological "science" and its attitude toward homosexual relations. In the Porfirian period social scientists had been obsessed with the problem of "order," which seemed the necessary first step toward capitalist economic development. Criminal activities represented a grave threat to public order, which in turn threatened economic development by disrupting commerce, encouraging capital flight, and discouraging foreign investment. Crime was therefore a source of considerable concern to Mexican policymakers. This concern translated into a scientific investigation not just of crime and criminals per se but of a generalized state of being, "criminality," that included sexual deviance. Roumagnac's special concerns about the disruptive potential of aggressive homosexuals—González's perverts—are a case in point and make this linkage with Porfirian fears of disorder quite clear. Thus Roumagnac's construction of "homosexuality" was far more ideological than scientific. This holds true for his successors as well.

Post-revolutionary criminologists shared Porfirian concerns about public order and capitalist economic development, but with one significant difference. Ideologically linked to the idea of an inclusive (if not democratic) modern state, their agenda stressed the redemptive possibilities of the new regime and thus doubly condemned congenital (probably unredeemable) states like homosexuality. Criminals might be the by-products of social injustice; homosexuals were (especially in the biological sense) unproductive sexual degenerates whose perversion threatened the moral health of the newly reborn Mexican nation. The wholesale transportation of "undesirable" homosexuals to the Islas Marías penal colony alluded to by Aguilar underscored this new attitude. In the new "revolutionary" Mexico the attitude was: criminals maybe, homosexuals definitely not!

Criminologists, however, were not the only group that politicized "homosexuality." Their male subjects, for example, constructed the politics of sexual deviance rather differently.[24] Coming for the most part from the popular classes, they generally took a position, common throughout Latin America, that heavily stigmatized effeminate sexual inverts (los jotos) but not necessarily their active (and thus more manly) sexual partners.[25] Although they also recognized different homosexual types, criminologists typically lumped criminal activity and all forms of sexual deviance under the rubric of "criminality." This conflation of deviances, given the lower-class origins of most Mexican criminals, amounted to a class distinction.[26] For male inmates, on the other hand, the stigma of homosexuality fractured along gender rather than class lines: men who inverted their gender by behaving like women were constantly mocked and harassed (and used) by their macho colleagues, while men who took the active (male) role in sexual relations usually escaped severe censure.[27]

Active partners denied their participation in homosexual acts when they spoke to criminologists; such behavior was never publicly acknowledged, even if it was expected. In any case, they rarely questioned their own manhood and vigorously rejected the criminologist's accusation of "homosexuality." For example, one of Roumagnac's adult male subjects felt compelled to "pray to God that in the time I'm here that I don't use one of those men." Another, although he too had resisted temptation, responded with a colorful euphemism—"I'm not saying I won't drink from that well" [de esta agua no beberé]—to express his position.[28] Nor did these attitudes change much. Years later an inmate informed another inquisitive criminologist that many fellow prisoners satisfied their sexual needs by making arrangements with "effeminate men" [los afeminados].[29] For active partners homosexual relations were a vice, even a sin, but not an indicator of their own homosexuality. And under these circumstances denying homosexual relations was no different than denying any other legal or moral transgression, a kind of denial convicted criminals likely understood quite well.

For most inmates, however, sexual inversion was a different matter altogether. Effeminate men were mercilessly teased and sometimes raped by other inmates. A 1931 account of conditions in Belén remarked that "male laundresses were *naturally* the object of ridicule from other inmates."[30] The situation was similar in the Federal Penitentiary, where prison authorities attempted to isolate effeminate inmates. In spite of their isolation, a inmate observer noted that "the others jeer at them." And, asked about sexual relations between active and passive partners in the Federal Penitentiary, another responded frankly that "sometimes the active one pays and other times the passive one; sometimes it's arranged free for reasons of sympathy and other times through the energetic imposition of the macho on the fairy [del macho sobre el joto]."[31]

Even through the criminologist's lens, the difference in inmates' attitudes is apparent. An anecdote related by criminologist Carlos Franco Sodi is especially revealing. In a short essay entitled "Meditating on the thought of a prisoner," Franco recalled encountering the following piece of graffiti, written in bad Spanish, on a wall in the Federal Penitentiary: "Padese sufre y sobrelleva sin perder la esperanza de reunirte con los tullos para aserlos felises y ser bueno." [Suffer, bear, and endure without losing the hope of being reunited with your loved ones in order to make them happy and to be good]. For Franco the message indicated the presence of "a normal individual, honorable and of moral sentiments," an "accidental" criminal whom the justice system could easily and profitably return to civil society. Beside this hopeful message, however, another inmate had boldly scrawled "los jotos."[32] The response, Franco noted, was "typical" because for most inmates "manliness consists in feeling at home behind bars, in being firmly resolved to lead a life of crime, and in feeling no remorse for the blood spilled or the deed committed that landed them behind bars."[33]

Franco's interpretation characterized the attitudes of guardians of public order. The inmate who scrawled "los jotos" next to the pious thoughts of his fellow prisoner clearly had a different take. And his take was as political as any criminologist's. Deciphering it, however, involves some speculation.

In his famous 1950 essay on "The sons of La Malinche," Mexican poet-philosopher Octavio Paz examined the various meanings of the Spanish verb *chingar* (to fuck). In his exposition of its meaning for Mexicans, the sexual politics were quite clear: "The *chingón* is the *macho*, the male: he rips open the *chingada*, the female who is pure passivity, defenseless against the exterior world."[34] In (relatively) polite conversation, *joder* (to screw) stands in for *chingar* and *jodido* (screwed) for *chingada*, but with one significant difference. *Jodido* carries the same political connotation as *chingada* but implies a less permanent, less explicitly sexual condition that allows for the possibility of resistance. On the other hand, *joto*—which resembles a bastardized past particle of *joder*—suggests the sexual "passivity" Paz attributes to the *chingada*. Thus, following Paz's construction of *chingar*, the *macho* inmate who scrawled "los jotos" was expressing deep disdain for the pious soul who accepted his punishment with resignation and remorse.

That disdain likely had little to do with sexual orientation and everything to do with the political situation of Mexico's lower classes: the sexual metaphor conveyed disgust for the complicitous *joto* who passively accepted being "screwed" by the dominant political and social system. Criminals might be *jodidos*—screwed by the legal system—but to accept that fate, to show remorse, was unmanly, the act of a *joto* or a "female who is pure passivity, defenseless against the exterior world."[35] Inmate slang (*calo*) for the sex act, *hostigar* (to harass or victimize), clarified the power relations involved in even normative sexual relations.[36] Passive acquiescence in this harassment was considered despicable.

The depreciation of passive femaleness in women and in men who acted like women represented a political (and obviously very sexist) position of resistance to arbitrary authority. The criminologists' construction, which lumped inverts and perverts into a single category of homosexual, attempted to symbolically transform the active, resistant *jodido* into the passive, complicitous *joto,* leaving him no space in which to act out the male rituals of domination (including sexual domination of other men) that gave existence and meaning to his political self. Machismo was thus the quintessential posture of political resistance, especially for otherwise downtrodden lower-class men. It was a posture learned at the feet of oppressive masters and entrenched by centuries of racism, economic exploitation, and political exclusion. Consequently, it was (and is) certainly not a position they would willingly relinquish at the behest of an elitist ideological construct like scientific criminology. Furthermore, if Paz is correct, the inmates' gendered construction of homosexuality was typical, even archetypical, of Mexican society in general. Regardless, its potent political symbolism made (makes) it a formidable adversary for modernizing criminologists.

By the same token, because it lacked a strongly politicized subtext, female homosexuality was effectively marginalized: by criminologists, because female criminality posed little threat to society, and by male inmates (and probably male society in general), because the female— women and *jotos*—had no political voice.[37] At the same time, the active male partner who "rips open" the *chingada,* the *joto,* or even the unwilling weaker inmate was not a homosexual (which would have lumped him with the *jotos*) but a *chingón* who imposed himself violently upon a hostile world. He resolutely refused to have it any other way.[38]

These distinct, often contradictory visions of homosexuality suggest the difficulty of discussing issues like homosexuality, sexuality, and criminality outside a political context: in the fluid medium of language and symbols categorical boundaries shift dramatically with the ideological tide. In Mexico criminologists and male inmates contested the meaning of homosexuality—the former constructed their vision around politicized notions of class legitimized by science, the latter around politicized notions of gender legitimized by resistance to arbitrary (male) authority. Both groups stressed homosexuality's ideological significance. For both, sex was politics—male politics. The complexities of lived experience became anecdotal evidence in the service of their different visions, or were left unspoken.[39]

# 7. FORJANDO PATRIA

Anthropology, Criminology,
and the Post-Revolutionary
Discourse on Citizenship

[I]t is necessary that the three big groups of our population—indigenous, mestizo, and white—come together, mix, and become confused [*se acerquen, se mezclan y confundan*] until they manage to homogenize and unify the racial type, procuring through the application of a sensible eugenics, to cultivate the satisfactory physical gifts and correct the defective ones. – Manuel Gamio, "Pueblos nuevos"

In 1916, in the midst of social revolution, the soon-to-be godfather of Mexican anthropology and self-proclaimed *indigenista* Manuel Gamio published an influential tract that he purposefully entitled *Forjando patria* (Forging the fatherland).[1] In this disparate collection of essays Gamio argued that true nationhood required all Mexicans, especially the much abused and much neglected indigenous peoples, to become the "children of a big family." With a bow to the ever-present specter of revolutionary violence, he nevertheless insisted that "the problem is not in avoiding the illusory collective aggressiveness of certain indigenous groups but in channeling their powerful energies, which are currently dispersed, attracting their members toward the other social group that they have always considered as enemies, incorporating them, building on them, tending finally to create a coherent, homogeneous national race, unified in language and convergent in culture."[2]

In the halcyon days that followed the Revolution, Secretary of Education José Vasconcelos borrowed Gamio's title and program for his ambitious campaign to forge a national culture. Vasconcelos envisioned a far-reaching, comprehensive education program that would remissionize Mexico's largely isolated, rural indigenous peoples and complete their long-overdue integration into the larger Mexican polity.[3] Put into practice, his program testified to vaulting ambition, nothing less than the forging of all Mexicans—the progenitors of a "cosmic race"—into a dynamic, modern, culturally unified nation-state. Previous attempts at national integration had floundered miserably; this time, revolutionary social reformers like Gamio and Vasconcelos confidently asserted, things would be different.[4]

Disillusion followed. Thirty-one years after the publication of Gamio's tract, Vasconcelos's great protégé, Diego Rivera, painted his crusading mentor into his last mural, "Dream of a Sunday Afternoon in the Central Alameda." Occupying center stage, hand in hand with the artist and his rediscovered predecessor and soul mate, José Guadalupe Posada, was the latter's ubiquitous grinning skeleton—a startlingly chic apparition sporting a fashionable late-nineteenth-century gown, an extravagant bonnet, a rattlesnake feather boa, and pince-nez glasses on a chain. White and mestizo elites dominated the mural's foreground, while the obviously indigenous carried trays of food and engaged in revolutionary struggle at its turbulent margins. The only significant exception proved the rule: an overdressed, scowling, "Indian" prostitute—a modern *la maliche*—arms akimbo and back turned to the viewer, confronted the promenaders. It was an unsettling symbol of Mexican nationhood.[5]

Painted in the 1940s, at the end of the self-proclaimed revolutionary era, these jarring images reflected still-unresolved tensions and exclusions in Mexican society. Rivera's vision recognized Mexico's tremendous diversity but denied the possibility of integration—of Gamio's "coherent, homogeneous national race, unified in language and convergent in culture." In spite of their passionate commitment, revolutionary social reformers, Rivera included, had again failed to realize the reoccurring dream of national consolidation; indigenous groups continued (and continue) to live, work, fight, and die at the margins of Mexican society.

The failure of the post-revolutionary dream/nightmare of national integration is the general theme of this chapter. The political, economic, and social causes of this failure—half-hearted post-revolutionary commitments to education and land reform, the "logic" of dependent capitalist development, a racist colonial legacy, to state some of the most obvious—are important (and immediately determinate), many (too many for a single chapter), and relatively well understood (at least in broad outline). The perceptual/discursive causes, however, are less clear. And yet they lie at the heart of the "Indian problem." Even when

the will was there (which it often was not), the very manner in which the
Mexican intelligentsia, professional social analysts, and official policymakers constructed that problem guaranteed that any solution would
be partial, difficult, and painful.

This chapter specifically examines the intersection of anthropological and criminological discourse in the context of post-revolutionary efforts to forge a modern nation-state. Anthropologists like Manuel
Gamio imagined an inclusive national community that revalued indigenous cultures, reincorporated indigenous peoples, and prepared them
for the responsibilities of citizenship.[6] Criminologists, as professional
analysts of society's excluded criminal elements—those legally denied
the rights of citizens—clarified and qualified the terms of acceptance.
The exclusions built into criminological discourse contributed a dis-
turbing countercurrent to anthropological inclusiveness. But, mixed
message aside, practitioners openly acknowledged and even welcomed
the methodological and discursive linkages between the two disciplines.
The implications of that linkage, however, they left unimagined or at
least unspoken. Covert or not, the criminological subtext of post-revolutionary anthropology contained the proverbial weak link, the fatal
flaw that exposed the big lie behind the inclusive rhetoric of *indigenista*
anthropologists and, by extension, of revolutionary nationalism itself.
After all, for indigenous groups, conditional acceptance was nothing
new.

### On Integrating Indians: A Brief Sketch

Elite concerns about the need to integrate Mexico's indigenous peoples
into national life took on a certain immediacy after the 1821 severing of
colonial ties with Spain. In his monumental *Historia antigua de México*,
Mexican-born Jesuit historian Francisco Javier Clavigero had blamed
Spanish colonial practice for the degraded state of the Indian population, arguing that "if their upbringing were carefully supervised, if they
were educated in schools by competent teachers, and if they were encouraged by rewards, one would see among the Indians philosophers,
mathematicians and theologians who would vie with the most famous
of Europe. But it is difficult if not impossible, to make progress in the
sciences in midst of a miserable and servile life full of continual vexa-
tions."[7] And two years before Father Hidalgo's 1810 Grito de Dolores
initiated the struggle for independence, Prussian scientist Alexander
von Humboldt had bluntly informed his international readership that

"Mexico is the country of inequality," its indigenous people "a picture of extreme misery" thanks to years of abuse, racial prejudice, and the misguided segregationist policies of the Spanish crown.[8] For self-consciously progressive Mexican elites independence offered the opportunity to redress the mistakes of the colonial past and to transform the fledgling nation into an enlightened modern state.[9]

The nature of that transformation was hotly contested. But in spite of the profound disagreements that plunged Mexico into a half century of political chaos, liberals and conservatives shared a common concern about the Indian problem. Both groups criticized the crown's segregationist policies, which, for all their humanitarian intent, had isolated indigenous groups, set them apart from dominant whites and mestizos, and thus exacerbated heterogeneous Mexico's already considerable social tensions. Conservative Lucas Alamán, for example, considered the Indians an "entirely separate nation" that in spite of their colonial privileges "looked at everyone else with hate and distrust." His liberal adversary Lorenzo de Zavala went further, proposing the "incorporation of those of indigenous descent into society, under the same laws and civil and political rights" with the caveat that they "be obliged to form regular societies or leave the territory of the Republic."[10] Similarly, a midcentury optimist welcomed the end of the "odious" colonial caste system and declared that "now we have only free Mexicans with no distinctions other than aptitude and merit."[11] In modern Mexico, conservative or liberal, Indians would be productive citizens or be damned!

Ironically, perhaps, just as citizenship was being thrust upon them, Indians also became important symbols of Mexican separateness from Spain. And although liberals lauded Aztec glories while conservatives propagated a Hispanic origin myth—Alamán hid Cortés's bones to protect them from liberal desecration—both agreed that contemporary Indians bore faint resemblance to their illustrious ancestors. The 1825 founding of the Museo Nacional Mexicano to display and preserve national antiquities thus had little to do with recognizing the contributions of contemporary indigenous peoples and everything to do with propagating the symbols of incipient nationalism.[12] More important, this incongruous dual construction—suspicious contemporary Indian as reluctant citizen, glorious pre-Conquest Indian as national symbol—which included a threat (of national disintegration) and a promise (of redemption), formed the basis for future approaches to the Indian problem. Proposals and even policies might reflect considerable differences among elites, but most accepted this fundamental construction of the Indian problem.

If nationalists had new plans for the Indians, they based those plans on longstanding racial prejudices. The Mexican origins of the stereotypical Indian likely began with the inevitable "othering" engendered by conquest and colonial domination.[13] Whatever its roots, by independence the stereotype was ubiquitous and quite well developed. Some commentators stressed the Indian's political apathy, primitive economy, and traditionalist culture:

> The native [indígena] is quiet, long suffering, apathetic when his interests are not involved, but when they are, he is obstreperous, insolent, and enterprising. Monotonous in his customs, he does today what he did yesterday and what he will do tomorrow. The plow and the hoe, these are the objects of his concern: corn and beans, and some of the spontaneous fruits of the earth, these are his fare. He is a superstitious believer and spends his savings on annual dances that he esteems as if they were the most august of ceremonies. Toward everything, finally, he is indifferent: fatherland, government, institutions; nothing moves him as long as it doesn't disturb his repose.[14]

According to this vision the Indian is not only disengaged but actively blocks engagement—the only circumstance that rouses "him" from his lethargy and causes him to become "obstreperous, insolent, and enterprising." Generally dull and apathetic, the Indian (like a wild animal) becomes clever and dangerous when cornered. Other commentators went further, accusing Indians of habitual drunkenness, which "is frequently the origin of personal attacks [atentados contra las personas]" and of being natural sneak thieves [rateros] "always and without exceptions."[15] Apathetic, alcoholic, backward, resistant (sometimes to the point of violence), and inherently criminal, Indians presented an imposing obstacle to the great desiderata of nineteenth-century Mexican elites: national consolidation and economic progress.

To make matters even worse, according to Emperor Maximilian's French scientists and contrary to appearances in a country where indigenous tamemes (bearers) carried most everything on their backs, Indians were a weak, degenerate race.[16] In an 1865 translation for the Boletín de la Sociedad Mexicana de Geografía y Estadística (Bulletin of the Mexican Geographical and Statistical Society), a Dr. Jourdanet warned that "although generally healthy and often long-lived, they are weak and can bring to field work only very modest forces." He blamed this condition on the degenerative effects of the central plateau's high altitude and poor living conditions.[17] Jourdanet's findings received further endorsement in an 1878 study of the "Influencia de altura sobre la vida y la salud del habitante de Anahuac" (Influence of altitude on the life and health of the inhabitant of Anahuac). Its author, after a careful study of relative lung capacity and oxygen in the blood, attempted to merge European science and Mexican prejudice. "The inhabitant of Anahuac," he advised, "is less robust than at lower elevations in the country, his constitution is generally weak, his muscles little developed and his material work relatively minimal. His complexion is pallid and yellowish, his face sullen, his air is sad and pensive, his step slow and always with a reflection of melancholy vacillation. . . . The great majority of the population is submerged in an undefinable apathy, takes no part in public life, and lives day to day without worrying about the future."[18] This new twist on the established stereotype not only provided scientific endorsement for longstanding racist attitudes but undermined hopes that Indians might some day be productive citizens. Even physical labor, their one solid historical claim to a place in Mexican society, was less than adequate: a perpetually exhausted race was hardly the foundation of a dynamic, modern nation. For elites, enamored of the "productive" capitalist economies of Western Europe and North America, these signs of degeneration were ominous.

Grounded in the evolutionary theories of Lamarck and Darwin via Comte and Spencer, turn-of-the-century Porfirian positivistism roused further fears of national decline (especially after a disastrous nineteenth century). Even while Porfirian elites gloried at home and abroad in Mexico's distinctive Indian heritage, concern about the current Indian problem grew apace.[19] Some social commentators, like Francisco Bulnes, gave in to blatant racism and despair. "The Indian," he lamented with more art than originality, "is disinterested, stoic, without enlightenment; depreciates death, life, gold, morality, work, science, sadness and hope. He loves four things seriously: the idols of his old religion, the earth that feeds him, personal liberty, and the alcohol that produces his dismal and dreary deliriums."[20] More optimistic analysts, like Porfirio Díaz's education minister Justo Sierra, sought to "convert the native into a social asset" through the traditional liberal combination of education and immigration. "We need to attract immigrants from Europe so as to obtain a cross with the indigenous race," he suggested, "for only European blood can keep the level of civilization that has produced our nationality from sinking, which would mean regression, not evolution."[21] Both visions reinforced longstanding prejudices, and even Sierra's relatively moderate reading of the Indian problem depreciated their potential contribution. Given general concerns about national survival in the international struggle for life (especially with a belligerent, expansionist United States on the northern border), these readings deliberately created a sense of impending crisis that boded ill for Mexico's indigenous peoples.

But while the Indian stereotype suffered ever greater indignities over the course of the nineteenth century, the fortunes of its mestizo counterpart gradually improved.[22] In the colonial and early national periods elite observers had commented repeatedly on the volatile mestizo: "easily upset, and once upset, tenacious in his judgments, terrible in his resolutions, and atrocious in his vengeance."[23] "It is well known," another observed, "that a higher level of culture [*la mayor cultura*] that is not grounded on a moral or religious base increases rather than diminishes crime."[24] More politically active than most indigenous peoples and the principal perpetrators of urban crime, mestizos (especially of the lower classes) were more familiar and more of an immediate threat to elites. Some analysts, like Porfirian criminologist Julio Guerrero, went so far as to contrast the immoral mestizo and Indian urban poor with the honorable rural Indians who "never live in sexual promiscuity, recognize their children, are affectionate with them and whose wives attend their husbands in their humble hut, keeping themselves faithful and loving."[25] But this was a secondary discussion about the corrupting influence of the city on family values that ignored larger issues of race and citizenship. Most observers agreed that mestizos, for all their many flaws, contributed far more to Mexican national life than did their Indian counterparts.

More than that, as the racial constructions of European Social Darwinism collided with Mexican nationalist discourse after midcentury, social commentators began to see the mestizo population as the foundation of a national race. Politicized biological metaphors that stressed the hybrid vigor of mixed races dominated the discourse. Even Ignacio Manuel Altamirano, who, like fellow *puro* liberal Benito Juárez, was of indigenous descent, praised the "homogenization of the conquering and conquered races . . . that should constitute physiologically and politically speaking the great force of the nation [*pueblo*]."[26] Another prominent liberal (and positivist), Justo Sierra, rejected European notions of racial purity and praised the "virility" of the "new race."[27] For

Sierra, the middle-class mestizo purified of the "sociopathogenic microbes" of alcoholism and superstition that bubbled up from the Indian underclass represented an end to the racial divisions that obstructed Mexico's "social evolution" and thus provided the key to national progress.[28] Not surprisingly, this newly constructed progressive mestizo was often contrasted with the weak, degenerate Indian. In his "Memorandum on the causes that have created the current situation of the indigenous race of Mexico . . . ," Francisco Pimentel, a prominent scholar and Second Empire functionary, gave the volatile mestizo stereotype a positive spin, noting that "it is easier to cure an excessively robust man than it is to revive an exhumed corpse, weakened by endless privations and overwork."[29] Positivist sociologist Andrés Molina Enríquez's "revolutionary" 1909 indictment of Mexican development, *Las grandes problemas nacionales* (The great national problems), echoed Pimentel's assessment. After deploring the moral and physical degradation of Mexico's Indian population, Molina Enríquez praised the energetic "mestizo, who [because he] has always been poor, is vulgar, crude, suspicious, restless and impetuous; but stubborn, faithful, generous and patient."[30] In the constructions of social analysts like Altamirano, Pimentel, Sierra, and Molina Enríquez, then, the mestizo symbolized a vigorous, new, autarkical Mexican race that reconciled a divisive racial and cultural heritage. The Indian, like the Spaniard, harked back to the tainted colonial past.

Homogenization, as Altamirano called it, became the leitmotiv of nineteenth-century nationalist discourse. Pimentel argued that "Indians [should] forget their customs and even their language . . . and form with the whites a homogeneous mass, a true nation."[31] Even historian Vincente Riva Palacio, who considered Indians more physically evolved than whites, argued that "in order for true nationality to exist it is indispensable that its individuals have relatively similar aptitudes, harmonious tendencies, similarly constituted organisms, that they be subject in general to the same morphologic and functional viscidities, to the same epidemic dangers, and that they not present within themselves anything more than individual anomalies and in their many intellectual manifestations a trait not possessed by the race in general."[32] Regardless of Riva Palacio's pro-Indian outlook, the call for a homogeneous national culture (if not race) invariably worked in favor of mestizos. Porfirian positivist Agustín Aragón, for example, lamented the incomplete racial fusion that had opened "this profound abyss that separates one class from another and produces the most serious of obstacles for the country's political development."[33] Once thought to possess all the bad traits of both parent races, mestizos now represented the obvious source of the racial/cultural unity that nationalists saw as Mexico's best hope for the future. The mestizo, as Dr. Jourdanet had declared, is "he who progresses"; the Indian (and after independence the creole as well) obstructed progress.[34]

## On Anthropologists and Indians

The long gestation of Mexican anthropology that began with the founding of the National Museum in 1825 was inextricably bound up with the nationalist discourse about Indians. The antiquarian investigation of pre-Conquest indigenous cultures, which romanticized the Indian past as the foundation of Mexican national identity, dominated early "amateur" anthropology. The study of contemporary Indians was left to "undisciplined" social commentators. Ironically, scientists from a Franco-Mexican Commission organized by the Paris-based Societé d'Anthropologie in the 1860s were the first self-identified professionals to attempt a systematic investigation of Mexico's indigenous peoples.[35] The untimely demise of Maximilian cut the project short, but not before inspiring Manuel Orozco y Berra's "Geography of the languages and ethnographic map of Mexico in 1864" and Francisco Pimentel's previously mentioned memorandum of the same year.[36] Both works set important precedents not only in their concern for living Indians but in their obvious attempt to inform government policies.

The practical need for information and especially for accurate statistics had been recognized earlier. An 1851 article for the *Boletín de la Sociedad Mexicana de Geografía y Estadística*, founded in 1839, called for a panoply of racial data (under the general rubric of "moral" statistics): "races: primitive or pre-Conquest, Spanish, mestizo, European immigrant, comparison of whites with the others, distinctive aptitudes of each, level of intelligence, respective civilization, educatability, means of teaching, relative physical strength of the races."[37] A subsequent article in the same journal argued that "without a practical knowledge of the [Mexican] peoples, one cannot calculate their civilization, their morality, their wealth, nor their specific needs."[38] The interest in statistics persisted. A 1902 study of "La estadística y sus funciones como lazo de unión entre los individuos y entre los pueblos" (Statistics and their function as bonds of union between individuals and peoples) even suggested making statistics the "Mexican national science."[39] The author argued optimistically: "Making known the state and the movement, the shape and the structure of the population, allows us to see who we are, ethnically or psychologically speaking, and even when distance separates us, sympathy unites us, and we join together in a common aspiration, a common tendency, a common ideal across boundaries of all kinds."[40] Like anthropology, statistics (and these were anthropological statistics) was thus a fundamentally nationalistic science with compelling ties to government needs. These ties between scientific study and public policy would become even stronger with the professionalization of anthropology during the late nineteenth and early twentieth centuries; the will to knowledge was inextricably interwoven with the will to power.

Not surprisingly, the positivist-inspired Porfirian era, with its commitment to "scientific politics," produced Mexico's first generation of professional anthropologists.[41] Physical anthropology with its compulsive measuring and comparing of racial bodies quickly carved out a professional space. Its ascendency to disciplinary status was marked by the 1887 establishment of the physical anthropology section at the National Museum, the museum's 1900 hiring of Nicolás León as director, and his 1903 appointment as its first professor of anthropology and ethnology.[42] León, in turn, would train the next generation of Mexican anthropologists.

North American physical anthropologists working in Mexico, Aleš Hrdlička (León's mentor) and Frederick Starr in particular, played a crucial role in this process, providing legitimacy and direction to the fledgling discipline. Neither was particularly racist by the European standards of Gustav Le Bon and Arthur de Gobineau: they attributed the apparent degeneration of Mexican Indians to environmental and social causes rather than to inherent racial inferiority.[43] Nevertheless the racial nature of their investigations and of those of their Mexican colleagues and protégés carried considerable baggage: degeneration was no less dangerous to national well-being because its causes came (at least initially) from outside the carefully measured body of the anthropological subject. As might be expected, this North American racial agenda and its colonialist subtext resonated powerfully with the social concerns of subsequent Mexican anthropologists.

Mexican anthropology's big break came with the Revolution. Porfirian scientific politics was, more than anything, an ideological construct designed to legitimize an undemocratic regime. In practice, most científicos showed little inclination to undertake serious social reform. The victorious revolutionaries, compelled by a populist ideology, had bigger plans. And the activist state that emerged from revolutionary struggle seemed an ideal vehicle for ambitious social scientists.[44]

The auspicious appearance of Manuel Gamio's *Forjando patria* in the midst of revolution thus marked a watershed in Mexican anthropology. "Today," he proclaimed, "it is up to Mexican revolutionaries to seize the hammer and tighten the blacksmith's apron so that from the miraculous anvil a new fatherland will arise from a combination of [Spanish] iron and [Indian] bronze."[45] Not surprisingly, in Gamio's vision of national consolidation, anthropology played the crucial role. "It is axiomatic," he insisted, "that Anthropology in its broadest sense should be fundamental to the discharge of good government."[46] The need for a comprehensive study of Mexico's indigenous peoples, prominent in nineteenth-century anthropological discourse, figured into Gamio's scheme as well: "We not only need to know how many men, women, and children there are in the Republic, the languages they speak, and how they control their ethnic groups. We need to know many other things: geography, geology, meteorology, flora and fauna . . . also language, religion, industry, art, commerce, folklore, clothing, food, strength, physical-anthropological type, etc., etc." This comprehensive knowledge, he insisted, would help "us understand our needs, aspirations, deficiencies and qualities," which would in turn allow "[us] to procure the betterment of [Mexico's] diverse ethnic groups."[47] In this context the collective pronoun could signify the Mexican people, the intelligentsia, bureaucratic policymakers, or professional anthropologists. These telescoping significations attempted to elide fundamental differences in power and agency; nevertheless the inevitable linkage between knowledge and power was plain to see. Just as positivist sociology had served the Porfirian regime, anthropology was to be the revolutionary science par excellence.[48]

According to Gamio, only the potent combination of anthropological knowledge and revolutionary fervor could span Mexico's vast cultural divides. In the conclusion to *Forjando patria*, he outlined a program for national integration: "*Fusion of races, convergence and fusion of cultural manifestations, linguistic unification and economic balance of social elements . . . ought to characterize the Mexican population, so* that it constitute and incarnate a powerful Fatherland and a coherent and defined nationality."[49] Aside from the nod to "economic balance," the line could have come from Pimentel or Sierra. Homogenization was still the heart and soul of Mexican nationalism; anthropologists were its latest prophets.

There were some differences. A disciple of renowned cultural relativist Franz Boas, Gamio was repelled by racist European anthropology.[50] "The Indian has the same aptitudes for progress as the white," he noted, "being neither superior or inferior." And, he added with typically liberal optimism, "with improvements in his food, clothing, education, and entertainments, the Indian will embrace contemporary culture the same as any other race."[51] Thus, although he rejected biologically based racism, Gamio still privileged a progressive, homogeneous national culture that could only come from *mestizaje* (race mixture).[52] Mestizo culture for all its "deficiencies" and "deformities" was "the national culture . . . of the future"; Indian culture (or Spanish culture for that matter) was not so much inherently inferior as inappropriate, divisive, and doomed to extinction.[53] Biological differences might persist for a while; cultural unity would first make them irrelevant and consequently—through increased intermarriage—break them down altogether. Complete integration seemed just a matter of a few generations. And the need was pressing. In Gamio's positivist vision, Mexico's national health and by extension its survival in the international struggle for life required the unity that only a national mestizo culture could bring. Justo Sierra had already said much the same thing.

This fundamentally positivist vision of national integration formed the basis of the post-revolutionary anthropological project. As head of the newly formed Department of Anthropology (1917) and founder-editor of a popular anthropological journal, *Ethnos* (1920–25), Gamio was well positioned to influence the direction of post-revolutionary anthropology. His 1922 chef-d'oeuvre, a comprehensive two-volume study of the population of the valley of Teotihuacán, which accompanied extensive archeological reconstruction, brought him international recognition and further consolidated his position, especially among professional anthropologists. The study brought together all the threads of Mexican anthropology, from antiquarian concerns about pre-Conquest societies to physical and cultural studies of the valley's contemporary residents. As usual, the positivist teleology was transparent. "The tendencies of all peoples," Gamio wrote in the opening of his introduction, "has been and always will be to strive to reach an equilibrium, vigorous and flourishing development, as much physical as intellectual and economic. To governments and governed together falls the task of imposing effective means for reaching these ends, making indispensable the foreknowledge of the factors necessary to promote that development as well as the obstacles that are opposed to it, that for that reason would be eliminated or at least transformed."[54] Gamio's stress on applied anthropology in the service of post-revolutionary nation building and his concern about possible "obstacles" took on deeper meaning in the more detailed studies that comprised the two volumes. For example, a study of the indigenous "physical type" noted that most indigenous subjects deviated from the round-headed norm, which indicated some race mixture (a good thing), but that mestizo subjects were generally taller, larger, stronger, and narrower headed than their indigenous counterparts.[55] Another study concluded that although the lack of protein in their diet could account for some of their deficiencies, "the indigenous people that currently inhabit the valley of Teotihuacán belong to a race in physiological decline."[56] Yet another study specified the environmental causes of this decline. The author noted that "the lack of cleanliness, the ignorance of the most elemental precepts of hygiene, the abundance of parasites, the poorly constructed houses, the monotonous diet, the unhealthy water of some of the water holes and wells, the alcoholic abuses and endemic nature of some diseases make the hygienic conditions of the inhabitants not at all favorable."[57] His unsurprising solution: the "socialization and education" of the indigenous population, leading to "spontaneous, progressive, and intense *mestizaje*."[58] Thus, even though post-revolutionary anthropologists (like their liberal predecessors) recognized the social, cultural, environmental, and historical causes of Indian "decline," this obstacle to national progress was an accomplished fact that could only be overcome through the redeeming powers of cultural unification and race mixture. The principal message was inclusive, but the conditional nature of inclusion remained a distant if persistent murmur.

The 1920 inauguration of *Ethnos*, an anthropology journal directed at the "general public," helped disseminate these ideas among a broader (if still mostly elite) audience of well-informed citizens, intellectuals, and enlightened bureaucrats.[59] Gamio's blend of disciplinary aggrandizement and revolutionary nationalism permeated the journal. By the second issue he was pushing hard for an anthropologically correct census that would include racial and cultural data. Incomplete data, he argued, "has hindered the development of the population instead of bettering it."[60] In 1923 the journal reappeared after a brief hiatus. Its new subtitle, "magazine dedicated to the study and betterment of the indigenous population of Mexico," further clarified its practical, proselytizing mission.

Nor did this mission develop in a vacuum. Gamio's 1920 selection as a vice president of the Second International Eugenics Congress in Washington DC recognized his often-stated commitment to "bettering" Mexico's indigenous peoples and to preparing them for the "racial fusion . . . cultural generalization and linguistic unification" that would spawn a vigorous, hybrid Mexican race.[61] In an article entitled "Nacionalismo e internacionalismo" (Nationalism and internationalism), he noted that Mexico might eventually become part of an international federation (a bureaucratization perhaps of Vasconcelos's "cosmic race") but that "at this moment, we ought first of all to form a nation."[62] A colleague observed that physical anthropology in particular applied "the principles of Eugenics for the racial betterment of populations" and lamented that Mexico still lacked a preliminary study of racial degeneration.[63] In Mexico's case international science again served a nationalist cause even as it continued to reinforce racial thinking among Mexican anthropologists.

The 1925 takeover of *Ethnos* by the Secretariat of Public Education in the wake of Plutarco Elías Calles's ascension to the presidency cemented even more strongly anthropology's ties to government-directed social reform. The new director, Lucio Mendieta y Núñez, surpassed even Gamio in his bluntness. Inspired perhaps by the new regime's more active (and sometimes brutal) approach to social reform, he baldly declared that the purpose of anthropological study was "to obtain a complete and as exact as possible knowledge of the principal indigenous populations of the Republic, past and present, in order to uncover the causes of their present vices and the scientific means of correcting them."[64] Calles's accelerated land-distribution program of the mid-1920s favored the communal *ejido* landholding system. This system both presupposed and sought to foster a cooperative (coopted), acculturated peasant class integrated into the national economy, and, as his response to the Cristero Revolt made clear, Calles brooked no resistance. In this political context and with the introduction of eugenics and the frank acknowledgment that anthropology's purpose was to uncover and correct vices, officially sanctioned anthropological discourse had crossed the fine line that separated anthropology and criminology. The essentially positive, inclusive thrust of Gamio's message (at least on the surface) had taken on a negative, exclusive tone. His vision had always tacitly assumed the need to change unprogressive attitudes; now that need had become the guiding principle of anthropological knowledge.

### On Reconstructing the Indian Criminal
The line dividing anthropology and criminology had never been particularly clear. Both fields of study took on "scientific" disciplinary status as offshoots of positivist sociology. Both owed a considerable debt to the nineteenth-century evolutionary paradigms of Lamarck and Darwin. Shared methodologies strengthened the bond. Physical anthropology benefited immensely from the pioneering work of self-described Italian criminal anthropologist Cesare Lombroso, who built an international reputation on his discovery of the hidden physiological "stigmata" (mostly cranial) of criminality. Lombroso's refinement of the methodology of early-nineteenth-century phrenologists, who had posited crude links between cranial development and personality, was based on earlier work by French physical anthropologist Paul Broca. Likewise, the internationalization of Parisian police clerk Alphonse Bertillon's elaborate system for measuring criminal bodies (derived from Broca and Lombroso) provided a useful example for physical anthropologists as they sought to standardize their own measuring procedures.[65] This cross-fertilization also provided a considerable amount of interpretive baggage, the most egregious examples being Broca's theories of racial inferiority based on brain structure and Lombroso's theory of "atavism," which linked criminality with the physical traits of "primitive" races. Intentional or not, this racist baggage increased the ideological potential of both anthropology and criminology because it legitimized longstanding social inequities.

The connections between cultural anthropology and criminology were nearly as strong. French criminologist Gabriel Tarde had insisted, in opposition to Lombroso's biological determinism, that milieu—living conditions, social status, cultural background, health, education, and so forth—rather than heredity was the crucial variable in determining criminality. Most criminologists, including Lombroso himself, responded by creating elaborate causal hierarchies and criminal typologies that factored in both heredity and milieu in varying degrees. And although focused on the criminal subject, both the data and methodol-

ogy of this more refined criminology borrowed heavily from anthropology, and vice versa. The subjects under investigation—criminal or Indian, for example—might differ (with some inevitable overlapping of
course); "scientific" methodologies did not.

For late-nineteenth-century Mexican criminal anthropologists Francisco Martínez Baca and Manuel Vergara the disciplinary connection
had seemed obvious. In their study of the skulls of indigenous criminals
who died in the Puebla penitentiary they noted that small craniums,
less-developed occipital regions, and "simple" sutures indicated inferiority "according to the observations of Broca."[66] This scientific verification of Indian inferiority was hardly surprising. The real problem, they
cautioned, was determining the specific stigmata of Mexican criminality in a country where European atavisms represented the norm.
Careful measurement of Indian subjects, then, would provide a baseline
"of the physiognomical features of this race that will allow us to distinguish the anomalies."[67]

In addition to compiling these cranial measurements they also collected information on each subject's personal, family, and cultural
background. Alcoholism, for example, indicated a predisposition to
crime because it lowered inhibitions and caused both personal and inherited degeneration.[68] But it was only one factor, and a fairly obvious
one at that. The combined data sets, however, would eventually allow
professional criminologists to identify even the previously hidden stigmata of the Indian criminal. The potential benefits to the forces of social
order were incalculable. The self-aggrandizing will to knowledge and
power (or at least bureaucratic positions), so evident in Mexican anthropology, was matched by its sister discipline. And the drive to determine physiological and behavioral norms in order to identify deviance
supplied a compelling raison d'être for subsequent anthropological
studies. In light of this disciplinary connection, studies on indigenous
peoples by physical and cultural anthropologists took on a more ominous tone not altogether suppressed even in Gamio's heyday.[69]

Strongly implicated (as a branch of scientific politics) in the Porfirian
criminalization of the urban lower classes, criminologists kept a low
profile in the years that immediately followed the Revolution. By the
late 1920s, as revolutionary populist fervor cooled under Calles's increasingly dour gaze, they were ready to reclaim their professional and
discursive spaces. And resurgent criminology quickly made its mark on
its sister discipline. A 1928 article recalled the inclusive optimism of the

first post-revolutionary decade, arguing for underlying affinities between Indian and Spanish culture—including a brachycephalic (roundheaded) love of ritual—that would allow the two cultures to mix easily.[70] But practical cynicism was the order of the day. A new popular anthropology journal, *Quetzalcoatl* (1929–31), demonstrated the more exclusive, pessimistic orientation of 1930s anthropology.[71] Paradoxically, perhaps, the founding of a broad-based National Revolutionary Party (PNR) in 1929 clearly delineated the parameters of political participation and thus clarified the requirements for citizenship. This delimitation of boundaries, which highlighted the inclusive/exclusive nature of the social contract, doubtless encouraged a criminological perspective. An article on "La redención del indio desde un nuevo punto de vista" (The redemption of the Indian from a new perspective) by editor Carlos Basauri noted the widespread presence of "various stigmata of degeneration" among Indians, which he attributed to "precocious sexual unions, defective alimentation, alcoholism and lack of hygiene." Moreover, these causes were more cultural than circumstantial. Regarding nutrition, for example, he asserted that "on many occasions the economic circumstances . . . the scant agricultural production and miserable living conditions impose this diet; but in *most* cases it is traditional custom and ignorance that cause [Indians] to persist in such a lamentable system."[72] Basauri's social consciousness, meant to spur reform, also reinforced classic stereotypes like the drunken Indian mother who weaned her children on pulque. And if the degenerate Indian male resisted criminality—congenital lassitude made even criminal acts difficult—his biological degeneration still presented an obstacle to national progress.

In a subsequent article on "El tipo nacional mexicano del porvenir" (The Mexican national type of the future), Basauri presented the inescapable solution: *mestizaje*. He argued that although education might raise the Indian's "moral level," the race had already reached the "limit of its biological development." On the other hand, he insisted that "the strongest races, the most beautiful and most talented, are the result of many ethnic combinations." And racial biology aside, this mestizo "psychological and social type" represented (yet again) the national future.[73] The message echoed Gamio's; the virulent attack on indigenous races and cultures, however, was even more pronounced. Indians might have a secondary place in the new Mexico; their culture, which encouraged degeneration and even criminality, did not.

Once again, foreign anthropologists helped reinforce and legitimize this trend. In 1933 an Italian-Mexican team that included Carlos Basauri measured and photographed nearly two thousand indigenous subjects.[74] The expedition's avowed purpose was to study the evolution of populations and race mixture in Mexico. Their new technique, biotyping, sought to categorize and map human populations according to various physical criteria, including the inevitable cranial and nasal indices. It seemed the perfect solution to the often-lamented but still unsolved problem of defining and delimiting Mexico's racially heterogeneous population. Mexican anthropologist José Gómez Robledo pointed out that "in Mexico, where the number of aboriginal groups, differentiated by somatic and ethnographic characteristics, passes fifty, biotypology can lead us to create a true ethnic inventory through which we will arrive at the knowledge of the value of the indigenous human material and the most adequate ways and means to manage their assimilation into modern society, which is the same as realizing national unity."[75] Better yet, even a partial analysis of the results offered no surprises. Expedition leader Corrado Gini noted of the Seri that "from a biological point of view, if one cannot deny their degenerative flaws, one should nevertheless allow that they are flaws caused by inbreeding, if not defective alimentation, flaws that will probably disappear with mestizaje and better living conditions." Not only would "incorporation" benefit the Seri but it "could only augment that extreme variety and multiple combinations . . . [that] after a rigorous selection, we suspect will result in the [racial] type that will create the future of this beautiful country."[76] This rigid eugenic approach left little room for a "degenerate" Seri culture that foolishly sought isolation to preserve "the purity of their customs and the individual and moral integrity of their race."[77] The latest innovation in anthropological science thus confirmed the widely accepted conclusion that physically degenerate, tradition-bound indigenous peoples hindered (often deliberately) national development.

Biotypology also bolstered the already strong ties between Mexican anthropologists and an increasingly corporatist state. The links between Italian fascism and criminology—renowned criminologist and Lombroso disciple Enrico Ferri wrote a "fascist" penal code—were well known. The push to biotype national populations was part of the same statist agenda in both Italy and Mexico. As we have seen, new Mexican federal penal codes promulgated in 1929 and 1931 promoted increased judicial discretion in the name of "social defense." And in-

creased judicial discretion required the "scientific" data that biotypology promised to provide as well as the experts (criminologists or anthropologists in this case) to interpret it accurately (see chapter 5). With
proper information and interpretation, criminologists argued, the criminal-justice system could identify and isolate dangerous "born" and career criminals while "occasional" and accidental criminals were rehabilitated or spared the corrupting prison experience altogether. This
statist agenda became even more pronounced after the 1934 ascension
of Lázaro Cárdenas to the Mexican presidency. Cárdenas broadened
the political base still further, created official sectors for the renamed
Mexican Revolutionary Party (PRM), and expanded the education and
transportation infrastructures. These efforts purposefully expanded the
reach of the state and thus the pressure to conform to national standards. As the intellectual vanguard of integrationist thought, anthropologists were hardly disinterested observers.

Given its scientific and professional attractions, biotypology retained
its fascination for Mexican criminologists and anthropologists. Gini's
disciple Ada D'Aloja even took up residence in Mexico, teaching biotypology, demographics, and human genetics at the National School of
Anthropology and History, the National University, and the University
of the Americas from 1939 until 1976.[78] With this kind of impetus the
new techniques expanded quickly in both disciplines. The results, however, were nothing new. Criminologist Anselmo Marino Flores, for example, remeasured a cache of Indian and mestizo skulls collected by
Martínez Baca at the Federal Penitentiary for a 1945 article for the Revista Mexicana de Estudios Antropológicos (Mexican journal of anthropological studies). He blithely admitted that "the different schools
of Biotypology . . . are not, in the final analysis, anything but continuers
and developers of the ideas of Lombroso," and went on to distinguish
between the cranial types of murders and thieves.[79] A cowritten 1963 article for Anales del Museo Nacional de Arqueología, Historia y Etnografía (Annals of the National Institute of Anthropology and History),
repeated the same procedure, this time using the Puebla skulls from
Martínez Baca and Vergara's original study![80] The appearance of criminological works in anthropology journals highlighted the (re)tightening
of disciplinary bonds.

Anthropologists also employed this new methodology both to refur-
bish old ideas about Indians and to demonstrate their usefulness to government functionaries. A 1945 article lamented the decline of physical

anthropology since the death of Nicolás León and called for an extensive anthropometrical study comparing rural Indians with their urban
counterparts.[81] Gómez Robledo, a student of D'Aloja's, was probably
the most active promoter of biotypology, authoring or coauthoring bio-
typical studies of Tarascans, Zapotecs, and Otomís. These studies not
only reinforced expectations but also served a practical end. "The bio-
typical orientation," he observed, "is very preoccupied with differen-
tiating racial groups and serves for that reason to opportunistically di-
agnose the predisposition to illness of the people examined, to know
aptitudes and ineptitudes for work, and to suggest teaching methods
and education programs."[82] Thus, in the guise of new science, biotypology reinforced longstanding anthropological and criminological traditions, cemented the ties between the two disciplines, and strengthened
the already tight bonds that bound these disciplines to an ever-more-
powerful one-party state. Martínez Baca and Vergara would have recognized the project as a continuation and development—to paraphrase
Marino Flores—of their own.

Anthropological studies that focused on indigenous cultures rather
than bodies also took on a criminological tone. This was especially true
of the ongoing debate about the social dangers of alcoholism, traditionally associated in the Spanish colonial imagination with Indian culture.[83] In 1929, with the moralistic Calles still lurking in the background, President Emilio Portes Gil sponsored a nationwide campaign
against alcoholism that "undermines the physical and moral strength of
our men; ends conjugal happiness and destroys with degenerate children all possibility of greatness in the future of the Fatherland."[84] His
fellow campaigners were more explicit, especially regarding the Indian
problem. One cited nineteenth-century French psychiatrist Benedict
Morel's theory of progressive "moral insanity"—alcoholism in the first
generation, criminality by the third, racial extinction by the fourth—
while noting widespread "drunkenness among our primitive peoples."[85] Ex-científico Enrique Creel repeated the Morel citation and
condemned "the customs of our people" that typically included the
heavy drinking "with which they mix all their sufferings and delights."[86]

In this moralistic context anthropologists redoubled their attacks on
Indian culture. In a 1939 "Ensayo sobre el alcoholismo entre las razas
indígenas de México" (Essay on alcoholism among the indigenous races
of Mexico), ex-editor of Ethnos Lucio Mendieta y Núñez underlined
the social dangers of this modern plague: "When a great number of per-

sons abandon themselves to the vice of drunkenness to such a degree that they produce organic hereditary degenerations, the evil oversteps the orbit of the individual life to become a social danger that manifests itself in damage to the economy, culture, and the vitality itself of the society in which it occurs."[87] Crime was one of those social dangers: "among the indigenous," he noted, "alcoholism provokes the commission of crimes of violence, from simple scuffles to frequent homicides."[88] And custom—"meetings, festivities, religious and magical ideas, the payment of wages with alcohol"—was largely to blame.[89] Many of his recommendations, especially the creation of sports leagues with game days scheduled for Sundays and traditional "fiesta days," thus attempted to break the stranglehold of tradition on indigenous cultures. Most required "the intervention of all the organs of the Federal and State governments." The need for more studies was, of course, a given.[90] At least in Mendieta's case, then, the fine line between anthropological knowledge and public policy had all but disappeared. In case any doubts remained, he followed up these recommendations with an edited "Etnografía de México" (Ethnology of Mexico) that included data on the criminal tendencies of various indigenous groups. Most, unsurprisingly, showed a predisposition to violent crimes involving alcohol.[91]

As these attacks on Indian alcoholism and Indian culture demonstrate, the criminological subtext, a bit player in earlier Mexican anthropology, had now taken center stage. The appearance of articles reviewing new criminological theories and techniques in journals like *Quetzalcoatl* made the disciplinary connection explicit.[92] Even Mexican criminologists, who generally left Indian affairs to anthropologists, got in a few digs. A 1939 article on "Las razas indígenas y la defensa social" ("The indigenous races and social defense) in *Criminalia*, the professional journal for Mexican criminologists, argued that while judicial discretion might take into account racial and cultural differences, Indians should be subject to the same laws as anyone else. Race, after all, was fundamentally "psychological and cultural," as was Indian "inferiority." In Mexico, the author insisted, "we are all mestizos, and on being mestizos, with a common tradition, with a common mestizo intellectual formation and culture, rests the great future of our country and the solution to ethnic problems." Refusal to assimilate, to adapt mestizo culture, thus transformed the tradition-bound Indian from reluctant citizen to "delinquent as a result of antisocial action."[93]

Prominent criminologist Carlos Franco Sodi explained the roots of these antisocial tendencies in an essay on "Delincuencia indígena" (Indigenous delinquency). He noted that in his experience as a Mexico City judge and former director of the Federal Penitentiary, Indians rarely understood the reasons for their imprisonment because they interpreted crime differently than did non-Indians. And he provided an illustrative anecdote in which the young men of a village kill a family of witches under orders from the council of elders. Their shock at being tried for a murder they freely admitted to and saw as completely justified symbolized the vast chasm that separated them from mainstream Mexican society. Nor was the perverse resilience of Indian traditions lightly overturned: even after their crime was explained and the remorseful men convicted and imprisoned, villagers murdered the last surviving witch. Aside from a lighthearted sense of irony, Franco Sodi might easily have been the reincarnation of Diego de Landa confronting Mayan idolatry in the sixteenth century.

His description of the uncomprehending Indian could have come straight from an earlier era as well: "There he sits, silent and taciturn, just like we see him on the edges of sidewalks or the sides of roads, look fixed on the ground, his face unexpressive and his spirit far away, very far away, from that filthy cell, melancholically remembering perhaps his beloved fields, nostalgically recalling his poor distant hovel and without understanding why some laws and strange men have deprived him of his liberty . . . and put between him and the luminous horizons that he always contemplates ecstatically, bars so tall and cold and walls so dismal and black."[94] This persistent stereotype of the apathetic and resistant Indian, Franco Sodi concluded, "bears in his breast the seeds of his own destruction, seeds *that will not disappear* while the Indian and ourselves are distinct, while that one [*aquél*] and the man of the city think and feel differently, while one and the other speak diverse languages, and understand family, society, and morality in such opposed ways."[95] For criminologists and increasingly also for anthropologists, Indianness itself was a tragedy; it was also a crime.

### *Plus Ça Change . . .*

The resemblance between Franco Sodi's 1951 description of an incarcerated Indian in Mexico City and Manuel Larrainzar's 1852 observations from Soconusco that opened the first section of this chapter is striking. Even the picturesque, quasi-poetic style carries across five hundred miles, the chasm between metropolis and periphery, and a hundred years of European scientific discourse. This discursive continuity in elite discourse dramatically highlights the continued failure to forge a fatherland for all Mexicans, "to create a coherent, homogeneous national race, unified in language and convergent in culture." *Mestizaje* had undoubtedly forged a dominant—Gramsci would call it "hegemonic"— national culture, but the remaining indigenous peoples faced (and face) considerable pressure to conform. Inclusion could only come with the unconditional surrender of cultural identity, which was, after all, what many elites had wanted all along.[96]

This discursive continuity also reflects an underlying continuity in social relations. After a century and a half of promises, Mexico's indigenous peoples remained (and remain) very much at the margins of the national fresco. Maybe completing the task was impossible; maybe Mexican policymakers lacked the financial wherewithal to solve the "Indian problem." Maybe they lacked the will. Maybe indigenous culture was too deeply rooted to allow for easy integration. Maybe demented elites forced downtrodden, intoxicated Indians up the steep stairs of their ancient pyramids and cut out their still-beating hearts so that the great god capitalism would permit the sun to rise on a new modern mestizo age. These explanations all contain an element of truth. Regardless, the manner in which elites constructed the Indian problem clouded their integration efforts.

This chapter has specifically examined the constructions of social commentators, anthropologist, and criminologists—the self-proclaimed experts on the Indian problem. For all their many differences—and the Indian problem was a much contested issue—the vast majority of these observers (the categories overlap) shared three basic assumptions: first, that Mexico's contemporary indigenous peoples were the tired, tattered, and besotted remnants of a once-great race (races for the more sophisticated); second, that they represented a substantial obstacle to national progress; and third, that only racial and cultural *mestizaje* could unify the nation and remove that obstacle.

Anthropology was the principal discourse. In a burst of post-revolutionary optimism, anthropological discourse seemed to favor its indigenous subjects, bestowing its blessings, insights, and prestige on their culture and on their bodies. Anthropological knowledge was the key to the kingdom, to the long-awaited redemption of the long-suffering Indian. But the discipline existed at the sufferance of politicians and bureaucrats and, in serving Caesar, lost its innocence. Applied anthropology with its promise to integrate indigenous peoples into a mestizo Mexico became an ideology in the service of the post-revolutionary state, and it was an elite, mestizo voice.

By 1930 the exclusionary criminological subtext embedded in the Mexican elite construction of national integration resurfaced with a vigor: the stubborn, tradition-bound Indian who resisted the responsibilities of citizenship became a criminal. And this shift from irresponsible citizen to violent criminal may have been the only real change in the Indian's discursive status: a discursive sleight of hand—from violent mestizo/thieving Indian to violent Indian/thieving mestizo—that symbolized the "evolution" of the mestizo in the elite imagination. In postrevolutionary Mexico the Indian who could not or would not adapt to the new mestizo national culture was likely to contemplate the future from behind "bars so tall and cold and walls so dismal and black."

"The Indian," Octavio Paz observed in *The Labyrinth of Solitude*, his 1950 masterwork on Mexican national identity, "blends into the landscape until he is an indistinguishable part of the white wall against which he leans at twilight, of the dark earth on which he stretches out to rest at midday, of the silence that surrounds him. He disguises his human singularity to such an extent that he finally annihilates it and turns into a stone, a tree, a wall, silence, and space."[97] He dons this mask, Paz tells us, to avoid confronting his condition. But like most elite observers, the authorial voice here identifies only one agent. In Paz's version, the Indian "annihilates" his own "human singularity." (Paz fails to tell us if Indian women—perennial objects of lust—have similar powers). Individual agency—at least on the part of the Indian—is only partly responsible for this disappearance. The Indian not only disappears (for protection in a hostile environment), he is also disappeared. He is an invisible man because his human singularity cannot be seen by elite observers. Elite discourses like anthropology and criminology eschew the individual to generalize about the group. Service to the state and the requirements of public policy exacerbate this tendency. The Mexican Indian, then, is not redeemed, because redemption requires the ability to see the human singularity behind the mask; to see the intimate articulations between cultural and individual identity. Cultural death is thus only the first in a series of unseen murders. But then, the scientific gaze is not dependent on sight.

# CONCLUSION

The nation-state is the most traveled and at the same time the most impenetrable domain of modern society. We all know that those black lines on the political maps are like the scars of unremitting war, plundering, and conquest; but we also suspect that, in addition to the state violence upon which nations are founded, there are strange, age-old forces of a cultural and psychological nature that trace the frontiers separating us from strangers. These subtle forces, subjected to the harshness of economic and political oscillations, are nevertheless responsible for the opacity of the phenomenon of nationhood. Among other things, this opacity obscures the profound motives that lead men to tolerate a system of domination and, by the forbearance they display, to give a seal of legitimacy to injustice, inequality, and exploitation. – Roger Bartra, *The Cage of Melancholy*

This study of elite discourse about criminality seeks—in the spirit of Roger Bartra's problematic—to penetrate "the opacity of the phenomenon of nationhood . . . [that] obscures the profound motives that lead men to tolerate a system of domination." It seeks to explain the failures of repeated elite efforts—some sincere, some cynical, most Machiavellian, all ideological—to transform traditional colonial subjects into modern national citizens and, in the process, to forge a Mexican national identity. It seeks to demonstrate that those failures were neither accidental nor circumstantial, that they were, in fact, fundamental to the construction of modern Mexico.

Mexico's failures were hardly unique. The elusive nature of the twin grails of nationalism and modernity, at least for the "developing" world, has always been recognized; their exclusive nature, everywhere, is becoming increasingly apparent. Recent scholarship has stressed the

centrality of race and gender exclusions to modern nation-state construction. In *Making Race and Nation,* for example, Anthony Marx
insists that "race made nation-states," that "specified racism was the
predominant logic of nation-state building in a century obsessed with
stability and growth."[1] And in an article on "The politics of identity and
gendered nationalism," V. Spike Peterson makes a similar claim for
gender, arguing that "In patriarchal societies (currently the norm
worldwide), group coherence and continuity is achieved through denial
of equality within the group. . . . As the inequality that is most naturalized, and therefore used to justify multiple hierarchies, gender hierarchy is central to the construction and reproduction of asymmetrical
social relations. The exclusivity and domination 'faces' of nationalism
typify such asymmetrical relations."[2] Apparently contradictory, these
two arguments—along with extensive literature linking nation building
and class relations—actually complement each other. Different historical circumstances produced different discursive (if not clearly ideological) responses—sometimes centered on race, other times on gender
or class—but "exclusivity and domination" characterized the project
everywhere.

The glue that bound these different responses together was criminological discourse. Race, gender, and class provided categories of exclusion; criminality provided the means for defining and policing those
categories. Thus, to paraphrase Anthony Marx: criminality refracted
through the lens of race, class, and gender "made nation-states." And,
far from being the arcane abstractions of minor social theorists, discourses like criminology, penology and anthropology represented the
opaque core of the nation-building project, a core that supplied "a seal
of legitimacy to injustice, inequality, and exploitation." Michel Foucault argues that sexuality constructs the modern self through the production, dissemination, and implantation of a "sexual science": criminality constructs the modern nation in much the same way.[3]

As conceived by proponents and practitioners, criminology and
penology (along with psychology, sociology, and anthropology) were
the quintessential discourses of modernity, the scientific products of a
profound epistemological shift—generally identified with the Enlightenment—that made possible the rational analysis and organization of
human societies. Scholars like Foucault have stressed this rupture in
perception and the modernity of its discursive products.[4] Certainly the

discursive aspects of this shift are undeniable; new words and new linkages (especially with rationalism and evolutionary science) figured prominently in post-Enlightenment discussions of crime and punishment. But whether or not this discursive shift was really epistemological or was merely a Gramscian re-articulation of traditional discursive elements that disguised fundamental continuities in Mexican social relations is far from clear.

Language inevitably colors perception. Public reaction to a problem like crime or a condition like criminality is unavoidably affected by its description. So as Mexican criminologists and penologists introduced new ways of talking about crime, public perceptions changed as well. These changes were especially apparent in their repeated calls for reform. Inspired by Enlightenment optimism, positivist science, or revolutionary aspirations to social justice (and often goaded into action by popular pressure), Mexican social reformers encouraged the development of a more equitable, more responsive criminal-justice system. And, successful or not, these reform efforts did indeed provide new standards of legitimacy that subalterns could and did use to pierce the opacity of nationhood and the system of domination it sought to disguise.

In spite of these demonstrable reforms, however, discursive changes were hardly the dramatic break with the past touted by generations of social reformers. From their inception and in spite of their self-proclaimed modernity, Mexican criminology and penology rearticulated traditional elite concerns about the nation's marginal groups. The classist, racist, and sexist elements of criminology and penology were inextricably bound up in a reformist critique of Mexican society that attempted, somewhat paradoxically, to ameliorate gross social inequalities and bestow national citizenship on previously excluded groups. These reformist critiques—even in the hands of subalterns—often denigrated the very groups they sought to integrate. Policymakers and theorists might submerge their classist, racist, and sexist assumptions under an opaque layer of Enlightenment egalitarianism, link them to the verities of evolutionary science, or invoke the sociological doctrine of social defense. Nonetheless, that discursive sleight of hand could not disguise underlying continuities in Mexican social relations over the *longue durée*.

Ultimately, the discursive ambiguities that permitted and even encouraged longstanding elite biases effectively precluded any dramatic restructuring of actual social relations. In a country wracked by over a century of civil wars, foreign invasions, revolution, and the endless structural adjustments that have accompanied national integration into an expanding global economy, a dramatic shift in social relations was (is) unthinkable. Thus, even in the face of considerable popular pressure, comprehensive citizenship was (is) a luxury that Mexican elite nation builders could (can) not or would (will) not afford. So, much like their colonial predecessors, they used (use) boundary-delimiting discourses like criminology, penology, and even anthropology to "legitimately" define and sanction the behavior of their marginalized fellow "citizens." And, in spite of (maybe even because of) their reformist potential, these discourses served (serve) to justify the continued exploitation, persecution, and disenfranchisement of *los de abajo,* and thus guaranteed (guarantee) their effective exclusion from full citizenship.

At bottom, perhaps, lies a failure of imagination. In *The Conquest of America* Tzvetan Todorov proposes three axes for "the problematic of alterity" that he employs to "account for the differences that exist in actuality [among different Spanish interactions with Indians]": "First of all, there is a value judgment . . . : the other is good or bad, I love him or do not love him . . . he is my equal or my inferior. . . . Secondly, there is the action of *rapprochement* or distancing in relation to the other . . . : I embrace the other's values, I identify myself with him; or else I identify the other with myself, I impose my own image upon him. . . . Thirdly, I know or am ignorant of the other's identity."[5] These same axes account equally well for the considerable differences among Mexican criminologists, penologists, and anthropologists. Like the early Spaniards confronted by Indians, their responses to the criminal "other" ranged from ignorant and sympathetic to knowledgeable and condemnatory (or, more often, ignorant and condemnatory to knowledgeable and sympathetic). But if—to paraphrase Todorov—in the best of cases, they speak well *of* criminals, women, Indians, or the lower classes, with very few exceptions they do not speak *to* them.[6] Western Europe, Todorov argues, has spent the last 350 years using its unique capacity to understand the other "to do away with . . . exterior alterity."[7] This is a gross oversimplification of a complex historical process, but it nevertheless gets at the root of the problem: the inability of Mexican elites (and they are not alone) to imagine an inclusive society that did not require—as Porfirio Díaz put it—that the "ideals and methods" of all citizens "be harmonized and the national identity intensified." According to these terms resistance was (is) not so much futile as constrained by the discursive (and ultimately perceptual) field in which it operated (operates). Continued failure to forge a fatherland for all Mexicans (was) is the inevitable result.

# NOTES

Unless otherwise noted, all translations are my own.

## Introduction

1. The "liberal" Maximilian also supported these goals, as did enlightened conservatives like Lucas Alamán. See Charles Hale, *Mexican Liberalism in the Age of Mora, 1821–1853* (New Haven CT: Yale University Press, 1968).

2. James Creelman, "President Díaz, Hero of the Americas," *Pearson's Magazine* 19, no. 3 (March 1908): 245.

3. Benedict Anderson, *Imagined Communities: Reflections on the Origin and Spread of Nationalism*, rev. ed. (New York: Verso, 1991), 7.

4. B. Anderson, *Imagined Communities*, 4.

5. Most scholars see French revolutionary liberalism as providing the ideological base for modern nationalism. See, for example, E. J. Hobsbawm, *The Age of Revolution, 1789–1848* (New York: New American Library, 1962), 163–77.

6. Anderson deals specifically with Latin America's "Creole pioneers" in *Imagined Communities*, chapter 4.

7. "Elites" is an unavoidably and, in this case, deliberately ambiguous choice. Included in this category is anyone with enough political, economic, or social clout to take an *active* role in *public* debates over Mexico's future.

8. Eric Hobsbawm stresses the connection between elite social engineering and nationalism in "Introduction: Inventing Tradition," in *The Invention of Tradition*, ed. Hobsbawm and Terence Ranger (Cambridge: Cambridge University Press, 1983), 13–14. The literature on Mexican nationalism is too extensive to allow me to include anything more than specifically historical studies. Post-Enlightenment Mexican nationalism as an elite construction is examined in some detail in David Brading, *The Origins of Mexican Nationalism* (New York: Cambridge University Press, 1985), and Frederick C. Turner, *The Dynamic of Mexican Nationalism* (Chapel Hill: University of North Carolina Press, 1968). The works are complementary: Brading focuses on the independence era, while Turner devotes most of his attention to revolutionary nationalism. Some

scholars, however, stress the colonial roots of Mexican national identity. See, for example, Peggy K. Liss, *Mexico under Spain, 1521–1556: Society and the Origins of Nationality* (Chicago: University of Chicago Press, 1975). For more recent scholarship see the essays in *El nacionalismo en México*, ed. Cecilia Noriega Elío (México: El Colegio de Michoacán, 1992). On the related history of Mexican national identity see Henry C. Schmidt, *The Roots of Lo Mexicano: Self and Society in Mexican Thought, 1900–1934* (College Station: Texas A & M University Press, 1978) and Roger Bartra, *The Cage of Melancholy: Identity and Metamorphosis in the Mexican Character*, trans. Christopher J. Hall (New Brunswick NJ: Rutgers University Press, 1992).

9. Anthony D. Smith makes a compelling case for the notion of "reconstruction" in "The Nation: Invented, Imagined, Reconstructed?" *Millennium* (winter 1991): 353–68.

10. Josefina Vázquez de Knauth, *Nacionalismo y educación en México*, 2nd ed. (México: El Colegio de México, 1975). The historiography on Mexican education is extensive. Vázquez de Knauth includes a good bibliography, as do Ernesto Meneses Morales, ed., *Tendencias educativas oficiales en México, 1821–1911* (México: Editorial Porrúa, 1983), and Mary Kay Vaughn, *The State, Education, and Social Class in Mexico, 1880–1928* (Dekalb IL: Northern Illinois University Press, 1982). Critiques of Mexican education efforts by Vaughn, *The State, Education, and Social Class in Mexico*; Ramón Eduardo Ruíz, *Mexico: The Challenge of Poverty and Illiteracy* (San Marino CA: Huntington Library, 1963); and James W. Wilkie, *The Mexican Revolution: Federal Expenditure and Social Change since 1910*, 2nd ed., rev. (Berkeley: University of California Press, 1970) suggest that education reform was not quite as high a priority as official rhetoric might imply.

11. William H. Beezley, *Judas at the Jockey Club and Other Episodes of Porfirian Mexico* (Lincoln: University of Nebraska Press, 1987); William H. Beezley, Cheryl English Martin, and William French, eds., *Rituals of Rule, Rituals of Resistance: Popular Celebrations and Popular Culture in Mexico* (Wilmington DE: Scholarly Resources, 1994); and Mauricio Tenorio-Trillo, "1910 Mexico City: Space and Nation in the City of the *Centenario*," *Journal of Latin American Studies* 28 (1996): 75–104.

12. Michel Foucault, in *Discipline and Punish: The Birth of the Prison*, trans. Alan Sheridan (New York: Vintage, 1979), argues with some justice that schools, penitentiaries, and military barracks were similarly conceived components of a disciplinary "carceral" system. This interpretation, however, ignores a functional difference. Public schools encourage the internalization of normative values and behaviors, while courts and prisons punish those who fail to "voluntarily" conform.

13. Philip Corrigan and Derek Sayer, *The Great Arch: English State Formation as Cultural Revolution* (New York: Oxford University Press, 1985).

Quoted in William Roseberry, "Hegemony and the Language of Contention," in *Everyday Forms of State Formation: Revolution and the Negotiation of Rule in Modern Mexico*, ed. Gilbert M. Joseph and Daniel Nugent (Durham NC: Duke University Press, 1994), 355—66, quote on 363.

14. For an in-depth exploration of royal legitimacy and Bourbon secularization see Colin MacLachlan, *Spain's Empire in the New World: The Role of Ideas in Institutional and Social Change* (Berkeley: University of California Press, 1988).

15. Clifford Geertz, "Primordial and Civic Ties," in *Nationalism*, ed. John Hutchinson and Anthony D. Smith (New York: Oxford University Press, 1994), 30.

16. For a succinct discussion of Gramscian hegemony see Chantal Mouffe, "Hegemony and Ideology in Gramsci," in *Culture, Ideology and Social Process: A Reader*, ed. Tony Bennett et al., (London: Open University, 1981), 219—34.

17. Florencia E. Mallon, *Peasant and Nation: The Making of Postcolonial Mexico and Peru* (Berkeley: University of California Press, 1995); *Everyday Forms of State Formation*, ed. Joseph and Nugent; and Marjorie Becker, *Setting the Virgin on Fire: Lázaro Cárdenas, Michoacán Peasants, and the Redemption of the Mexican Revolution* (Berkeley: University of California Press, 1995) are three important recent examples of ongoing scholarly efforts to introduce subalterns into the historical record. The internalization of and resistance to normative values regarding criminality is still largely uncharted territory. Elite efforts to exploit the popular appeal of criminology, penology, and anthropology will be explored in later chapters.

18. Roseberry, "Hegemony," 361.

19. A well-known example that does both is Judith Adler Hellman, *Mexico in Crisis*, 2nd ed. (New York: Holmes and Meier, 1988). For general overviews see David C. Bailey, "Revisionism and the Recent Historiography of the Mexican Revolution," *Hispanic American Historical Review* 58, no. 1 (February 1978): 62—79, and William Dirk Raat, "Recent Trends in the Historiography of the Mexican Revolution," *The Mexican Revolution: An Annotated Guide to Recent Scholarship* (Boston: G. K. Hall and Co., 1982), xxiii—xxxvi.

20. The historiographies on nationalism and education were cited earlier. The classic intellectual histories of Leopoldo Zea (on positivism); Jacqueline Covo, Jesús Reyes Heroles, and Charles Hale (on liberalism); and Arnaldo Córdova (on revolutionary nationalism) generally ignore the issue of criminality, although most recognize the inherent exclusions of these different political ideologies. The major works include Arnaldo Córdova, *La ideología de la Revolución Mexicana: La formación del nuevo régimen* (México: Ediciones Era, 1973); Jacqueline Covo, *Las ideas de la Reforma en México (1855—1861)* (México: Universidad Nacional Autónoma de México, 1983); Hale, *Mexican Liberalism* and *The Transformation of Liberalism in Late Nineteenth-Century Mex-*

*ico* (Princeton: Princeton University Press, 1989); Jesús Reyes Heroles, *El liberalismo mexicano*, 3 vols. (México: Universidad Nacional Autónoma de México, 1957–61); and Leopoldo Zea, *El positivismo en México* (México: El Colegio de México, 1943) and *Apogeo y decadencia del positivismo en México* (México: El Colegio de México, 1944).

21. François Xavier Guerra argues, for example, that Díaz's inability to live up to the 1857 Constitution created an ideological double bind that led to a legitimation crisis, which in turn contributed to his downfall. See his *Le Mexique: De l'ancien régime à la révolution*, 2 vols. (Paris: L'Harmattan, 1985).

22. Teresa Lozano Armendares, *La criminalidad en la ciudad de México, 1800–1821* (México: Universidad Nacional Autónoma de México, 1987); Sergio García Avila and Eduardo Miranda Arrieta, *Desorden social y criminalidad en Michoacán, 1825–1850* (Morelia: Supremo Tribunal de Justicia del Estado de Michoacán de Ocampo, 1994); Gabriel Haslip-Viera, "Crime and the Administration of Justice in Colonial Mexico City, 1689–1810" (Ph.D. diss., Columbia University, 1980); Pablo Piccato, "Criminals in Mexico City, 1900–1931: A Cultural History" (Ph.D. diss., University of Texas at Austin, 1997); Laurence J. Rohlfes, "Police and Penal Correction in Mexico City, 1876–1911: A Study of Order and Progress in Porfirian Mexico" (Ph.D. diss., Tulane University, 1983); Michael C. Scardaville, "Crime and the Urban Poor: Mexico City in the Late Colonial Period" (Ph.D. diss., University of Florida, 1977); Paul J. Vanderwood, *Disorder and Progress: Bandits, Police, and Mexican Development* (Lincoln: University of Nebraska Press, 1981). This situation is changing quickly; the growing periodical literature is cited in appropriate chapters.

23. Mauricio Tenorio-Trillo, *Mexico at the World's Fairs: Crafting A Modern Nation* (Berkeley: University of California Press, 1996), xi.

## 1. Classic Criminology

1. Both Hidalgo and Morelos showed considerable interest in judicial legitimacy. See Ernesto de la Torre Villar, "La génesis del poder judicial en el México independiente," *Historia Mexicana* 35, no. 1 (julio–septiembre 1985): 131–72.

2. Beccaria and Bentham's impact on criminology are examined in Elio Monachesi, "Cesare Beccaria," and Gilbert Geis, "Jeremy Bentham," in *Pioneers in Criminology*, ed. Hermann Mannheim (London: Stevens and Sons, 1960), 36–67. On Bentham's utility principle see especially Jeremy Bentham, *An Introduction to the Principles of Morals and Legislation* (New York: Hafner, 1948). For Michel Foucault, Bentham's panopticon provided a paradigm for post-Enlightenment surveillance of civil society. See Foucault's *Discipline and Punish*, 195–228. The history of Mexican prison reform is explored in chapter 4.

3. Used this way, "officially sanctioned texts" refer simply to those texts written by acknowledged experts, recognized as authoritative and considered,

within the context of Enlightenment epistemology, as "objective" rather than as deliberately polemical. This study uses the term "lower classes" in its very loosest sense to include the many different social groups that elites usually lumped together as "la clase ínfima" or "las clases inferiores." The category is much larger, for example, than that of the much-maligned *léperos*, or street people. And, since elites generally perceived the lower classes as mestizo or *indio*, the class designation clearly carried strong, if unacknowledged, racial connotations. For more precise discussions of Mexico City's complex class structure see Scardaville, "Crime and the Urban Poor"; Patricia Seed, "Social Dimensions of Race: Mexico City, 1753," *Hispanic American Historical Review* 62, no. 4 (November 1982): 569–606; and Gabriel Haslip-Viera, "The Underclass," in *Cities and Society in Colonial Latin America*, ed. Louisa Schell Hoberman and Susan Migden Socolow (Albuquerque: University of New Mexico Press, 1986), 285–312. See also Gabriel Haslip-Viera, "Crime and the Administration of Justice."

4. See, for example, Torcuato S. di Tella, "The Dangerous Classes in Early Nineteenth-Century Mexico," *Journal of Latin American Studies* 5, no. 1 (May 1973): 99–104; and Virginia Guedea, "México en 1812: Control político y bebidas prohibidas," *Estudios de Historia Moderna y Contemporánea de México* 8 (1980): 23–55.

5. Michel Foucault, *The Archeology of Knowledge and the Discourse on Language*, trans. A. M. Sheridan Smith (New York: Harper Colophon, 1972), 34. The issue of intertextuality in relation to criminology is discussed in Marie-Christine Leps, *Apprehending the Criminal: The Production of Deviance in Nineteenth-Century Discourse* (Durham NC: Duke University Press, 1992), 3–4. Text, in this broad usage, would include the "text" of public policies.

6. Francisco Blasco y Fernández de Moreda, *Lardizábal: El primer penalista de América española* (México: Imprenta Universitaria, 1957), 27. For additional biographical information on Lardizábal see Luis Garrido, "El primer penalista de México," *Criminalia* 13, nos. 1–12 (1947): 356–58; and Constancio Bernaldo de Quirós, "Lardizábal y Olavide, dos ilustres magistrados criollos del siglo XVIII," *Criminalia* 14, nos. 1–12 (1948): 19–26. It is indicative of profound continuities in post-Enlightenment criminology that all three authors—Garrido was a prominent Mexican criminologist, Bernaldo de Quirós an internationally renowned Spanish criminologist, and Blasco y Fernández a distinguished Spanish penologist—found Lardizábal's discourse both congenial and prophetic.

7. Manuel de Lardizábal y Uribe, *Discurso sobre las penas* (México: Editorial Porrúa, 1982), viii–ix.

8. Enlightenment rationalism did not always contradict Catholic teaching. Post-Tridentine insistence on "free will" (as opposed to Protestant predestination) stressed individual choice, which, if not always rational, nonetheless admitted the responsibility of the the human agent. See Patricia Seed, *To Love,*

*Honor, and Obey in Colonial Mexico: Conflicts Over Marriage Choice, 1574–1821* (Stanford CA: Stanford University Press, 1988), 32–46.

9. By public, Lardizábal probably meant legally sanctioned, although, unlike later penologists, he also favored punishment in public, including the judicious use of whippings (but not mutilation), especially for lower-class criminals (*la gente del pueblo inferior*). Lardizábal *Discurso sobre las penas*, 192.

10. Lardizábal *Discurso sobre las penas*, 55.

11. Lardizábal *Discurso sobre las penas*, 213.

12. On paradigms see Thomas S. Kuhn, *The Structure of Scientific Revolutions*, 2nd ed., enlarged (Chicago: University of Chicago Press, 1970). These issues are also discussed in the introduction to chapter 2.

13. See, for example, Leon Radzinowicz, *Ideology and Crime* (London: Heineman, 1966).

14. Blasco y Fernández boldly asserts that "Lardizábal is the first eclectic," in *Lardizábal: El primer penalista*, 52. This eclecticism would make Lardizábal the prototypical Mexican criminologist.

15. Lardizábal, *Discurso sobre las penas*, 103.

16. Lardizábal, *Discurso sobre las penas*, 106–18.

17. Lardizábal, *Discurso sobre las penas*, 93.

18. As a loyal functionary of the Spanish crown, Lardizábal rejected some of the more egalitarian aspects of Enlightenment criminal justice. For example, other mitigating circumstances in punishment included "the class, estate, occupation, etc." of the criminal. Proportional punishment (punishment that suited the crime), Lardizábal argued, dictated that a noble be punished differently than a plebian (*plebeyo*). *Discurso sobre las penas*, 144–45.

19. Lardizábal, *Discurso sobre las penas*, 3–4.

20. Lardizábal, *Discurso sobre las penas*, 4.

21. Lardizábal, *Discurso sobre las penas*, 206.

22. Lardizábal, *Discurso sobre las penas*, 115–16. For Lardizábal, criminals with records of habitual public drunkenness merited a harsher sentence.

23. Lardizábal, *Discurso sobre las penas*, 143.

24. Lardizábal, *Discurso sobre las penas*, 199.

25. Hipólito Villarroel, *Enfermedades políticas que padece la capital de esta Nueva España en casi todos los cuerpos de que se compone y remedios que se le deben aplicar para su curación si se quire que sea útil al Rey y al público* (México: Miguel Ángel Porrúa, 1982), 142. As the three introductions to this edition attest, very little is known about either Villarroel or his intended audience, but he was clearly well connected and knowledgeable about the public administration of Mexico City.

26. Villarroel, *Enfermedades políticas*, 89.

27. Villarroel, *Enfermedades políticas*, 245–46.

28. Villarroel, *Enfermedades políticas*, 283.

29. Villarroel, *Enfermedades políticas*, 121. His italics.

30. Villarroel, *Enfermedades políticas*, 233–34. The themes of alleged upper-class decadence and social disintegration in the late-colonial period are explored in depth in Juan Pedro Viqueira Albán, *Relajados o reprimidos? Diversiones públicas y vida social en la ciudad de México durante el Siglo de las Luces* (México: Fondo de Cultura Económico, 1987).

31. Villarroel, *Enfermedades que padece*, 265.

32. Villarroel, *Enfermedades que padece*, v–vii. On Bustamante's centralist, pro-Catholic republicanism see David Brading, *The First America: The Spanish Monarchy, Creole Patriots, and the Liberal State, 1492–1867* (New York: Cambridge University Press, 1991), 634–46.

33. Vincente Rocafuerte, "Ensayo sobre el nuevo sistema de carceles," *Colección Rocafuerte*, ed. Neptalí Zúñiga, vol. 9, *Rocafuerte y las doctrinas penales* (Quito: Edición del gobierno de Ecuador homenaje a Don Vincente Rocafuerte en el primer centenario de su muerte, 1947). For a history of Mexican prison reform see chapter 4.

34. Rocafuerte, "Ensayo sobre el nuevo sistema de carceles," iv.

35. Rocafuerte, "Ensayo sobre el nuevo sistema de carceles," 5. Ironically, Rocafuerte advised the nominally conservative government of Anastasio Bustamante.

36. Rocafuerte, "Ensayo sobre el nuevo sistema de carceles," 6.

37. Rocafuerte was involved in the opening of the first Lancasterian primary school in Mexico City in 1822. See Jaime E. Rodríguez O., *The Emergence of Spanish America: Vincente Rocafuerte and Spanish Americanism, 1808–1832* (Berkeley: University of Californian Press, 1975), 57; and Hale, *Mexican Liberalism*, 168–69.

38. Rocafuerte, "Ensayo sobre el nuevo sistema de carceles," 9. This liberal insistence on the despotic nature of colonial criminal justice is contradicted by Michael Scardaville in "Crime and the Urban Poor," chapter 6.

39. Rocafuerte, "Ensayo sobre el nuevo sistema de carceles," 11. Rocafuerte's role in Mexican economic development is explored in Rodríguez, *The Emergence of Spanish America*, 196–203.

40. Rocafuerte, "Ensayo sobre el nuevo sistema de carceles," 20–22.

41. Rocafuerte, "Ensayo sobre el nuevo sistema de carceles," 23.

42. Rocafuerte, "Ensayo sobre el nuevo sistema de carceles," 13.

43. Rocafuerte, "Ensayo sobre el nuevo sistema de carceles," 11–12.

44. The standard works on Mora and early-nineteenth-century Mexican liberalism are Hale, *Mexican Liberalism*, and Jesús Reyes Heroles, *El liberalismo mexicano*.

45. José María Luis Mora, "Discurso sobre la necesidad e importancia de la observancia de las leyes," *Obras completas*, vol. 1, *Obra política* (México: Secretaría de Educación Pública, 1986), 273.

46. José María Luis Mora, "Política. Ideas sueltas sobre la arbitrariedad en los procedimientos judiciales," *Obras completas,* 1:201−5.

47. José María Luis Mora, *Obras sueltas de José María Luis Mora, ciudadano mexicano,* 2nd ed. (México: Editorial Porrúa, 1963), 57.

48. José María Luis Mora, "Memoria sobre carceles inglesas," *Obras completas,* vol. 7, *Obra diplomática* (México: Secretaría de Educación Pública, 1988), 60.

49. J. M. L. Mora, "Memoria sobre carceles inglesas," 72−73. Mora's observations on British criminals were part of a report on the British prison system commissioned by the Mexican government. His frank criticisms of the British prison system is refreshing, but there is no indication that he saw Mexican criminals any differently than he did their British counterparts.

50. J. M. L. Mora, "Memoria sobre carceles inglesas," 73.

51. Otero's works on penal reform are found in Mariano Otero, *Obras,* vol. 2, ed. Jesús Reyes Heroles (México: Editorial Porrúa, 1967), 651−722. Most of these works have also been collected in Mariano Otero, "Indicaciones sobre la importancia y necesidad de la reforma de las Leyes Penales," "Carta sobre penitenciarias de Don Mariano Otero al Señor Licenciado Juan B. Cevallos, en Morelia, Michoacán," and "Mejora del pueblo: Casas de corrección," *Criminalia* 28, no. 8 (31 agosto 1962): 474−513.

52. Otero, "Mejora del pueblo," *Obras,* 2:686.

53. On page 22 of "Crime and the Urban Poor" Scardaville argues convincingly that "*léperos* were not a distinct group within the urban poor, as their contemporaries believed, but represented instead a cross section of the lower social sectors of Mexico City." Criminology, however, generally reflected elite perceptions rather than social "reality." The term is thus used in this study to indicate a perceived (rather than actual) category.

54. Scardaville, "Crime and the Urban Poor," 272−316. According to Scardaville, criminal cases in the formal courts were often unnecessarily lengthy. On the continuities and changes involved in the shift from Hapsburg to Bourbon criminal justice see Michael C. Scardaville, "(Hapsburg) Law and (Bourbon) Order: State Authority, Popular Unrest, and the Criminal Justice System in Bourbon Mexico City," in *Reconstructing Criminality in Latin America,* ed. Carlos Aguirre and Robert Buffington (Wilmington DE: Scholarly Resources, forthcoming). For more on colonial justice in general see Haslip-Viera, "Crime and the Administration of Justice." The infamous Tribunal of the Acordada was created during the eighteenth century in part to bypass the formal legal bureaucracy. On this question and other aspects of institutionalized Bourbon criminal justice see Colin MacLachlan, *Criminal Justice in Eighteenth-Century Mexico: A Study of the Tribunal of the Acordada* (Berkeley: University of California Press, 1974).

55. Lozano, *La criminalidad,* 187. For a detailed exploration of the politics of

vagrancy in the post-independence period see Richard Warren, "Mass Mobilization versus Social Control: Vagrancy and Public Order in Early Republican Mexico," in *Reconstructing Criminality*, ed. Aguirre and Buffington.

56. Eduardo Báez Macías, ed., "Ordenanzas para el establecimiento de alcaldes de barrio en la Nueva España," *Boletín del Archivo General de la Nación* 10, nos. 1–2 (1969): 121.

57. Facsimile in Jorge Nacif Mina, *La policía en la historia de la Ciudad de México (1524–1928)* (México: Desarrollo Social SocioCultur, 1986), 23.

58. Viquiera Albán argues that "extravagance and the good life became inseparable in the upper classes at the same time as they became intolerable in the people [pueblo]" in *Relajados o reprimidos?* 268.

59. Patricia Seed makes a convincing case for expanded internal migration into Mexico City after 1749 in "The Social Dimensions of Race." In "Alcohol Abuse and Tavern Reform in Late Colonial Mexico City," *Hispanic American Historical Review* 60, no. 4 (1980): 644, Michael C. Scardaville estimates that 85 percent of the 112,926 people who lived in Mexico City in 1790 could be considered "poor."

60. Quoted in Enrique Florescano and Isabel Gil Sánchez, "La época de las reformas borbónicas y el crecimiento económico, 1750–1808," in *Historia general de México*, vol. 2 (México: El Colegio de México, 1976), 220. On Bourbon-era efforts to regulate factory workers see Susan Deans-Smith, "The Working Poor and the Eighteenth-Century Colonial State: Gender, Public Order, and Work Discipline," in Beezley et al., *Rituals of Rule*, 47–75.

61. José Gómez de la Cortina, "Población," *Boletín del Instituto de Geografía y Estadística de la República Mexicana* 1 (marzo 1839): 32. Gómez includes 1836 criminal conviction statistics for the Federal District, but these are less revealing than arrest records, and the class status of these convicted criminals can only be surmised.

62. Scardaville, "Crime and the Urban Poor," 38.

63. Haslip-Viera, "The Underclass," 289. Haslip-Viera also notes the connection between certain occupations—shoemaking, textiles, construction—and the likelihood of arrest. Haslip-Viera, "The Underclass," 290.

64. Bando, February 24, 1772, AGN, Bandos, vol. 8, fol. 53. Quoted in Scardaville, "Crime and the Urban Poor," 123, n. 2.

65. The spatial dimensions of efforts to control public drunkenness are analyzed by Guedea in "México en 1812." Efforts to control public behavior outside Mexico City are examined in Anne Staples, "Policía y Buen Gobierno: Municipal Efforts to Regulate Public Behavior," in Beezley et al., *Rituals of Rule*, 115–26. On the repression of public festivals in this period see Linda A. Curcio-Nagy, "Giants and Gypsies: Corpus Christi in Colonial Mexico," in Beezley et al., *Rituals of Rule*, 1–26.

66. Lozano, *La criminalidad*, 123. Lozano notes that arrests were based more

on class than on race. Although research on the early national period remains to be done, there is no reason to believe that elite concerns about lower-class criminality underwent any significant changes. The impact of independence on legal institutions is examined in Linda Arnold, *Bureaucracy and Bureaucrats in Mexico City, 1742–1835* (Tucson: University of Arizona Press, 1988).

67. Nacif Mina, *La policía en la historia*, 75.

68. For a history of pre-independence efforts to regulate drinking see Guedea, "México en 1812," 23–64. Guedea links 1812 efforts to control alcohol consumption directly to concerns about Hidalgo's revolt. On colonial regulations see also Scardaville, "Alcohol Abuse," 643–71, and Scardaville, "Crime and the Urban Poor," chapter 5. Bourbon concerns about lower-class alcohol abuse are also addressed in José Jesús Hernández Palomo, *El aguardiente de caña en México* (Sevilla: Escuela de Estudios Hispano-Americanos de Sevilla, 1974).

69. "Informe sobre pulquerías y tabernas el año de 1784," *Boletín del Archivo General de la Nación* 18, no. 2 (1947): 216.

70. "Discurso sobre la policía de México, 1788," in Sonia Lombardo de Ruíz, ed., *Antología de textos sobre la ciudad de México en el período de la Ilustración (1788–1792)* (México: Instituto Nacional de Antropología e Historia, Departamento de Investigaciones Históricas, 1982), 60 and 63. The italics are in the anonymous original.

71. Scardaville, "Crime and the Urban Poor," 208.

72. Lozano, *La criminalidad*, 73.

73. Scardaville, "Crime and the Urban Poor," 228–31. See also Lozano, *La criminalidad*, 149.

74. Scardaville, "Crime and the Urban Poor," 100–103; and Lozano, *La criminalidad*, 147.

75. Scardaville, "Crime and the Urban Poor," 247–50; and Guedea, "México en 1812," 55. Ironically, reformers as late as the 1930s encountered the same obstacles as did their Bourbon counterparts. See, for example, "La campaña contra el alcoholismo: Iniciativa presidential," *Boletín de la Sociedad Mexicana de Geografía y Estadística* 42, no. 1 (abril 1930): 5–83.

76. During the late colonial period Mexico City police generally ignored the vagrancy laws because the problem was too vast to address. See Scardaville, "Crime and the Urban Poor," 10. The arrest rates for vagrancy (and drunkenness) picked up considerably, however, in the wake of Hidalgo's failed insurrection. See Lozano, *La criminalidad*, 107.

77. Scardaville, "Crime and the Urban Poor," 149–71. For specific cases see Lozano, *La criminalidad*, 86–95.

78. In *Apprehending the Criminal*, Marie-Christine Leps argues that novelists Emile Zola, Arthur Conan Doyle, and Robert Louis Stevenson challenged the restricted vision of criminality presented in criminological texts and the popular press. Leps seems a little reverential about the redeeming insights of the

great nineteenth-century novelists. Fernández de Lizardi's insights into criminality did not diminish his underlying class prejudices, nor did they subvert the criminological project in any meaningful way.

79. There are many editions of this work, including José Joaquín Fernández de Lizardi, *Periquillo Sarniento*, ed. L. Sainz de Medrano (Madrid: Editor Nacional, 1976). Likewise, a later novel, *La Quijotita*, chronicles the fall of a frivolous upper-class girl into prostitution. See Jean Franco, *Plotting Women: Gender and Representation in Mexico* (New York: Columbia University Press, 1989), 81–92.

80. José Joaquín Fernández de Lizardi, "Diálogo entre un francés y un italiano sobre la América septentrional," *El Pensador Mexicano*, ed. Agustín Yáñez (México: Universidad Nacional Autónoma de México, 1940), 28.

81. José Joaquín Fernández de Lizardi, "Conversaciones del payo y el sacristán," *El Pensador Mexicano*, 140.

82. Fernández de Lizardi, "Conversaciones del payo," 173–75.

83. José Joaquín Fernández de Lizardi, "Propónense los medios de extirpar la mendicidad de este reino," *Obras*, vol. 3, *Periódicos* (México: Universidad Nacional Autónoma de México, Centro de Estudios Literarios, 1968), 206. His italics.

84. Fernández de Lizardi, "Conversaciones del payo," 148–55. Fernández de Lizardi was especially hard on women, insisting that a woman convicted of indecent exposure be forced to work in prison to earn money for respectable clothing and, if that failed, that she remain in prison forever "because only in this way will she be covered." Likewise, female vagrants were to be imprisoned until they found employment. His idea for neighborhood informers may have been inspired by late colonial *alcaldes de barrio*. See Guedea, "México en 1812," 29.

85. José Fernándo Ramírez, "Noticias históricas y estadísticas de Durango, 1849–1850," *Boletín de la Sociedad Mexicana de Geografía y Estadística* 5 (1857): 39–40.

86. Alexander von Humboldt, *Political Essay on the Kingdom of New Spain*, vol. 1, trans. John Black (New York: AMS Press, 1966), 149–50, 235. This reprint is from the four-volume 1811 London edition of Humboldt's work, which testifies to its enormous popularity and prestige.

87. Joel Roberts Poinsett, *Notes on Mexico Made in the Autumn of 1822* (New York: Frederick A. Praeger, 1969), 49.

88. Jean Louis Berlandier, *Journey to Mexico during the Years 1826 to 1834*, 2 vols., trans. Sheila M. Ohlendorf (Austin: Texas State Historical Association and Center for Studies in Texas History, c. 1980), 2:143.

89. Quoted in N. Ray Gilmore, "The Condition of the Poor in Mexico, 1834," *Hispanic American Historical Review* 37, no. 2 (May 1957): 222–23.

90. F. R., "De la mendicidad y de los medios que deben adaptarse para hacerla desaparecer," *La Ilustración Mexicana* 3 (1852): 189.

91. F. R., "De la mendicidad," 137. Prison reformers like Rocafuerte and Otero also commented unfavorably on the lack of private philanthropy in Mexico.

92. J. F. Ramírez, "Noticias históricas," 43.

93. F. R. "De la mendicidad," 138.

94. F. R. "De la mendicidad," 138.

95. Diego Alvarez, "La familia," *La Ilustración Mexicana* 4 (1853): 149. This midcentury concern about the family is clearly related to ongoing state efforts to mobilize women. See Sylvia Arrom, "The Mobilization of Women," in *The Women of Mexico City, 1790–1857* (Stanford CA: Stanford University Press, 1985), 14–52.

96. F. R., "De la mendicidad," 140. The war with the United States profoundly influenced liberal social critics, including Otero. See Hale, *Mexican Liberalism*, 11–16.

97. Seed, "The Social Dimensions of Race," 569–74; and Scardaville, "Crime and the Urban Poor," 6.

98. José Ramón Pacheco, "Necesidad de la estadística: Puntos que debe contener y modo de formarla," *Boletín de la Sociedad Mexicana de Geografía y Estadística* 4 (septiembre 1851): 13.

99. "Estadística de Yucatán," *Boletín de la Sociedad Mexicana de Geografía y Estadística* 3 (1852): 293–94.

100. "Noticias estadísticas del Distrito de Acapulco de Tabares perteneciente al estado de Guerrero," *Boletín de la Sociedad Mexicana de Geografía y Estadística* 7 (1859): 410.

101. Manuel Larrainzar, "Noticia histórica de Soconusco y su incorporación a la República Mexicana," *Boletín de la Sociedad Mexicana de Geografía y Estadística* 3 (1852): 232.

102. Mora also wrote about the influence of climate on behavior and race. See José María Luis Mora, "Población de la República Mexicana. Su extensión, calidad y aumento. Carácter de los mexicanos. Progresos que han hecho en todos los ramos que constituyen a un pueblo culto y civilizado," *Obras completas*, vol. 4, *Obra histórica* (México: Secretaría de Educación Pública, 1987), 56–123.

103. For biographical data on Martínez de Castro see José Angel Ceniceros, "Vida y pensamiento de Antonio Martínez de Castro," *Criminalia* 30, no. 3 (31 mayo 1964): 182–85; and Raúl Carrancà y Trujillo, "Don Antonio Martínez de Castro y la Escuela Nacional Preparatoria," *Criminalia* 34, no. 3 (30 marzo 1968): 108–15.

104. Antonio Martínez de Castro, "Exposición de motivos del Código Penal," *Criminalia* 34, no. 3 (30 marzo 1968): 133.

105. Quoted in Javier Piña y Palacios, "Una cláusula del testamento del Presidente Juárez sobre la administración de justicia que aún no se cumple," *Criminalia* 34, no. 3 (30 marzo 1968): 121. Piña y Palacios includes the entire text of an 1868 *memoria* from Antonio Martínez de Castro to Congress on the need to reform criminal procedures. Again, as with Lardizábal, the fact that a prominent modern criminologist like Piña y Palacios would recognize the currency of Martínez de Castro's basic agenda argues strongly for fundamental perceptual continuities in Mexican criminology.

106. Piña y Palacios, "Una cláusula," 129.

107. Justo Sierra, "La mendicidad en México," *Obras completas del Maestro Justo Sierra*, vol. 4 (México: Universidad Nacional Autónoma de México, 1948), 306–8.

108. Enrique M. de los Ríos, *El Monitor Republicano*, 10 diciembre 1889.

109. "Juvenal," *El Monitor Republicano*, 23 julio 1889 and 22 noviembre 1889.

110. See, for example, *El Monitor Republicano*, 26 abril 1889, 16 mayo 1889, 12 junio 1889, 22 junio 1889, 2 julio 1889, 24 agosto 1889, 28 agosto 1889, 25 octubre 1889, 30 octubre 1889, and 27 diciembre 1889.

111. "Juvenal," *El Monitor Republicano*, 26 abril 1889.

112. On Porfirian efforts to improve public health see Moisés González Navarro, *El Porfiriato. La vida social*, vol. 4, *Historia moderna de México*, ed. Daniel Cosío Villegas (México: Editorial Hermes, 1957), 52–134. González Navarro deals specifically with anti-alcohol campaigns on pages 72–82.

113. Charles Darwin's *Descent of Man, and Selection in Relation to Sex* had been published seven years earlier, in 1871.

114. Justo Sierra, "Contestación a la carta del Doctor Fenelon," *Obras completas*, 4:358–61. This article first appeared in *La Libertad*, 12 octubre 1878.

115. Internal migration during the late nineteenth century had its greatest impact in the larger cities, especially the capital. See González Navarro, *El Porfiriato. La vida social*, 26–27.

116. This transition is extensively analyzed in Hale, *Transformation of Liberalism*.

117. Fernández de Lizardi, "Diálogo entre un francés y un italiano," 22.

118. Fernández de Lizardi, "Conversaciones del payo," 181.

## 2. Scientific Criminology

1. The literature on Porfirian modernization is extensive. The classic work is still Moisés González Navarro, *El Porfiriato. La vida social*. See also Beezley, *Judas at the Jockey Club*. What Beezley calls the Porfirian "persuasion" was not just confined to Mexico City. See, for example, his "The Porfirian Smart Set Anticipates Thorsten Veblen in Guadalajara," in *Judas at the Jockey Club*; William French, "Progreso Forzado: Workers and the Inculcation of the Capitalist Work

Ethic in the Parral Mining District," in Beezley et al., *Rituals of Rule*; and Allen Wells and Gilbert M. Joseph, "Modernizing Visions, *Chilango* Blueprints, and Provincial Growing Pains: Mérida at the Turn of the Century," *Mexican Studies/Estudios Mexicanos* 8, no. 2 (summer 1992): 167–215.

2. See especially Tenorio-Trillo, *Mexico at the World's Fair* and "1910 Mexico City."

3. For a broad overview of Porfirian attitudes toward crime see Pablo Piccato, "Understanding Society: Porfirian Discourse about Criminality and Alcoholism," unpublished manuscript. For a brief review of the criminological debate see Javier MacGregor Campusano, "Historiografía sobre criminalidad y sistema penitenciario," *Secuencia: Revista de Historia y Ciencias Sociales* 22 (1992): 232–34. For more on the larger phenomenon of criminality see Piccato, "Criminals in Mexico City."

4. Kuhn, *The Structure of Scientific Revolutions*.

5. Kuhn, *The Structure of Scientific Revolutions*, 15.

6. Kuhn, *The Structure of Scientific Revolutions*, 177.

7. Kuhn, *The Structure of Scientific Revolutions*, 193.

8. In fairness to Kuhn, he repeatedly expresses strong reservations about the applicability of his model to social sciences like criminology and even medicine, because of their links to "external social need." See *The Structure of Scientific Revolutions*, viii, 15, 18, 164, 209.

9. Kuhn considered this situation rare, at least in the physical sciences. See *The Structure of Scientific Revolutions*, ix. Nancy Leys Stepans, in *The Hour of Eugenics: Race, Gender, and Nation in Latin America* (Ithaca NY: Cornell University Press, 1991), argues that Latin American eugenics (including Mexican eugenics) favored a "soft" neo-Lamarckian approach based on French environmentalism that she contrasts with the "hard" Mendelian eugenics of the United States, England, and Nazi Germany. Her own evidence, however, demonstrates that Latin American eugenists used both hereditarian and environmental theories. Rather than a dominant paradigm, neo-Lamarckian eugenics represented the shifting middle ground in a theoretically unstable field. Mexican criminology exhibits the same theoretical schizophrenia. On the European dispute see Robert A. Nye, "Heredity or Milieu: The Foundations of Modern Criminological Theory," *Isis* 67, no. 238 (September 1976): 335–55.

10. The division of anthropology into physical and cultural subdisciplines represents a similar "solution" to potentially contentious etiologies. Both solutions support Foucault's description of the often contradictory nature of discourses in *The Archeology of Knowledge* (see the introduction to chapter 1).

11. Kuhn uses the term "gestalt" to signify mode of perception. See, for example, *The Structure of Scientific Revolutions*, 111–12.

12. The philosophical implications of social science paradigms are explored in Hayden White, "The Politics of Historical Interpretation: Discipline and De-

Sublimation," in *The Content of the Form: Narrative Discourse and Historical Representation* (Baltimore MD: The Johns Hopkins University Press, 1987). On page 59 White notes the importance of understanding the disciplinary nature of modern social sciences, which "have been promoted to the status of disciplines without having attained to the theoretical and methodological regimentation that characterizes the physical sciences."

13. Kuhn recognized the need for a broader construction of the paradigm, which he called the "disciplinary matrix" in the postscript to the second edition of *The Structure of Scientific Revolutions*, 182–85.

14. On focusing the scientific "gaze" see the preface to Michel Foucault, *The Birth of the Clinic: An Archeology of Medical Perception*, trans. A. M. Sheridan Smith (New York: Vintage, 1975).

15. The practical details of the Porfirian war on crime have been well documented by Laurence J. Rohlfes, who notes that the Mexico City police budget quadrupled during the Porfiriato. "Police and Penal Correction," 76.

16. Rafael de Zayas Enríquez, *Fisiología del crimen: Estudio jurídico-sociológico*, 2 vols. (Veracruz: Imprenta de R. de Zayas, 1885). Zayas was one of the most cosmopolitan Porfirians. He served as consul in San Francisco and promoted Mexico at the 1889 Paris World's Fair. See Tenorio-Trillo, *Mexico at the World's Fairs*, 21 and 34. Like many early criminologists Zayas also had literary ambitions and an enthusiasm for statistics. See especially his 1893 *Los Estados Unidos Mexicanos: Sus condiciones naturales y sus elementos de prosperidad* (México: Facultad de Economía, UNAM, 1989).

17. Zayas, *Fisiología del crimen*, 1:4–5.

18. Zayas, *Fisiología del crimen*, 1:10.

19. The death penalty was much debated in nineteenth-century Mexico. During the 1857 Constitutional Convention debates, for example, some delegates like Melchor Campo and Ignacio Ramírez argued that Mexico was not yet socially or institutionally advanced enough to desist, while others like José Antonio Gamboa declared it barbaric and unworthy of a modern society. See Francisco Zarco, *Historia del Congreso Extraordinario Constituyente, 1856–1857* (México: El Colegio de México, 1956), 754–89.

20. For a brief summary of Lombroso's theories see Marvin E. Wolfgang, "Cesare Lombroso," in *Pioneers in Criminology*, ed. Mannheim, 168–227.

21. Zayas, *Fisiología del crimen*, 1:19.

22. One compelling reason for an eclectic approach was the underlying similarity of the competing French and Italian schools of criminology. See, for example, Ruth Harris, *Murders and Madness: Medicine, Law, and Society in the Fin de Siècle* (Oxford: Clarendon Press, 1989), 88. Harris argues that both schools proposed "deterministic explanations of criminal behavior," both constructed elaborate criminal typologies, and both "regarded crime as a social pathology rather than as an individual moral failing." Some scholars have noted

an inherent determinism in the "scientific world view" in general. See Martin J. Wiener, *Reconstructing the Criminal: Culture, Law, and Policy in England, 1830–1914* (New York: Cambridge University Press, 1990), 162.

23. On presupposition in nineteenth-century criminological discourse see Leps, *Apprehending the Criminal*, 10–11.

24. Zayas, *Fisiología del crimen*, 1:19. On the flawed nature of the nineteenth-century human sciences see Stephen Jay Gould, *The Mismeasure of Man* (New York: W. W. Norton, 1981).

25. The theory of moral insanity is generally associated with French psychiatrist Prosper Despine and his more famous English counterpart Henry Maudsley. See C. Bernaldo de Quirós, *Modern Theories of Criminality*, trans. Alfonso de Salvio (New York: Agathon Press, 1967), 7–9; and Peter Scott, "Henry Maudsley," in *Pioneers in Criminology*, ed. Mannheim, 144–67. Zayas cites both Despine and Maudsley.

26. Zayas, *Fisiología del crimen*, 2:46. His italics.

27. Zayas, *Fisiología del crimen*, 2:81.

28. Zayas, *Fisiología del crimen*, 2:195.

29. Zayas, *Fisiología del crimen*, 1:14.

30. Zayas, *Fisiología del crimen*, 1:18.

31. On page 96 of *Apprehending the Criminal* Marie-Christine Leps contends that "objective information—up-to-the-minute, full, worldwide, and above all true—was not just a new commodity thrown on the market by mass journalism, but its most central concept, its proclaimed raison d'être." Leps explores the connections between scientific and journalistic objectivity in *Apprehending the Criminal*, 96–134.

32. Zayas, *Fisiología del crimen*, 2:15.

33. Zayas, *Fisiología del crimen*, 2:170–93.

34. The links between journalism and science in Porfirian criminology are examined in more detail in chapter 3.

35. Francisco Martínez Baca and Manuel Vergara, *Estudios de antropología criminal* (Puebla: Imprenta, Litografía y Encuadernación de Benjamin Lara, 1892).

36. On the Mexican presence at world's fairs and especially on the use of scientific studies to appear modern see Tenorio-Trillo, *Mexico at the World's Fairs*.

37. Martínez and Vergara, *Estudios de antropología criminal*, iii.

38. Martínez and Vergara, *Estudios de antropología criminal*, vi.

39. Martínez and Vergara, *Estudios de antropología criminal*, 22.

40. Martínez and Vergara, *Estudios de antropología criminal*, 33–34.

41. Martínez and Vergara, *Estudios de antropología criminal*, viii–ix.

42. For Leopoldo Zea local applicability explained positivism's tremendous appeal for Latin American intellectuals. See *The Latin American Mind*, trans. James H. Abbott and Lowell Dunham (Norman: University of Oklahoma Press, 1963). Nevertheless, the critique of inappropriate foreign models dates

back at least to the independence period. On Haeckel's influence on positivists like Andrés Molina Enríquez see Agustín Basave, "El mito del mestizo: El pensamiento nacional de Andrés Molina Enríquez," in *El nacionalismo en Mexico*, ed. Noriega Elío, 223. Bartra also refers to Haeckel's influence in *Cage of Melancholy*, 7, 120.

43. Martínez and Vergara, *Estudios de antropología criminal*, 2. The contrast with Lardizábal's unfathomable soul is indicative of the optimism and presumption of late-nineteenth-century science.

44. See, for example, Liss, *Mexico Under Spain, 1521–1556*; and the introductory chapter of Schmidt, *Roots of Lo Mexicano*.

45. Martínez and Vergara, *Estudios de antropología criminal*, 15.

46. Martínez and Vergara, *Estudios de antropología criminal*, 68. Lacassagne is most famous for his rebuttal of Lombroso at the 1885 First International Congress of Criminal Anthropology in Rome: "Les sociétés ont les criminels qu'elles méritent." See Nye, "Heredity or Milieu," 338–41. Lacassagne's theory indicates the intense interest of French criminologists in criminal physiology in spite of their opposition to Lombrosian determinism.

47. Martínez and Vergara, *Estudios de antropología criminal*, 97.

48. Martínez and Vergara, *Estudios de antropología criminal*, 84. For a concise history and critique of various cranial indices see Gould, "Measuring Heads," in *The Mismeasure of Man*, 73–112.

49. Martínez and Vergara, *Estudios de antropología criminal*, 95.

50. Martínez and Vergara, *Estudios de antropología criminal*, 101–2.

51. Martínez and Vergara, *Estudios de antropología criminal*, 99.

52. Martínez and Vergara, *Estudios de antropología criminal*, 41. Martínez and Vergara were likely influenced in these ideas by Cesare Lombroso, although he was by no means the only prominent criminologist to suggest the specificity of anomalies or to use folk sayings to imply a link between positivist science and traditional wisdom.

53. Martínez and Vergara, *Estudios de antropología criminal*, 17–18.

54. Agustín Verdugo, *La responsibilidad criminal y las modernas escuelas de antropología* (México: Oficina Tip. de la Secretaría de Fomento, 1895), 46.

55. Verdugo, *La responsibilidad criminal*, 76.

56. This was the case in France, for example, and it explains in part French criminologists' refusal to accept the more extreme Italian positions—Enrico Ferri, for example, argued that only a scientifically trained expert could effectively judge and punish a criminal. The accommodation between nineteenth-century French "progressives" who saw in criminology a chance to expand judicial discretion, and "conservatives" who feared the growing power of scientific experts, is discussed in Harris, *Murders and Madness*, 120–25.

57. Miguel S. Macedo, *La criminalidad en México: Medios de combatirla* (México: Oficina Tip. de la Secretaría de Fomento, 1897).

58. Macedo, like most prominent, scientifically minded Mexican elites, was a member of the Sociedad Mexicana de Geografía y Estadística, which was founded in 1833 to encourage the statistical studies necessary to economic and social development. Crime statistics were one component of that project. See "Síntesis histórica del Boletín de la Sociedad Mexicana de Geografía y Estadística," *Boletín de la Sociedad Mexicana de Geografía y Estadística* 49, nos. 1–12 (marzo 1939): 9–18. On the intellectual formation of científicos, including Macedo see Alfonso de María y Campos, see "Porfirianos prominentes: Orígenes y años de juventud de ocho integrantes del grupo de los científicos, 1846–1876," *Historia Mexicana* 34, no. 4 (abril–junio 1985): 610–61.

59. Macedo, *La criminalidad en México*, 4.

60. Macedo, *La criminalidad en México*, 28.

61. Macedo, *La criminalidad en México*, 23.

62. Macedo, *La criminalidad en México*, 5–6. Criminal statistics for the Federal District were first collected in 1886 by Emilio Rebasa. These and subsequent figures suggesting that "the Mexican people were the most criminal in the world" were rejected as misleading and incomplete by Carlos Roumagnac in *La estadística criminal en México* (México: Imp. de Arturo García Cubas Sucesores Hermanos, 1907), 10, 27. Roumagnac's critique demonstrates the difficulty of using crime statistics to evaluate criminality, especially for the late nineteenth century. Laurence Rohlfes argues, for example, that crime actually decreased in Mexico City during the Porfiriato, although "police intolerance of public order violations" increased. Rohlfes, "Police and Penal Correction," 167.

63. Macedo, *La criminalidad en México*, 9–10. On Porfirian efforts to encourage immigration see González Navarro, *El Porfiriato. La vida social*, 134–52.

64. Macedo, *La criminalidad en México*, 4–5.

65. Macedo, *La criminalidad en México*, 37.

66. Macedo, *La criminalidad en México*, 6.

67. Macedo, *La criminalidad en México*, 10–11.

68. Macedo, *La criminalidad en México*, 11.

69. Macedo, *La criminalidad en México*, 28–35. According to Macedo's proposal parents (generally lower-class parents) could abandon their children both physically and morally. Moral abandonment meant that their lifestyle "condemned [their children] to follow a career of vagrancy, begging, and crime." Macedo, *La criminalidad en México*, 29. In 1897 the death penalty was still constitutional and allowed by the penal code but had fallen into disuse because most jurists considered it barbaric. Many of these reforms, including the transportation of recidivists to the Valle Nacional, Quintana Roo, and later Islas Marías, were attempted during the Porfiriato. See Rohlfes, "Police and Penal Correction," 237–84.

70. Macedo, *La criminalidad en México*, 28.

71. Julio Guerrero, *La génesis del crimen en México: Ensayo de psiquiatría social* (México: Imprenta de la Vda de Ch. Bouret, 1901).

72. Guerrero, *Génesis del crimen en México*, v. His italics.

73. Guerrero, *Génesis del crimen en México*, vii. English positivist and Social Darwinist Herbert Spencer argued that altruism—the willingness to sacrifice oneself for the collective good—was typical of the highest stages of human evolution. Spencer was not, however, a great believer in public charities (welfare), which he felt unnaturally preserved the unfit.

74. Guerrero, *Génesis del crimen en México*, xi–xii. His italics.

75. Guerrero, *Génesis del crimen en México*, xiii. His italics. Guerrero's contribution to the formulation of a Mexican national identity is examined in Schmidt, *Roots of Lo Mexicano*, 50–51. Roger Bartra explores Guerrero's contribution to the "imagining" of Mexican national character in *Cage of Melancholy*, 31–32. The quotations from Guerrero that follow amply support Bartra's point about the melancholic aspects of that mythical construction.

76. Guerrero, *Génesis del crimen en México*, 4.

77. Guerrero, *Génesis del crimen en México*, 17–20. Alcohol is, of course, generally considered a depressant, but Guerrero is right in noting its heightened effects at higher altitudes.

78. Guerrero, *Génesis del crimen en México*, 24.

79. Guerrero shared Macedo's preoccupation with comparative statistics, noting that Mexico City's 1896 ratio of violent crimes was 242 per 10,000 inhabitants, while Spain's was only 81.9 per 10,000 and Italy's only 23.4 per 10,000. Guerrero, *Génesis del crimen en México*, 22–23.

80. Guerrero, *Génesis del crimen en México*, 131.

81. Guerrero, *Génesis del crimen en México*, 154–55. Guerrero included women in his discussion of Mexican workers, arguing specifically that surplus labor and low wages encouraged prostitution. Guerrero, *Génesis del crimen en México*, 139.

82. Guerrero, *Génesis del crimen en México*, 314.

83. Guerrero, *Génesis del crimen en México*, 376.

84. Guerrero, *Génesis del crimen en México*, 319–20.

85. Guerrero, *Génesis del crimen en México*, 235.

86. Guerrero, *Génesis del crimen en México*, 230.

87. In his discussion of nineteenth-century elite English views of criminality Martin J. Weiner argues for "the replacement of a Victorian image of humanity by a less potentially dangerous but also less powerful image" of human nature by the turn of the century. Mexican criminologists like Guerrero presented contradictory images, arguing that the lower classes were degenerate and weak while at the same time insisting that degeneracy increased their potential for violence. As Weiner points out, the English had successfully addressed the threat of lower-class violence; the Mexican Revolution makes it clear that Mexican

policymakers had not. See *Reconstructing the Criminal*, 381. On the pervasive and ambiguous concept of degeneration see J. Edward Chamberlin and Sander L. Gilman, eds., *Degeneration: The Dark Side of Progress* (New York: Columbia University Press, 1985).

88. Guerrero, *Génesis del crimen en México*, 157–58.

89. Guerrero, *Génesis del crimen en México*, 158–60.

90. Guerrero, *Génesis del crimen en México*, 177–78.

91. Guerrero, *Génesis del crimen en México*, 333.

92. Roumagnac, *Estadística criminal en México*, 21.

93. Roumagnac, *Criminales en México: Ensayo de psicología criminal* (Mexico: Tipografía "El Fénix," 1904), 7–8.

94. Roumagnac, *Criminales*, 10.

95. Roumagnac, *Estadística criminal en México*, 6.

96. In his works Roumagnac cites only Martínez and Vergara, Guerrero, and Macedo, ignoring Zayas, whose pioneering work his own most closely resembles. Roumagnac, *Estadística criminal en México*, 27, and *Criminales*, 9.

97. For a brief biography and exposition of Ferri's ideas see Thorsten Sellin, "Enrico Ferri," in *Pioneers of Criminology*, ed. Mannheim, 277–300.

98. Roumagnac, *Criminales*, 59–60.

99. Roumagnac, *Criminales*, 22.

100. Roumagnac, *Criminales*, 47.

101. Roumagnac, *Criminales*, 58.

102. In *Estadística criminal en México*, for example, Roumagnac pushed for the collection of two crucial criminal statistics: "recidivism and the state of drunkenness at the time of the crime," 14.

103. Roumagnac, *Criminales*, 69–72. These comprehensive individual examinations were a favorite if rarely employed criminological technique. Martínez and Vergara had proposed a similar set of questions in *Estudios de antropología criminal*, 6–8. Roumagnac, however, was the first to actually compile extensive data on individual criminals.

104. The intricate narratives that comprise the bulk of Roumagnac's criminology are examined in detail in chapter 3.

105. The obvious exception is Julio Guerrero, whose *Génesis del crimen en México* is very much in the French environmentalist tradition of Tarde (and Hippolyte Taine, for that matter).

106. This attitude is reflected in Porfirian police records. According to Laurence Rohlfes, 93 percent of those apprehended by the Mexico City *gendarmería* in 1910 were from the lower classes. See his "Police and Penal Correction," 172.

107. Unfortunately, the history of modern Mexican criminology has yet to be written. Some sense of chronology can be gleaned from Antonio Sánchez Galindo, "Mexico," in *International Handbook of Contemporary Developments*

*in Criminology*, vol. 1, *Issues and the Americas*, ed. Elmer H. Johnson (Westport CT: Greenwood Press, 1983), 251–66; and Rosa del Olmo, *América latina y su criminología* (México: Siglo Veintiuno Editores, 1981).

### 3. Popular Criminology

1. Roumagnac, *Criminales*, 104–23. Roumagnac supplies only the last initial of the women's names, ostensibly to protect their identity, although he includes María's photograph. Her male lover is identified only as "X." For a more detailed exploration of this case see Pablo Piccato and Robert Buffington, "Tales of Two Women: The Narrative Construal of Porfirian Reality," *The Americas* 55, no. 3 (January 1999): 391–424.

2. On the lenient treatment of crimes of passion see Harris, *Murders and Madness*.

3. This concern was hardly confined to Mexico. See, for example, *Degeneration: The Dark Side of Progress*, ed. Chamberlin and Gilman.

4. This literature continues to grow. See, for example, Susan K. Besse, "Crimes of Passion: The Campaign against Wife Killing in Brazil, 1910–1940," *Journal of Social History* 22, no. 4 (1989): 653–66; Katherine Elaine Bliss, "Prostitution, Revolution and Social Reform in Mexico City, 1918–1940" (Ph.D. diss., University of Chicago, 1996), and "'Guided by an Imperious Moral Need': Prostitutes, Motherhood and Nationalism in Revolutionary Mexico," in *Reconstructing Criminality*, ed. Aguirre and Buffington; Sueann Caulfield, "Getting into Trouble: Dishonest Women, Modern Girls, and Women-Men in the Conceptual Language of Vida Policial, 1925–1927," *Signs* 19, no. 1 (1993): 146–76; Sueann Caulfield and Martha de Abreu Esteves, "Fifty Years of Virginity in Rio de Janeiro: Sexual Politics and Gender Roles in Juridical and Popular Discourse, 1890–1940," *Luso-Brazilian Review* 30, no. 1 (1993): 47–74; William French, "Prostitutes and Guardian Angels: Women, Work, and the Family in Porfirian Mexico," *Hispanic American Historical Review* 72, no. 4 (1992): 529–53; Donna Guy, *Sex and Danger in Buenos Aires: Prostitution, Family, and Nation in Argentina* (Lincoln: University of Nebraska Press, 1991); David McCreery, "'This Life of Misery and Shame': Prostitution in Guatemala City, 1880–1920," *Journal of Latin American Studies* 18 (1987): 333–53; Cristina Rivera Garza, "The Masters of the Streets: Bodies, Power and Modernity in Mexico, 1867–1930" (Ph.D. diss., University of Houston, 1995); Kristen Ruggiero, "Honor, Maternity, and the Disciplining of Women: Infanticide in Late Nineteenth-Century Buenos Aires," *Hispanic American Historical Review* 72, no. 3 (August 1992): 353–73, and "Not Guilty: Abortion and Infanticide in Nineteenth-Century Argentina," in *Reconstructing Criminality*, ed. Aguirre and Buffington; Ricardo D. Salvatore, "Criminology, Prison Reform, and the Buenos Aires Working Class," *Journal of Interdisciplinary History* 23, no. 2 (autumn 1992): 279–99; and Steve J. Stern, *The Secret History of Gender:*

*Women, Men and Power in Late Colonial Mexico* (Chapel Hill: University of North Carolina Press, 1995).

5. One exception is Donna Guy, "Tango, Gender, and Politics," in *Sex and Danger in Buenos Aires*, 141–74. Another is Benigno Trigo, "Crossing the Boundaries of Madness: Criminology and Figurative Language in Argentina (1878–1920)," *Journal of Latin American Studies* 6, no. 1 (1997): 7–20, although Trigo is interested primarily in the changes in criminological discourse.

6. This is especially true of the great historian of Mexican positivism Leopoldo Zea, whose principal works include *El positivismo en México* and *Apogeo y decadencia del positivismo en México*.

7. This generalized elite vision was sometimes modified to address class differences among women, especially lower-class women's need to work outside the home. Their civic obligations were nonetheless fundamentally unchanged. See Arrom, *The Women of Mexico City*; and Mary K. Vaughn, "Women, Class, and Education in Mexico, 1880–1928," *Latin American Perspectives* 4 (1977): 63–80.

8. The most prominent expression of this concern for Mexico's national survival is in Justo Sierra's *The Political Evolution of the Mexican People*, trans. Charles Ramsdell (Austin: University of Texas Press, 1969).

9. Roumagnac, *Criminales*, 7.

10. Antonio Gramsci's dispersed writings on the role of specialized intellectuals in consolidating cultural hegemony are collected in "Antonio Gramsci," in *Culture, Ideology and Social Process*, ed. Bennett et al. (London: Open University Press, 1989), 191–218; and Antonio Gramsci, *Cuadernos de la cárcel: Los intelectuales y la organización de la cultura* (México: Juan Pablos Editor, 1975).

11. On penitentiaries and other technologies of social control in Mexico see the next chapter of this book; Piccato, "Criminals in Mexico City"; and Rivera Garza, "The Masters of the Streets."

12. *Diccionario Porrúa: Historia, biografía y geografía de México*, vol. 2, 3rd ed. (México: Editorial Porrúa, 1971), 1810. Nor was he alone; Luis Lara y Pardo, author of a well-known Porfirian treatise on prostitution, was one of his collaborators on this work.

13. For a straightforward discussion of symbolic languages see Carroll Smith-Rosenberg, "Hearing Women's Words: A Feminist Reconstruction of History," in *Disorderly Conduct: Visions of Gender in Victorian America* (New York: Oxford University Press, 1985), 11–52.

14. Roumagnac, *Criminales*, 105.

15. Concern about the morality of working women was typical of late-nineteenth-century elites. See, for example, Donna J. Guy, "Public Health, Gender, and Private Morality: Paid Labor and the Formation of the Body Politic in Buenos Aires," *Gender and History* 2, no. 3 (autumn 1990): 297–317. Per-

ceived links between prostitution (which was not, however, illegal) and criminality were even more apparent. The classic Porfirian work on prostitution is Luis Lara y Pardo, *La prostitución en México* (Mexico City: Librería de la Vda. de Ch. Bouret, 1908). See also Bliss, "Prostitution, Revolution and Social Reform in Mexico City, 1918–1940" and "'Guided by an Imperious, Moral Need'"; French, "Prostitutes and Guardian Angels"; and Rivera Garza, "The Masters of the Streets."

16. Roumagnac, *Criminales*, 111.

17. Roumagnac, *Criminales*, 112.

18. Roumagnac, *Criminales*, 191. Roumagnac explains the hidden symbolism of hair parting (right side equals masculine, left side equals feminine) in a footnote on page 174.

19. Roumagnac, *Criminales*, 194–99.

20. Roumagnac's concern about homosexual practices was not confined to women. He asked his male subjects similar questions and received similar responses. On sexuality in Mexican prisons see chapter 6, and Pablo Piccato, "La experiencia penal en la ciudad de México: Cambios y permanencias tras la revolución," in *La experiencia institucional en la ciudad de México, 1821–1929*, ed. Carlos Illades (Universidad Autónoma Metropolitana–El Colegio de Michoacán, forthcoming).

21. Roumagnac, *Criminales*, 113.

22. Alphonse Bertillon, *Instructions for Taking Descriptions for the Identification of Criminals and Others by the Means of Anthropometric Indications*, trans. Gallus Muller (New York: AMS Press, 1977). A Spanish manual that circulated in Mexico around this time was Joaquín García Plaza y Romero, *Manual del señalamiento antropométrico (Método de Mr. Alf. Bertillón)* (Madrid: Librería Editorial de Bailly-Bailliere é Hijos, 1902).

23. The standard work is Magnus Morner, *Race Mixture in the History of Latin America* (Boston: Little, Brown, 1967).

24. See Foucault, *The Birth of the Clinic*. The use of photographic images is analyzed in John Tagg, "Power and Photography—A Means of Surveillance: The Photograph As Evidence in Law," in *Culture, Ideology and Social Process*, ed. Bennett et al., 285–308.

25. For an early colonial example see William B. Taylor, *Drinking, Homicide and Rebellion in Colonial Mexican Villages* (Stanford CA: Stanford University Press, 1979). For later colonial and national efforts see chapter 1.

26. Roumagnac, *Criminales*, 112.

27. For a critique of Porfirian education see Vaughn, *State, Education, and Social Class in Mexico*.

28. Roumagnac, *Criminales*, 33.

29. For a discussion of equilibrium and the nervous system see Harris, *Murders and Madness*, 37–41.

30. On Emile Zola see Sander L. Gilman, "Black Bodies, White Bodies," in *Degeneration: The Dark Side of Progress*, ed. Chamberlin and Gilman.

31. Franco, *Plotting Women*, 95–98. Early in his career revolutionary muralist José Clemente Orozco painted a series of watercolors depicting Mexico City prostitutes. See James B. Lynch Jr., "Orozco's House of Tears," *Journal of Interamerican Studies* 3, no. 3 (July 1961): 367–83. Coincidentally, Gamboa shared many of Roumagnac's traits, having worked as a court clerk, journalist, and translator of French literature. His second major novel, *Suprema ley*—the story of a young clerk in love with a murderess—opens in the offices of Mexico City's notorious jail, Belén, where Roumagnac conducted his interviews.

32. Carlos Roumagnac, *Crimenes sexuales y pasionales: Estudio de psicología morbosa* (México: Librería de Ch. Bouret, 1906).

33. Roumagnac, *Criminales*, 376–82.

34. Roumagnac, *Criminales*, 105.

35. The dangers of the "street" are discussed in François Giraud, "Viol et société coloniale: Le cas de la Nouvelle-Espagne au XVIIIe siècle," *Annales: Economies, Sociétés, Civilisations* 41, no. 3 (mai–juin 1986): 625–37; Staples, "Policía y Buen Gobierno"; and S. J. Stern, *The Secret History of Gender*.

36. Roumagnac, *Criminales*, 10.

37. See Roland Barthes, "Introduction to the Structural Analysis of Narratives," in *Image, Music, Text*, trans. Stephen Heath (New York: Noonday Press, 1977), 79–124. Barthes identifies these strategies as "the progressive integration of levels of description" and the alteration of "two systems of signs."

38. Roumagnac, *Criminales*, 107.

39. Roumagnac, *Criminales*, 104.

40. Roumagnac, *Criminales*, 116.

41. This point is one of the central themes of Cesare Lombroso and William Ferraro, *The Female Offender* (New York: D. Appleton, 1916).

42. Roumagnac, *Criminales*, 113.

43. This linkage between female physiology and criminality was typical of late-nineteenth-century criminology. See, for example, Harris, *Murders and Madness*, 35–36. Harris also examines the connection between romantic melodrama and women's accounts of crimes of passion in *Murders and Madness*, 222–23.

44. See Gilman, "Black Bodies, White Bodies," and Guy, *Sex and Danger in Buenos Aires*.

45. For a concise discussion of the Gramscian notion of rearticulation see Mouffe, "Hegemony and Ideology."

46. On the purported "objectivity" of narrative see White, "The Value of Narrativity in the Representation of Reality," in *The Content of the Form*, 1–25. On page 24 White warns that "this value attached to narrativity in the representation of real events arises out of a desire to have real events display the co-

herence, integrity, fullness, and closure of an image of life that is and can only be imaginary."

47. Freudian psychology and medical technologies like endocrinology (which emphasized the role of hormones in criminal behavior) further reinforced the notion of a specifically female criminality. See Félix Pichardo Estrada, "Criminología y delincuencia femenina," *Criminalia* 22, nos. 1–12 (enero–diciembre 1956): 167–74.

## 4. Revolutionary Reform

Earlier versions of this chapter appeared as "Revolutionary Reform: The Mexican Revolution and the Discourse on Prison Reform," *Mexican Studies/Estudios Mexicanos* 9, no. 1 (winter 1993): 71–93, and as "Revolutionary Reform: Capitalist Development, Prison Reform, and Executive Power in Mexico," in *The Birth of the Penitentiary in Latin America: Essays on Criminology, Prison Reform, and Social Control, 1830–1940*, ed. Ricardo D. Salvatore and Carlos Aguirre (Austin: University of Texas Press, 1996), 169–93. The latter volume contains several essays on penitentiaries and prison reform in Latin America, including an introductory essay that explores the regional implications.

1. For an account of the credential's fight see E. V. Niemeyer Jr., *Revolution at Querétaro: The Mexican Constitutional Convention of 1916–1917* (Austin: University of Texas Press, 1974), 44–59. A transcription of the proceedings recorded by a participant can be found in Félix F. Palavicini, *Historia de la Constitución de 1917* (México: n.d.), 57–143.

2. México, XLVI Legislatura de la Camara de Diputados, *Derechos del pueblo mexicano: México a través de sus constituciones*, vol. 4, *Antecedentes y evolución de los artículos 16 a 27 constitucionales* (México: XLVI Legislatura de la Camara de Diputados, 1967), 86–143. The legislative debates without commentary and antecedents can also be found in *Diario de los debates del Congreso Constituyente, 1916–1917*, 2 vols. (México: Talleres Gráficos de la Nación, 1960).

3. *Derechos del pueblo mexicano*, 4:91.

4. For another example of a discursive revolution see Keith Michael Baker, *Inventing the French Revolution: Essays on French Political Culture in the Eighteenth Century* (New York: Cambridge University Press, 1990), 18. Baker provides a useful definition of discourse as "a set of linguistic patterns and relationships that defined possible actions and utterances and gave them meaning" (24). Also germane is Joan Scott's reminder that discourse analysis should not reduce "the idea of meaning to instrumental utterances—words that people say to one another—rather than conveying the idea of meaning as the patterns and relationships that constitute understanding or a 'cultural system.'" Joan Wallach Scott, *Gender and the Politics of History* (New York: Columbia University Press, 1988), 59.

5. Although he uses the term ideology rather than discourse, Arnaldo Córdova reaches a similar conclusion in *La ideología*.

6. On the temperance debate see Niemeyer, *Revolution at Querétaro*, 181–97.

7. On the diverse late-nineteenth-century liberal agendas see Alan Knight, "El liberalismo mexicano desde la Reforma hasta la Revolución (una interpreatación)," *Historia Mexicana* 35, no. 1 (julio–septiembre 1985): 59–91. For analytical purposes Knight disaggregates liberalism into three categories—political, institutional, and developmentalist—that sometimes complement and sometimes contradict each other. Both tendencies are clearly represented in the debate over prison reform, especially during the revolutionary period.

8. Córdova, *La ideología*, 28.

9. For an analysis of revisionist historiography see Bailey, "Revisionism and the Recent Historiography of the Mexican Revolution"; and Raat, "Recent Trends."

10. Charles Hale, for example, ignores prison reform, even though most liberals saw modern penitentiaries as an essential disciplinary component of economic and social development. See his *Mexican Liberalism* and *Transformation of Liberalism*.

11. Lardizábal, *Discurso sobre las penas*, 197. Concern about rationalizing punishment was typical of enlightened absolutist monarchs. Lardizábal, for example, cites a 1781 memorandum on the subject by Louis XVI's controversial finance minister, Jacques Necker. Lardizábal, *Discurso sobre las penas*, 215–18.

12. Lardizábal, *Discurso sobre las penas*, 214.

13. Rocafuerte, "Ensayo sobre el nuevo sistema de cárceles," 8.

14. Rocafuerte, "Ensayo sobre el nuevo sistema de cárceles," ii and 14. The treading mill (treadwheel) and its relation to incipient industrialization is discussed in Michael Ignatieff, *A Just Measure of Pain: The Penitentiary in the Industrial Revolution, 1750–1850* (New York: Pantheon, 1978), 177–87. Ignatieff includes illustrations. On the links between capitalist development and prison reform see also Dario Melossi and Massimo Pavarini, *The Prison and the Factory: Origins of the Penitentiary System* (London: MacMillan, 1981).

15. Mariano Otero, "Iniciativa dirigida a la Cámara de Diputados, por el Ministerio de Relaciones sobre la adapción y establecimiento del régimen penitenciario en el Distrito y territorios (1848)," *Obras*, 2:665.

16. Mariano Otero, "Indicaciones sobre la importancia y necesidad de la reforma de las leyes penales (1844)," *Obras*, 2:657. Otero's observations about Mexico City penal facilities and his recommendations for reform were seconded by conservative Ignacio Cumplido, who had been traumatized by spending thirty-three days in the Acordada for publishing the monarchist opinions of José María Gutiérrez de Estrada. Cumplido's appeal is included in "La vida en

NOTES TO PAGES 91–92    197

la cárcel de la Acordada: Apuntes históricos de Manuel Orozco y Berra y relato de un impresor preso en ella," *Criminalia* 25, nos. 1–12 (enero–diciembre 1959): 530–57.

17. J. M. L. Mora, "Memoria sobre cárceles inglesas," 102–3. Interestingly, liberals like Rocafuerte, Otero, and Mora accepted the church's moralizing role in Mexican society even as they denounced its political and economic influence. The prominent role of religion in North American and English prison reform and a belief that the superstitious lower classes could still benefit from a depoliticized Catholicism probably encouraged tolerance.

18. J. M. L. Mora, "Memoria sobre cárceles inglesas," 66–67; and Mariano Otero, "Mejora del pueblo (1859)," *Obras*, 2:685–93.

19. The attitudes of Lardizábal, Rocafuerte, Otero, and Mora toward crime in general are examined in chapter 1.

20. For additional details on liberal and Porfirian prison reform efforts see Rohlfes, "Police and Penal Correction." On prison reform efforts in the state of Puebla see Nydia E. Cruz Barrera, "Confines: El desarrollo del sistema penitenciario poblano en el siglo XIX" (tesis de maestría en ciencias sociales, Universidad Autónoma de Puebla, 1989). On Jalisco's penitentiary see Rodney D. Anderson, "Las clases peligrosas: Crimen y castigo en Jalisco, 1894–1910," *Relaciones: Estudios de Historia y Sociedad* 7, no. 28 (otoño 1986): 5–32.

21. Rohlfes, "Police and Penal Correction," 292.

22. Peruvian penologists directly concerned with disciplining Native Americans took a different approach. See Carlos Aguirre, "The Penitentiary and the 'Modernization' of Penal Justice in Nineteenth-Century Peru," paper presented at the American Historical Association Annual Meeting, Chicago, December 28, 1991.

23. Henry C. Schmidt provides a detailed history of racial consciousness in Mexico in *Roots of Lo Mexicano*.

24. As was typical, a separate building for female inmates at the federal penitentiary in Mexico City was planned but never constructed. See Rohlfes, "Police and Penal Correction," 14.

25. Gregorio Cárdenas Hernández, *Adiós, Lecumberri* (México: Editorial Diana, 1979), 22.

26. Sergio García Ramírez, *El artículo 18 constitucional: Prisión preventiva, sistema penitenciaría, menores infractores* (México: Universidad Nacional Autónoma de México, 1967), 63.

27. José Enrique Ampudia, ed., *Boletín del Archivo General de la Nación* 5, no. 4 (octubre–diciembre 1981) and 6, no. 1 (enero–marzo 1982): 15. See also Otero, "Iniciativa y ley para el establecimineto del sistema penitenciario," *Obras*, 2:665–84.

28. Felipe Teña Ramírez, *Leyes fundamentales de México, 1808–1964*, 2nd ed. (México: Editorial Porrúa, 1964), 610.

29. In keeping with Maximilian's reputation as an enlightened monarch, Mexico City's principal jail, Belén, was remodeled and made somewhat more sanitary during his regime. A report to his prison commission, however, despaired of rehabilitating prisoners and suggested instead that inmates be forced to work and be whipped regularly to keep them from idleness and mutual contamination. "El imperio de Maximiliano y las prisiones en México en 1864," *Criminalia* 25, nos. 1-12 (enero-diciembre 1959): 388-96.

30. Miguel S. Macedo, "Los establecimientos penales," *Criminalia* 20, no. 7 (julio 1954): 429.

31. *Código Penal para el Distrito Federal y Territorio de la Baja-California sobre delitos del fuero común, y para toda la República sobre delitos contra la Federación* (Madrid: Establecimiento Tipográfico de Pedro Núñez, 1890), 5.

32. Sanchez Galindo, "Mexico," 263.

33. Enoch C. Wines, *The State of Prisons and of Child-Saving Institutions in the Civilized World* (Cambridge: University Press, John Wilson and Son, 1880), 42.

34. Sanchez, "Mexico," 263; Francisco Javier Peña, "Cárceles en México en 1875," *Criminalia* 25, no. 5 (agosto 1959): 468-503.

35. Peña, "Cárceles en México," 469.

36. Wines, *The State of Prisons*, 538.

37. Leopoldo Zea makes this point in a number of works including *El positivismo en México* and *Apogeo y decadencia del positivismo en México*.

38. Quoted in Jesús Silva Herzog, *El pensamiento económico, social y político de México, 1810-1964* (México: Fondo de Cultura Económica, 1974), 281.

39. William Dirk Raat, *El positivismo durante el Porfiriato* (México: Secretaría de Educación Pública, 1975), 21. Raat also notes that during the Reforma liberal positivist Gabino Barreda had replaced "love" with "liberty."

40. Guerrero, *Génesis del crímen en México*, 310.

41. Guerrero, *Génesis del crímen en México*, 390.

42. Roumagnac, *Criminales*, 54.

43. Sierra, *Obras Completas*, vol. 4: *Periodismo político*, 308.

44. Peña, "Cárceles en México," 497.

45. "Estado de la cárcel nacional conocida como Cárcel de Belén en el año de 1882" (from Manuel Rivera Cambas, *México pintoresco*), *Criminalia* 25, no. 8 (agosto 1959): 398.

46. Miguel S. Macedo, "La condena condicional. Inovaciones y reformas necesarias para establecerla en México. Discurso leído en la session de 17 de Diciembre de 1900 por el Lic. Miguel S. Macedo, delegado del I. Y. N. Colegio de Abogados de México," *Criminalia* 20, no. 7 (julio 1954): 387.

47. "Estado de la cárcel nacional," 401.

48. Macedo, "Establecimientos penales," 437.

49. Ampudia, ed., *Boletín del Archivo General de la Nación*, 46-50.

50. Ampudia, ed., *Boletín del Archivo General de la Nación*, 12.

51. Ampudia, ed., *Boletín del Archivo General de la Nación*, 13.

52. Ampudia, ed., *Boletín del Archivo General de la Nación*, 16.

53. See Rohlfes, "Police and Penal Correction"; and Vanderwood, *Disorder and Progress*.

54. Roumagnac, *Criminales*, 40.

55. Ampudia, ed., *Boletín del Archivo General de la Nación*, 17.

56. Ampudia, ed., *Boletín del Archivo General de la Nación*, 12.

57. Ampudia, ed., *Boletín del Archivo General de la Nación*, 23–25.

58. Ampudia, ed., *Boletín del Archivo General de la Nación*, 102–20.

59. Ampudia, ed., *Boletín del Archivo General de la Nación*, 24–25.

60. Ampudia, ed., *Boletín del Archivo General de la Nación*, 26.

61. Ampudia, ed., *Boletín del Archivo General de la Nación*, 13. Penitentiary regulations were formalized in 1902 and modified only slightly by presidential decree in 1927. See "Reglamento general de los establecimientos penales del Distrito Federal," *Criminalia* 18, nos. 1–12 (enero–diciembre 1952): 532–79.

62. Ampudia, ed., *Boletín del Archivo General de la Nación*, 26.

63. Ampudia, ed., *Boletín del Archivo General de la Nación*, 28.

64. García Ramírez, *El artículo 18 constitucional*, 45–46.

65. Javier Piña y Palacios, ed., "Las Islas Marías al principios de este Siglo," *Criminalia* 36, no. 5 (mayo 1970): 211–27.

66. Piña y Palacios, ed., "Islas Marías," 216.

67. Piña y Palacios, ed., "Islas Marías," 223.

68. Piña y Palacios, ed., "Islas Marías," 224.

69. Piña y Palacios, ed., "Islas Marías," 222.

70. On the continuities underlying "scientific politics" see Hale, *Transformation of Liberalism*.

71. *El Monitor Republicano* (Mexico City), 22 noviembre 1889.

72. *El Monitor Republicano*, 29 mayo 1889 and 27 diciembre 1889.

73. *El Monitor Republicano*, 10 diciembre 1889.

74. *El Monitor Republicano*, 15 febrero 1889.

75. *El Monitor Republicano*, 10 diciembre 1889.

76. Daniel Cosío Villegas, *Historia moderna de México*, vol. 9, *El Porfiriato. La vida política interior*, part 2 (México: Editorial Hermes, 1972), 221.

77. *El Monitor Republicano*, 9 marzo 1889.

78. Wines, *The State of Prisons*, 534.

79. *El Monitor Republicano*, 12 enero 1889.

80. Ampudia, ed., *Boletín del Archivo General de la Nación*, 84.

81. Quoted in Silva Herzog, *Pensamiento*, 22.

82. Antonio Martínez Báez, "Sarabia en San Juan de Ulúa," *Historia Mexicana* 10, no. 2 (octubre–diciembre 1960): 342–60.

83. The first draft, published in April 1906, made no mention of prison re-

form. See *El programa del Partido Liberal Mexicano de 1906 y sus antecedentes* (México: Ediciones Antorcha, 1985), 219–25.

84. Isidro Fabela, ed., *Documentos históricos de la Revolución Mexicana*, vol. 10, *Actividades políticas y revolucionarias de los hermanos Flores Magón* (México: Editorial Jus, 1966), 57.

85. Fabela, ed., *Documentos históricos*, 10:62.

86. Armando Bartra, ed., *Regeneración, 1900–1918* (México: Ediciones Era, 1977), 150.

87. Silva Herzog, *Pensamiento*, 555–56.

88. A. Bartra, ed., *Regeneración*, 270.

89. Fabela, *Documentos históricos*, vol. 4, *El Plan de Guadalupe*, 86–87.

90. Fabela, *Documentos históricos*, 4:161–80.

91. Palavicini, *Historia de la Constitución de 1917*, 119–20.

92. *Derechos del pueblo mexicano*, 4:95.

93. *Derechos del pueblo mexicano*, 93.

94. *Derechos del pueblo mexicano*, 118.

95. *Derechos del pueblo mexicano*, 138.

96. *Derechos del pueblo mexicano*, 113.

97. Felix F. Palavicini, *Mi vida revolucionaria* (México: Ediciones Bota, 1937), 183–4.

98. *Derechos del pueblo mexicano*, 4:116.

99. Quoted in García Ramírez, *El artículo 18 constitucional*, 68.

100. *Derechos del pueblo mexicano*, 4:127.

101. *Derechos del pueblo mexicano*, 4:107.

102. Palavicini, *Historia de la Constitución de 1917*, 203.

103. *Derechos del pueblo mexicano*, 4:134.

104. *Derechos del pueblo mexicano*, 4:141–43.

105. *Derechos del pueblo mexicano*, 4:106.

106. *Derechos del pueblo mexicano*, 4:141–42.

107. *Derechos del pueblo mexicano*, 4:143.

108. *Derechos del pueblo mexicano*, 4:91.

109. Sanchez, "Mexico," 254.

110. Casmiro Cueto, "Consideraciones generales y apuntes para la crítica, estadística de la criminalidad habida en el Distrito Federal durante el año de 1922," *Boletín de la Sociedad Mexicana de Geografía y Estadística* 37, nos. 1–6 (1928): 40–41.

111. German Fernández del Castillo, "La obra histórica de don Miguel S. Macedo," *Criminalia* 11, no. 8 (agosto 1945): 460–61.

112. Beezley, *Judas at the Jockey Club*.

113. For the role of education in the Mexican carceral system see Vaughn, *State, Education, and Social Class in Mexico*.

## 5. Looking Forward, Looking Back

A shorter version of this chapter can be found in *Crime, Histoire & Sociétés/ Crime, History & Societies* 2, no. 2 (1998): 15–34.

1. This historiography is extensive. See, for example, Margarita de la Villa and José Luis Zambrano, *Bibliografía sumaria de Derecho Mexicano* (México: Universidad Nacional Autónoma de México, 1957), and the bibliography in María del Refugio González, "Historia del Derecho Mexicano," *Introducción al Derecho Mexicano* (México: Universidad Nacional Autónoma de México, La Gran Enciclopedia Mexicana, 1983), 96–108.

2. The Mexican federal system, like its North American counterpart, gives individual states the right to promulgate penal codes within constitutional guidelines. In practice, the Federal District penal code provides the model for most state codes.

3. On this shift in Mexican liberalism see Hale, *Transformation of Liberalism*.

4. The actual role of the "people" in Mexican politics is a contested issue. Virginia Guedea argues convincingly that they began to play a prominent role in the capital during the independence period. See her "El pueblo de México y la política capitalina, 1808–1812," *Mexican Studies/Estudios Mexicanos* 10, no. 1 (winter 1994): 27–61.

5. See Michael C. Scardaville, "(Hapsburg) Law and (Bourbon) Order."

6. On popular efforts by prostitutes and criminals to solicit state intervention see Katherine Elaine Bliss, "'Guided by an Imperious Moral Need': Prostitutes, Motherhood and Nationalism in Revolutionary Mexico," in *Reconstructing Criminality in Latin America*; and Pablo Piccato, "Criminals in Mexico City."

7. Jürgen Habermas, *The Structural Transformation of the Public Sphere: An Inquiry into a Category of Bourgeois Society*, trans. Thomas Burger and Frederick Lawrence (Cambridge MA: MIT Press, 1989), 195.

8. On constitutional guarantees see Emilio O. Rabasa, *Historia de las constituciones Mexicanas* (México: Universidad Nacional Autónoma de México, Instituto de Investigaciones Jurídicas, 1990).

9. For histories of Mexican colonial and early national criminal law see Miguel S. Macedo, *Apuntes para la historia del Derecho Penal Mexicano* (México: Editorial "CULTURA," 1931); Refugio González, "Historia del Derecho Mexicano," 12–108; and Jorge Vera Estañol, "La evolución jurídica," in *México: Su evolución social*, ed. Justo Sierra, 2:725–73. Perversely, Spain had a modern liberal penal code by 1848, while Mexican jurists continued to use colonial criminal laws.

10. Manuel de Lardizábal y Uribe, *Discurso sobre las penas*, iii.

11. Quoted in R. González, "Historia del Derecho Mexicano," 49–50.

12. José María Luis Mora, "Escritos del Obispo electo de Michoacán Don

Manuel Abad y Queipo," in *Obras completas*, vol. 3, *Obra política* (México: Secretaría de Educación, 1986–88), 63.

13. Mariano Otero, "Indicaciones sobre la importancia y necesidad de la reforma de las leyes penales," *Obras*, 2:653–54.

14. José María Luis Mora, "Disertación formada y leída por don José María Luis Mora, ante el Supremo Tribunal de Justicia del Estado de México para examinarse de abogado," *Obras completas*, vol. 2, *Obra política*, 250.

15. Francisco Zarco, *Historia del Congreso*, 316.

16. Francisco Zarco, *Historia del Congreso*, 351. Mexico's relative backwardness also served to justify keeping the death penalty until a reformative penitentiary system had been developed. Capital punishment was, however, restricted to serious crimes, like murder, and political criminals, excepting traitors, were no longer eligible for execution. Francisco Zarco, *Historia del Congreso*, 1347.

17. Rafael Rebollar, *Exposición de motivos con que fué presentado a la Secretaria de Justicia el proyecto de reformas al código de procedimientos penales* (México: Imp. y Lit. de F. Díaz de Leon Sucesores, 1894), xlix–l, and *Código de procedimientos penales para el distrito y territorios federales* (México: Imp. y Lit. de F. Díaz de Leon Sucesores, 1894), 8–9.

18. Transcendental punishment was directed not just at the individual but at the family as well. The typical transcendental punishment in Spanish colonial law was infamy, which carried down to the fourth generation, denying the condemned access to royal favors and to public employment.

19. Zarco, *Historia del Congreso*, 1345–48.

20. Ceniceros, "Vida y pensamiento de Castro," 182–85. Background on the penal-code commission is also included in Antonio Martínez de Castro, "Exposición de motivos del Código Penal," *Criminalia* 34, no. 3 (30 marzo 1968): 132–33.

21. Quoted in Piña y Palacios, "Una cláusula," 131.

22. The grammatical errors are noted in José Almaraz, *Exposición de motivos del Código Penal promulgado el 15 de diciembre de 1929. Parte general* (México, 1931), 15–16.

23. Martínez de Castro, "Exposición de motivos del Código Penal," 132.

24. Martínez de Castro, "Exposición de motivos del Código Penal," 133.

25. See especially Jeremy Bentham, *An Introduction to the Principles of Morals*. This work was first published in 1789.

26. *Código Penal para el Distrito Federal*, 7. My italics.

27. *Código Penal para el Distrito Federal*, 13–14. If they represented a danger to society, they could, under certain circumstances, be institutionalized in asylums or special juvenile facilities (47).

28. *Código Penal para el Distrito Federal*, 10.

29. *Código Penal para el Distrito Federal*, 14–21.

30. *Código Penal para el Distrito Federal*, 58–59.

31. *Código Penal para el Distrito Federal*, 221–36. The ideological impact of these provisions would have been greatly enhanced had Mexican educators realized Martínez de Castro's vision of a literate general public.

32. *Código Penal para el Distrito Federal*, 34. Preparatory liberty could include up to half of the inmate's original sentence.

33. Miguel S. Macedo and José Angel Ceniceros, *Derecho Penal y Procedimientos Penales, programa y conferencias de 1926* (México: Escuela Libre de Derecho, 1928), 26.

34. Secretaría de Justicia, Comisión Revisora del Código Penal, *Trabajos de revisión del Código Penal*, vol. 3 (México: Tip. de la Oficina Impresora de Estampillas, 1913), 28, (gambling), 57–60 (public disturbances), 71–90 (drunkenness). The commission recommended that habitual criminals, including vagrants and beggars, be transported to a penal colony (3:383). And even those convicted of habitual drunkenness were allowed only two attempts at rehabilitation before being transported (3:90).

35. Quoted in Francisco González de la Vega, *El Código Penal comentado precedido de la reforma de las leyes penales en México* (México: Editorial Porrúa, 1981), 22.

36. Revolutionary turmoil prevented the incorporation of the Porfirian revisions into the penal code, although the publication of the four-volume *Trabajos de revisión del Código Penal* ensured that they played a role in later revision efforts. See Ignacio Villalobos, *La crisis del derecho penal en México* (México: Editorial Jus, 1948), 155.

37. Vera Estañol, "Evolución jurídica," 772.

38. Macedo, "Condena condicional," 381. In this speech Macedo argued in favor of "conditional" punishments but added that Mexico lacked the institutional infrastructure—modern prisons, trained personnel, effective criminal procedures—to support a parole system (394–95).

39. José Angel Ceniceros, "Miguel S. Macedo, maestro y jurista," in *Glosas históricas y sociológicas* (México: Ediciones Bota, 1966), 142.

40. On the practical implications of revolutionary penal reform see Piccato, "Experiencia penal."

41. Javier Pina y Palacios, "El maestro Antonio Ramos Pedrueza," *Criminalia* 27, nos. 1–12 (enero–diciembre 1961): 636; and Antonio Ramos Pedrueza, "Derecho Penal (Lecciones)," *Criminalia* 27, nos. 1–12 (enero–diciembre 1961): 637–55. In 1921 UNAM rector José Vasconcelos dismissed Ramos from his professorship in penal law for publicly eulogizing Agustín de Iturbide to students at the Escuela Nacional Preparatoria. Both Macedo and Ramos were among that school's illustrious alumni.

42. Pedrueza, "Derecho Penal (Lecciones)," 641, 653. My italics.

43. Macedo and Ceniceros, *Derecho Penal*, 219.

44. Almaraz, *Exposición de motivos del Código Penal*, 11–12.

45. Almaraz, *Exposición de motivos del Código Penal*, 14–15.

46. Almaraz, *Exposición de motivos del Código Penal*, 18.

47. Almaraz, *Exposición de motivos del Código Penal*, 18–19.

48. Almaraz, *Exposición de motivos del Código Penal*, 20.

49. Almaraz, *Exposición de motivos del Código Penal*, 12. His italics.

50. Almaraz, *Exposición de motivos del Código Penal*, 100.

51. Almaraz, *Exposición de motivos del Código Penal*, 54.

52. Almaraz, *Exposición de motivos del Código Penal*, 53.

53. Almaraz, *Exposición de motivos del Código Penal*, 49.

54. Juan José González Bustamante, "El Código Penal de 1931," *Criminalia* 33, no. 2 (1 febrero 1957): 110.

55. Fernando Anaya Monroy, "El Código Penal de 1931 y la realidad mexicana," *Criminalia* 22, nos. 1–12 (1 noviembre 1956): 794.

56. González de la Vega, *Código Penal comentado*, 23–24.

57. Juan José González Bustamante, "Las reformas penales," *Universal Gráfico*, 23 agosto 1948.

58. Anaya, "Código Penal de 1931," 795–96.

59. Luis Garrido, "Celestino Porte Petit y el Código Penal de 1931," *Notas de un penalista* (México: Ediciones Bota, 1947), 58.

60. From Alfonso Teja Zabre, "Exposición de Motivos presentada al Congreso Jurídico Nacional reunido en la ciudad de México en mayo de 1931 a nombre de la Comisión Revisora de las Leyes Penales." Quoted in Anaya, "Código Penal de 1931," 799.

61. Quoted in Jorge A. Vivo, "Reforma penal en México," *Criminalia* 3, nos. 1–12 (1937): 452.

62. Anaya, "Código Penal de 1931," 800.

63. Quoted in González Bustamante, "Código Penal de 1931," 112.

64. Quoted in Vivo, "Reforma penal en México," 452.

65. Quoted in Anaya, "Código Penal de 1931," 803.

66. González de la Vega, *Código Penal comentado*, 31.

67. On royal mercy see MacLachlan, *Spain's Empire in the New World*, 1–20. On informal justice see Piccato, "Criminals in Mexico City," chapter 5.

68. Garrido, "Celestino Porte Petit," 64–65.

69. Juan José González Bustamante, "Las reformas penales," *El Universal Gráfico*, 16 agosto 1948.

70. Garrido, "Celestino Porte Petit," 67.

71. José Almaraz referred sarcastically to the new code as an "accumulation of narrow empiricisms" in his *Algunos errores y absurdos de la legislación penal de 1931* (México: n.p., 1941), 14.

72. Quoted in Lozano, *La criminalidad*, 175.

73. Archivo General de la Nación, Secretaría de Justicia, vol. 273, case no. 4439.

74. Reclusorio Oriente, Segundo Corte Penal, Juzgado Quinto, México D. F., Expediente 2046343.

75. See, for example, Lardizábal's list of mitigating circumstances in chapter 1.

## 6. Los Jotos

This chapter first appeared as "Los Jotos: Contested Visions of Homosexuality in Modern Mexico," in *Sex and Sexuality in Latin America*, ed. Daniel Balderston and Donna Guy (New York: New York University Press, 1997), 118–32.

1. On this obsession with national survival see, for example, Justo Sierra, "The Present Era," in *Political Evolution of the Mexican People*, 342–68.

2. The transition from the broadly defined conceptual category of "sexual inversion" to the narrower "medical model of homosexuality" and the categorical confusion that resulted is explored in George Chauncey Jr., "From Sexual Inversion to Homosexuality: The Changing Medical Conceptualization of Female Deviance," in *Passion and Power: Sexuality in History*, ed. Kathy Peiss and Christina Simmons (Philadelphia PA: Temple University Press, 1989), 87–117.

3. Other aspects of Roumagnac's criminology are dealt with in chapters 2 and 3. For a more thorough treatment of his investigation into inmate sexuality and its role in prison life see Pablo Piccato, "Sexuality in the Prison: Mexico City, 1897–1919," unpublished manuscript, 1995.

4. Roumagnac, *Criminales*, 10. His introduction provided a review of European criminology that further developed the implied theoretical link between criminal and sexual deviance.

5. Michel Foucault, among others, argues that Victorians were obsessed with sex even as they pretended to deny it a place in polite society. Peter Gay and Michael Mason also dispute the image of sexually repressed Victorians. See Michel Foucault, *The History of Sexuality*, vol. 1, *An Introduction*, trans. Robert Hurley (New York: Vintage, 1978); Peter Gay, *The Bourgeois Experience: Victoria to Freud*, vol. 1, *The Education of the Senses* (New York: Oxford University Press, 1984); and Michael Mason, *The Making of Victorian Sexuality* (New York: Oxford University Press, 1994).

6. Roumagnac, *Criminales*, 41.

7. Roumagnac, *Criminales*, 77. The word *mayate* is apparently derived from the Nahuatl *mayatl*, an iridescent green beetle. (Marcos A. Morínigo, *Diccionario manual de americanismos* [Buenos Aires: Muchnik Editores, 1965], 405). Also, in classic Nahuatl *mazatl* connotes a "bestial . . . sexual or lascivious person" (John Bierhorst, *A Nahuatl-English Dictionary and Concordance to the Cantares Mexicanos* [Stanford CA: Stanford University Press, 1985], 208). For a glossary of Latin American terms for homosexual acts and actors see Stephen O. Murray and Wayne R. Dynes, "Hispanic Homosexualities: A Spanish Lexicon," in *Latin American Male Homosexualities*, ed.

Stephen O. Murray (Albuquerque: University of New Mexico Press, 1995), 180–92. Murray and Dynes note that the term *mayate* also signifies a "flashy dresser" and, in Chicano Spanish, a "black pimp." (p. 188). Their translation of *caballo* as "mare" seems dubious: the usual word for mare is *yegua*, and rural Mexicans, at least, clearly distinguished between male *caballos* and female *yeguas*. More likely, the imagery reflects the domesticated male animal that is ridden (dominated) by a male rider. Another possible derivation: in Spanish playing cards, the *caballo* corresponds to the "queen" in the standard deck. Although the etymology of these terms is far from clear, my suspicion is that these multiple connotations probably reinforced the use of these particular terms. As we will see, the word *joto* also had many connotations.

   8. Roumagnac, *Criminales*, 97.

   9. Roumagnac, *Criminales*, 77.

   10. Roumagnac, *Criminales*, 210.

   11. Homosexual subcultures centered around sexual inversion thrived (and continue to thrive) in many Latin American cities. See, for example, Jorge Salessi, "The Argentine Dissemination of Homosexuality, 1890–1914," *Journal of the History of Sexuality* 4, no. 3 (1994): 337–68; Daniel Bao, "Invertidos Sexuales, Tortilleras, and Maricas Machos: The Construction of Homosexuality in Buenos Aires, Argentina, 1900–1950," *Journal of Homosexuality* 24, nos. 3–4 (1993): 183–219; Rommel Mendès-Leite, "The Game of Appearances: The 'Ambigusexuality' in Brazilian Culture of Sexuality," *Journal of Homosexuality* 25, no. 3 (1993): 271–82; and Richard G. Parker, *Bodies, Pleasures and Passions: Sexual Culture in Contemporary Brazil* (Boston: Beacon Press, 1991).

   12. Roumagnac, *Criminales*, 219–20.

   13. Roumagnac, *Criminales*, 307.

   14. Roumagnac, *Criminales*, 312.

   15. Roumagnac, *Criminales*, 296–303.

   16. Roumagnac, *Criminales*, 191. He explains the significance of hair parting on page 174.

   17. Roumagnac, *Criminales*, 104–15. See chapter 3 for more on this case and on female deviancy in general.

   18. Pablo Piccato argues that women inmates generally had more stable, "supportive" homosexual relationships than the men and boys did. See his "Sexuality in the Prison," 25.

   19. Female homosexuality was also a problem for national reproduction. See especially Salessi, "The Argentine Dissemination of Homosexuality." However, in Mexico, fear of female criminality and working women in the public sphere was apparently less of an issue than it was in Argentina. Roumagnac was one of the few criminologists to give women equal time.

   20. Alfonso Millán, "Carácter antisocial de los homosexuales," *Criminalia* 2

(diciembre 1934): 53–59. Millán was the medical director of a Mexico City insane asylum, the Manicomio General de la Casteñeda.

21. Susana Solano, "El homosexualismo y el estado peligroso," *Criminalia* 2 (junio 1935): 148–150. The use of the verb "to be," *ser* in the original Spanish, indicates that these are permanent rather than temporary states.

22. José Raúl Aguilar, *Los métodos criminales en México: Como defendernos* (México: Ediciones Lux, n.d.), 180–81. The penal colony at Islas Marías was specifically designed by the Porfirian regime to hold undesirables, which in the post-revolutionary period included everyone from political prisoners like Madre Conchita (who allegedly masterminded the assassination of President Alvaro Obregón) to pimps, homosexuals, and communists. For more information on the penal colony project see chapter 4.

23. Raúl González Enríquez, *El problema sexual del hombre en la penitenciaría* (Veracruz: Editorial Citlaltepetl, 1971), 94–96. As Roumagnac did, González conducted his research in Belén and the Federal Penitentiary. He won *El Universal's* annual Miguel Lanz Duret prize for the work in 1942, which suggests that it circulated fairly broadly. This was one of advantages of a titillating topic, as Roumagnac had discovered earlier.

24. On the political awareness of penitentiary inmates see Pablo Piccato, "Mexico City Prisoners: Between Social Engineering and Popular Culture," paper delivered at the Conference on Latin American History 1996 annual meeting, Atlanta, Georgia.

25. Most anthropologists who study Latin American attitudes toward homosexuality argue that this stigma against sexual inversion is typical, even normative. For an excellent overview of this literature see Tomás Almaguer, "Chicano Men: A Cartography of Homosexual Identity and Behavior," in Henry Abelove, Michèle Aina Barak, and David M. Halperin, eds., *The Lesbian and Gay Studies Reader* (New York: Routledge Press, 1993), 255–73. Unfortunately, these studies often ignore the specific historical contexts—political repression, economic exploitation, and social/racial discrimination—that reinforce this "Mediterranean" construction of homosexuality, especially for lower-class men. Almaguer also explains the semantics of the various "contemptuous" Spanish terms for male homosexuals—*maricón, joto, puto*—noting that the two latter words "are infinitely more derogatory and vulgar in that they underscore the sexually non-conforming nature of their passive/receptive position in the homosexual act" ("Chicano Men," 260). Translating "joto" into English is problematic because, although "faggot" carries the contempt it implies, it lacks the Spanish word's specificity. For that reason I have used the somewhat less derogatory "fairy," which stresses sexual inversion. According to some scholars, the word *joto* comes from the cell block "j" (*jota* in Spanish) of the Federal Penitentiary in Mexico City, where prison authorities attempted to isolate overtly homosexual inmates. (see Sergio García Ramírez, *El final de*

*Lecumberri: Reflexiones sobre la prisión* [México: Porrúa, 1977], 27), but the word appeared in the popular penny press before 1900, the year Lecumberri opened, and William B. Taylor notes its appearance—as an insult that sometimes led to homicide—in colonial court cases, in *Drinking, Homicide and Rebellion*, 82–83.

26. Mexican criminologists, most of them from the professional middle classes, did point out that the overly refined upper class contained many effeminate men. Thus the image of sexual deviance did double duty by damning the two classes that threatened the rising middle classes.

27. Jorge Salessi argues that even though Argentine criminologists used the broader conceptual category of homosexuality, they preserved the distinction between passive and active roles, with the passive "pederast" becoming the "stigmatized category of male sexual deviance." The point is debatable for Mexico as well, but I would argue for a greater difference between the vision of criminologists and that of the general population. See Salessi, "The Argentine Dissemination of Homosexuality," 367. Richard G. Parker analyzes Brazilian attitudes toward gender in considerable depth in "Men and Women," in *Bodies, Pleasures and Passions*, 30–66.

28. Roumagnac, *Criminales*, 275, 279.

29. Raúl Carrancà y Trujillo, "Sexo y penal," *Criminalia* 1 (septiembre 1933–agosto 1934): 26–31. Group activities like movies apparently provided ample opportunities for homosexual relations to take place.

30. Guillermo Mellado, *Belén por dentro y por fuera* (México: Cuadernos "Criminalia," 1959), 32. My italics. This was Belén's final year as a jail.

31. Carrancà y Trujillo, "Sexo y penal," 28.

32. Carlos Franco Sodi, *Don Juan Delincuente y otros ensayos* (México: Ediciones Bota, 1951), 12.

33. Franco Sodi, *Don Juan Delincuente*, 19.

34. Octavio Paz, "The Sons of La Malinche," in *The Labyrinth of Solitude: Life and Thought in Mexico*, trans. Lysander Kemp (New York: Grove Press, 1961), 65–88, quote on 77. There are numerous feminist critiques of Paz's heavily gendered construction of Mexican identity. See, for example, Norma Alarcón, "Chicana's Feminist Literature: A Re-vision through Malintzin/or Malintzin: Putting the Flesh Back on the Object," in *This Bridge Called My Back: Writings by Radical Women of Color*, ed. Cherríe Moraga and Gloria Anzaldúa (Watertown MA: Persephone, 1981), 182–90.

35. On medical discourses and sexual deviance see Chauncey, "From Sexual Inversion to Homosexuality," 108.

36. Roumagnac, *Criminales*, 379.

37. Jorge Salessi suggests that concern about working women and immigration (foreign penetration) fueled turn-of-the-century homophobia in Argentina. See Salessi, "The Argentine Dissemination of Homosexuality," 338. Some of

this doubtless occurred in Mexico, but not to the same extent; other than his observation about hair parting, Roumagnac evinced little interest in the gendered roles of "sapphists," and other observers disregarded women altogether. This marginalization of female homosexuality has persisted. Stephen O. Murray laments the lack of scholarship on "female homosexualities" in his introduction to *Latin American Male Homosexualities*, xiii, n. 3. He also provides a short bibliography on pages 178–79.

38. This reinforces Piccato's argument that "in Belén, male sexuality tended to express itself in violent ways and to be closer to the structure of power." See his "Sexuality in the Prison," 34. Interestingly, although "butch" women probably adopted many overtly male behaviors, extreme violence was rare. This, of course, does not preclude an aggressive sexuality. See, for example, Almaguer's discussion of Cherrié Moraga's work in "Chicano Men," 268.

39. For a contemporary ethnography that explores the complexities of the homosexual experience see Joseph Carrier, *De los otros: Intimacy and Homosexuality among Mexican Men* (New York: Columbia University Press, 1995).

### 7. Forjando Patria

1. The connection between *indigenistas* and Edward Said's Orientalists will I think become obvious, but since in this case both *indigenistas* and *indígenas* (indigenous peoples) are Mexican, the colonial relationship central to Said's formulation is a bit more incestuous and complex. See his *Orientalism* (New York: Pantheon, 1978). On Gamio's *indigenismo* see David Brading, "Manuel Gamio and Official Indigenismo in Mexico," *Bulletin of Latin America Research* 7, no. 1 (1988): 75–89.

2. Gamio, *Forjando Patria*, 11–12. Choosing the proper term to describe Mexico's heterogeneous indigenous groups and deciding who might fit the category is extremely difficult. For an extended discussion of these issues see Alan Knight, "Racism, Revolution, and *Indigenismo*: Mexico, 1910–1940," in *The Idea of Race in Latin America, 1870–1940*, ed. Richard Graham (Austin: University of Texas Press, 1990), 72–78. In this chapter I use "indigenous peoples" as the generic term but "Indians" either to translate *indios* or when the frame of reference reflects deliberate lumping. The commonly used "Native Americans" reflects a reverse lumping that plays no part in elite narratives, and I have avoided it for that reason. The use of the masculine pronoun follows the same logic.

3. The difference (more obvious in Spanish) between instruction, which passes on information and skills, and education, which seeks to fundamentally transform the student, is at the heart of post-revolutionary education programs (and some of their liberal predecessors) at least through the Cárdenas experiment with "socialist education." See especially Vázquez de Knauth, *Nacionalismo y educación en México*; Vaughn, *State, Education, and Social Class in Mexico*; and Becker, *Setting the Virgin on Fire*.

4. For a typology of Mexican nationalisms see Alan Knight, "Peasants into Patriots: Thoughts on the Making of the Mexican Nation," *Mexican Studies/ Estudios Mexicanos* 10, no. 1 (winter 1994): 135–61. The types of nationalism discussed in this essay were elite discourses on Mexican culture and nation building.

5. Octavio Paz explores the meaning of *La Malinche*—Cortez's Indian mistress, translator, and the violated mother of mestizo Mexicans—in his essay "The Sons of La Malinche," in *The Labyrinth of Solitude*, 65–88. See also Roger Bartra's "A la Chingada," in *Cage of Melancholy*, 147–62.

6. Reconstructing an "official" *indigenista* discourse (for the sake of analytical clarity) implies a somewhat artificial center for a complex, contested discursive field. The range of positions on the Indian problem is explored in Knight, "Racism, Revolution, and *Indigenismo*"; and in Alexander S. Dawson, "From Models for the Nation to Model Citizens: '*Indigenismo*' and the 'Revindication' of the Mexican Indian, 1920–1940," *Journal of Latin American Studies* 30 (May 1998): 279–308. Dawson sees offical *Indigenismo* as fundamentally inclusive if "restrictive in that it demanded a certain modernistic orientation." Dawson, "From Models for the Nation to Model Citizens," 295.

7. Quoted in John Leddy Phelan, "Neo-Aztecism in the Eighteenth Century and the Genesis of Mexican Nationalism," in *Culture in History: Essays in Honor of Paul Rabin*, ed. Stanley Diamond (New York: Columbia University Press, 1960), 765. Written from exile after the 1767 explusion of the Jesuit order, Clavigero's work was published in 1780–81 and widely disseminated throughout Europe and America. Phelan, "Neo-Aztecism in the Eighteenth Century," 763.

8. Humboldt, *Political Essay on the Kingdom of New Spain*, 184–85.

9. The most thorough scholarly investigations of elite efforts to construct a Mexican national identity are Brading, *First America*; and Schmidt, *Roots of Lo Mexicano*. The most charming is probably R. Bartra, *Cage of Melancholy*.

10. Both quoted in Jorge Chávez Chávez, "El pensamiento indigenista decimonónico," in *La antropología en México: Panorama histórico*, vol. 3, ed. Carlos García Mora, (México: Colección Biblioteca del INAH, 1988), 667–68. The complexities that characterized elite attitudes toward Indians, especially regarding social policy, are explored in David Brading, "Liberal Patriotism and the Mexican *Reforma*," *Journal of Latin American Studies* 20 (1988): 27–48; and Brading, *First America*.

11. Larrainzar, "Noticia histórica de Soconusco," 232.

12. On the connection between museums and nationalism see B. Anderson, *Imagined Communities*, chapter 10.

13. For an interesting, somewhat controversial discussion of "othering" indigenous peoples see Tzvetan Todorov, *The Conquest of America: The Question of the Other*, trans. Richard Howard (New York: HarperPerennial, 1984).

14. Larrainzar, "Noticia histórica de Soconusco," 234.

15. "Estadística de Yucatán," 294.

16. On French anthropology in nineteenth-century Mexico see Carlos Serrano Sánchez and Sergio López Alonso, "Los aportes de la antropología física europea," in *La antropología en México*, 5:203–22.

17. Dr. Jourdanet, "De la estadística de México considerada en sus relaciones con los niveles del suelo y con la aclimatación de las diferentes razas humanas que lo habitan," *Boletín de la Sociedad Mexicana de Geografía y Estadística* 11, no. 4 (1865): 240.

18. Dr. de Belina, "Influencia de altura sobre la vida y la salud del habitante de Anahuac," *Boletín de la Sociedad Mexicana de Geografía y Estadística* 4, nos. 4 and 5 (1878): 303.

19. On científico attitudes toward Indians see Moisés González Navarro, "Las ideas raciales de los científicos, 1890–1910," *Historia Mexicana* 37, no. 4 (abril–junio 1988): 565–83; T. G. Powell, "Mexican Intellectuals and the Indian Question, 1876–1911," *Hispanic American Historical Review* 48, no. 1 (February 1968): 136; William Dirk Raat, "Los intelectuales, el positivismo y la cuestión indígena," *Historia Mexicana* 20, no. 3 (enero–marzo 1971): 412–23; Martin S. Stabb, "Indigenism and Racism in Mexican Thought: 1857–1911," *Journal of Inter-American Studies* 1, no. 4 (October 1959): 405–23; and Hale, *Transformation of Liberalism*, chapter 7. On the propagandistic uses of the Indian past see Tenorio-Trillo, *Mexico at the World's Fairs*; and Barbara A. Tenenbaum, "Mexico and the Royal Indian: The Porfiriato and the National Past," working paper no. 8, Latin American Studies Center, University of Maryland at College Park, 1994.

20. Francisco Bulnes, *Páginas escogidas* (México: Universidad Nacional Autónoma de México, 1968), 155.

21. Sierra, *Political Evolution of the Mexican People*, 368.

22. The consequences of the cultural hegemony of *mestizaje* for indigenous peoples in Latin America has sparked a flurry of recent scholarly activity. *The Journal of Latin American Anthropology* 2, no. 1 (1996) is devoted entirely to the problem. See especially Carol A. Smith, "Myths, Intellectuals and Race/Class/Gender Distinctions in the Formation of Latin American Nations," 148–69; and Florencia E. Mallon, "Constructing *Mestizaje* in Latin America: Authenticity, Marginality and Gender in the Claiming of Ethnic Identities," 170–81. See also Virginia Tilley, "Indigenous People and the State: Ethnic Meta-Conflict in El Salvador" (Ph.D. diss., University of Wisconsin–Madison, 1997). Most, if not all, of these scholars note the considerable influence of Mexican intellectuals in the construction and promotion of *mestizaje* as a nationalist discourse.

23. Larrainzar, "Noticia histórica de Soconusco," 234. One important exception was Fray Servando Teresa y Mier, who argued that "all we creoles are

mestizos," but even he was careful to accept only "the pure blood of the native lords of the country." Quoted in Brading, *First America*, 595.

24. "Estadística de Yucatán," 294.

25. Guerrero, *La génesis del crimen en México*, 161.

26. Quoted in Graciela González Phillips, "Ignacio Manuel Altamirano," in *La antropología en México*, 9:104.

27. Justo Sierra, "Discurso de clausura pronunciado por el Sr. Lic. D. Justo Sierra en la sesión solemne del 18 de Agosto de 1895, en la Cámara de Diputados" (México: Oficina Tip. de la Secretaría de Fomento, 1895), 11. Not all Europeans favored racial purity. Dr. Jourdanet, for example, repeated the "well-known truths" about "the decadence of the pure races and the progressiveness of the men of mixed blood." The mestizo, he stated (before Sierra), "is [the group] that progresses." This European endorsement published in a Mexican journal may well have influenced the científico francophiles. Jourdanet, "De la estadística de México," 244.

28. Sierra, *Political Evolution of the Mexican People*, 360.

29. Quoted in Stabb, "Indigenism and Racism in Mexican Thought," 407.

30. Andrés Molina Enríquez, *Las grandes problemas nacionales* (México: Era, 1981), 110. For an analysis of Molina Enríquez's influential position on *mestizaje* see Agustín Basave, "El mito del mestizo: El pensamiento nacionalista de Andrés Molina Enríquez," in *El nacionalismo en México*, ed. Noriega Elío, 221–58.

31. Quoted in Blas Román Castellón Huerta, "Francisco Pimentel," in *La antropología en México*, 9:199.

32. Quoted in Carlos Serrano Sánchez and Martha Eugenia Rodríguez, "Vincente Riva Palacio," in *La antropología en México*, 11:311–12. Riva Palacio based his argument for Indian superiority on the lack of facial hair and less prominent canine teeth.

33. Agustín Aragón, "El territorio de México y sus habitantes," in *México: Su evolución social*, vol. 1, ed. Justo Sierra (México: Ballescá, 1900–1902), 29–30.

34. Sierra, *Political Evolution of the Mexican People*, 360.

35. Serrano Sánchez and Rodríguez, "Los aportes de la antropología física europea," 204–5.

36. Chávez, "El pensamiento indigenista decimonónico," 671.

37. Pacheco, "Necesidad de la estadística," 13.

38. Larrainzar, "Noticia histórico de Soconusco," 232.

39. Roberto A. Esteva Ruiz, "La estadística y sus funciones como lazo de unión entre los individuos y entre los pueblos," *Boletín de la Sociedad de Geografía y Estadística de la República Mexicana* (quinta época) 1, no. 1 (1902): 15.

40. Esteva Ruiz, "La estadística y sus funciones," 19. In spite of persistent interest, political instability and perennial lack of funds hindered effective action.

Finally, in 1881, during the Manuel González interregnum, an official census bureau was established, and the second Porfirian regime was the first with access to statistical data (although its accuracy was dubious) for formulating public policy.

41. The phrase is Charles Hale's. See his *Transformation of Liberalism*, chapter 2.

42. Nicolás León, "Historia de antropología física en México," *American Journal of Physical Anthropology* 2, no. 3 (July–September 1919): 231–35.

43. On racism in European and North American anthropology see Jacques Barzun, *Race: A Study in Superstition* (New York: Harper Torchbooks, 1937), and Gould, *The Mismeasure of Man*.

44. "Seemed" because according to many scholars the revolutionary commitment was largely rhetorical as well. See especially Wilkie, *Mexican Revolution*.

45. Gamio, *Forjando Patria*, 6.

46. Gamio, *Forjando Patria*, 23.

47. Gamio, *Forjando Patria*, 50–51.

48. The larger role of intellectuals, including Gamio, in the construction of a post-revolutionary nation-state is examined in Annick Lempérière, *Intellectuels, etats et société au Mexique: Les clercs de la nation (1910–1968)* (Paris: Editions L'Harmattan, 1992). On the role of local intellectuals see Claudio Lomnitz-Adler, *Las salidas del laberinto: Cultura e ideología en el espacio nacional mexicano* (México: Joaquín Mortiz, 1995).

49. Gamio, *Forjando patria*, 325. His italics.

50. Gamio studied with Franz Boas at Columbia from 1909 to 1911 and participated in the Boas-spearheaded International School of American Archeology and Ethnography in Mexico City. Boas directed the school and taught classes in Mexico City in 1910. His cultural relativism rejected racial/cultural comparisons as scientifically irrelevant and attacked the racist notions imbedded in European physical anthropology. While in Mexico, Boas, typically, refused to teach his physical anthropology classes to measure bodies. León, "Historia de antropología física en México," 243–44. Boas's internationalist project (funded in part by the U.S. and Prussian governments) floundered in the hypernationalistic revolutionary years. See Ricardo Godoy, "Franz Boas and His Plans for an International School of American Archeology and Ethnography in Mexico," *Journal of the History of the Behavioral Sciences* 13 (1977): 228–42.

51. Gamio, *Forjando patria*, 38.

52. David Brading argues convincingly that Gamio was a modernizing, liberal nationalist who saw little value in contemporary indigenous culture beyond its aesthetic sense and its arts and crafts. See his "Manuel Gamio and Official Indigensimo in Mexico," 88. Alan Knight explores the paternalistic, racist under-

pinnings of the *indigenista–mestizaje* cult in "Racism, Revolution, and *Indigenismo*," 86–87.

53. Gamio, *Forjando patria*, 175.

54. Manuel Gamio, *Introducción, síntesis y conclusiones de la obra "La población del valle de Teotihuacán"* (México: Secretaría de Educación Pública, 1922), ix.

55. Paul Siliceo Pauer, "Tipo físico," in Manuel Gamio, ed., *La población del valle de Teotihuacán: El medio que se ha desarrollado, su evolución étnica y social: Iniciativas para procurar su mejoramiento por la Dirección de Antropología* (México: Secretaría de Educación Pública), 165.

56. José Joaquín Izquierdo, "Estudio fisiológico del indígena adulto del valle de Teotihuacán," in Pauer, "Tipo físico," 186.

57. Paul Siliceo Pauer, "Datos sobre las condiciones higiénicos de la población," in "Tipo físico," 195.

58. Pauer, "Datos sobre las condiciones higiénicos," 201, his italics.

59. "Introducción," *Ethnos* 1, no. 1 (abril 1920): 2. For a brief history of *Ethnos* see María de la Luz del Valle Berrocal, "Ethnos," in *La antropología en México*, 8:468–72.

60. Manuel Gamio, "El censo de la población mexicana desde el punto de vista antropológica," *Ethnos* 1, no. 2 (mayo 1920): 46.

61. "El Segundo Congreso Internacional de Eugenesia," *Ethos* 1, no. 5 (agosto 1920): 128–130, and "La segunda época de Ethnos," *Ethnos*, segunda época 1, no. 1 (enero 1922): 2. For a history of post-revolutionary Mexican eugenics see Alexandra Stern, "Unraveling the History of Eugenics in Mexico," *Mendel Newsletter*, forthcoming; "Responsible Mothers and Normal Children: Eugenics and Nationalism in Postrevolutionary Mexico, 1920–1940," unpublished manuscript; and "Reproduction, Sexuality, and the State: Eugenics and Paternity in Mexico, 1900–1950," unpublished manuscript.

62. Manuel Gamio, "Nacionalismo e internacionalismo," *Ethnos*, segunda época 1, no. 2 (abril 1923): 3.

63. Paul Siliceo Pauer, "Conocimiento antropológico de la agrupaciones indígenas de México," *Ethnos*, segunda época 1, no. 1 (noviembre 1922–enero 1923): 15 and 18. On the Mexican eugenics movement see Stepans, *Hour of Eugenics*.

64. Lucio Mendieta y Núñez, "Importancia científica y práctica de los estudios etnológicos y ethnográficos," *Ethnos*, tercera época 1, nos. 3–4 (marzo y abril 1925): 46.

65. Concern about proper technique (crucial to international racial comparisons) eventually led to an "International Convention for the Unification of Craneo- and Cephalo-metric Measurements" in Monaco. The guidelines were translated and published in the *Boletín del Museo Nacional de Arqueología, Historia y Etnología* 2, no. 9 (marzo 1913): 174–83.

66. Martínez Baca and Vergara, *Estudios de antropología criminal*, 10.

67. Martínez Baca and Vergara, *Estudios de antropología criminal*, 98.

68. Martínez Baca and Vergara, *Estudios de antropología criminal*, 33–34.

69. Nicolas León's brief "Historia de antropología física en México" (235–40) devotes a third of its pages to the history of criminal anthropometry, including Martínez Baca and Vergara's study.

70. Miguel Galindo, "Le alma de la raza: Afinidades hispano-americanas," *Boletín de la Sociedad Mexicana de Geografía y Estadística*, quinta época 12, nos. 7–12 (1928): 331. Gustav Le Bon had argued that similar races could assimilate, while dissimilar races created systems of domination that resulted in the eventual extinction of the weaker race. The categorization of races by cephalic index (brachy-, dolicho-, mesati-, orthocephalic) based on the head ratio of width to length was popularized by Broca in the 1860s.

71. For a brief history of *Quetzalcoatl* see María Guadalupe González González, "Quetzalcoatl," in *La antropología en México*, 8:572–78.

72. Carlos Basauri, "La redención del indio desde un nuevo punto de vista," *Quetzalcoatl* 1, no. 1 (mayo 1929): 8–9. My italics.

73. Carlos Basauri, "El tipo nacional mexicano del porvenir," *Quetzalcoatl* 2, no. 1 (septiembre 1930): 6–7.

74. Carlos Serrano Sánchez and Mercedes Mejía Sánchez, "Misión italiana para el estudio de la población indígena y mestiza de México," in *La antropología en México*, 8:102–6.

75. José Gómez Robledo et al., *Pescadores y campesinos tarascos* (México: Secretaría de Educación Pública, 1943), xvi–xvii. Quoted in Javier Romero, "De la biotipología a la psicobiología," *Anales del Instituto Nacional de Antropología e Historia* 19 (1966): 80.

76. Corrado Gini, "Premiers resultats d'une expédition italo-mexicaine parmi les populations indigènes et métisses du Mexique," *Boletín de la Sociedad Mexicana de Geografía y Estadística* 45, nos. 3–4 (noviembre–diciembre 1935): 133–34. Gini was Gamio's counterpart on the Italian Committee for the Study of Population Problems and a fellow vice president of the Second International Eugenics Congress.

77. Gini, "Premiers resultats d'une expédition italo-mexicaine," 119.

78. Johanna Faulhaber, "Ada D'Aloja," in *La antropología en México*, 9:621–25.

79. Anselmo Marino Flores, "La criminología y una nueva técnica de craneología constitucionalista," *Revista Mexicana de Estudios Antropológicos* 7, nos. 1–3 (enero–diciembre 1945): 128, 146–47.

80. Anselmo Marino Flores and Carlos Serrano Sánchez, "Craneología y criminología," *Anales del Instituto Nacional de Antropología e Historia* 16 (1963): 123–33.

81. Javier Romero, "El Departamento de Antropología Física del Museo Nacional," *Anales del Museo Nacional de Arqueología, Historia y Etnografía* 5, no. 3 (1945): 201–2.

82. José Gomez Robledo et al., *Estudio biotipológico de los Otomí* (México: Instituto de Investigaciones Sociales, UNAM, 1961), 10. Quoted in Romero, "De la biotypología a la psicobiología," 81.

83. Porfirian concerns about alcoholism and criminality (the immediate source for post-revolutionary discussions) are examined in Pablo Piccato, "El Paso de Venus por el disco del Sol: Criminality and Alcoholism in the Late Porfiriato," *Mexican Studies/Estudios Mexicanos* 11, no. 2 (summer 1995): 203–42.

84. "La campaña contra el alcoholismo," 4. Mexican policymakers were concerned enough to flirt with a U.S.-style prohibition. See Robert Buffington, "Prohibition in the Borderlands," *Pacific Historical Review* 43, no. 1 (February 1994): 19–38.

85. Miguel Galindo, "La patria enferma: Memoria sobre el alcoholismo," *Boletín de la Sociedad Mexicana de Geografía y Estadística* 42, no. 1 (abril 1930): 24, 42.

86. Enrique C. Creel, "Alcoholismo," *Boletín de la Sociedad Mexicana de Geografía y Estadística* 42, no. 1 (abril 1930): 51, 58.

87. Lucio Mendieta y Núñez, "Ensayo sobre el Alcoholismo entre las Razas Indígenas de México," *Revista Mexicana de Sociología* 1, no. 3 (julio–agosto 1939): 77.

88. Mendieta y Núñez, "Ensayo sobre el Alcoholismo," 89.

89. Mendieta y Núñez, "Ensayo sobre el Alcoholismo," 78. Environment (including climate) and economic exploitation were the other causes.

90. Mendieta y Núñez, "Ensayo sobre el Alcoholismo," 92–93.

91. Alfonso Quiroz Cuaron, "Etnografía de México," *Criminalia* 25, nos. 1–12 (1959): 649–53.

92. José Gómez Robledo, "Algunas consideraciones sobre antropología criminal," *Quetzalcoatl* 2, no. 3 (septiembre 1930): 8–10; and Francisco Núñez Chávez, "Las relaciones de la clínica criminológica con la antropología," *Quetzalcoatl* 3, no. 4 (enero 1931): 10–11.

93. Gilberto Loyo, "Las razas indígenas y la defensa social," *Criminalia* 1, no. 1 (septiembre 1939): 517–21.

94. Carlos Franco Sodi, "Delincuencia indígena," in *Don Juan Delincuente y otros ensayos* (México: Ediciones Bota, 1951), 137–38.

95. Franco Sodi, "Delincuencia indígena," 137.

96. Serge Gruzinski's provocative work on the "colonization" of the indigenous imaginary during the colonial period testifies to the deep roots of the acculturation process. See his *La colonización de lo imaginario: Sociedades indí-*

*genas y occidentalización en el México español, siglos XVI–XXVII* (México: Fondo de Cultura Económica, 1991).

97. Paz, *Labyrinth of Solitude*, 43.

## Conclusion

1. Anthony Marx, *Making Race and Nation: A Comparison of South Africa, the United States and Brazil* (New York: Cambridge University Press, 1998).

2. V. Spike Peterson, "The Politics of Identity and Gendered Nationalism," in *Foreign Policy Analysis: Continuity and Change in Its Second Generation*, ed. Laura Neack, Jeanne A. K. Hey, and Patrick J. Haney (Englewood Cliffs NJ: Prentice Hall, 1995), 183. For a review of this literature see Sylvia Walby, "Woman and Nation," *International Journal of Comparative Sociology* 32, nos. 1–2 (1992): 81–100.

3. Foucault, *History of Sexuality*, 1:12–13.

4. This theme permeates nearly all of Foucault's work, especially his histories: *Madness and Civilization: A History of Insanity in the Age of Reason*, trans. Richard Howard (New York: Vintage, 1965); *Discipline and Punish*; and *The Birth of the Clinic*. The well-known opening of *Discipline and Punish*, in which a public execution is juxtaposed against a private prison schedule, dramatically illustrates this fundamental shift in the nature of punishment. For a discussion of the post-Enlightenment epistemological shift and its implications for the history of criminality in Latin America see the introduction to *Reconstructing Criminality*, ed. Aguirre and Buffington.

5. Todorov, *The Conquest of America*, 185.

6. Todorov, *The Conquest of America*, 132. His italics.

7. Todorov, *The Conquest of America*, 247–48.

# BIBLIOGRAPHICAL ESSAY

Scholarly work on the history of crime in Mexico is scarce. Fortunately, the quality of what exists is quite good. Works on crime in the colonial period include three splendid monographs: William B. Taylor's *Drinking, Homicide and Rebellion in Colonial Mexican Villages* (Stanford: Stanford University Press, 1979); Colin MacLachlan's *Criminal Justice in Eighteenth-Century Mexico: A Study of the Tribunal of the Acordada* (Berkeley: University of California Press, 1974); and Juan Pedro Viqueira Albán's *Relajados o reprimidos? Diversiones públicas y vida social en la ciudad de México durante el Siglo de las Luces* (México: Fondo de Cultura Económico, 1987), and two excellent dissertations, Gabriel Haslip-Viera's "Crime and the Administration of Justice in Colonial Mexico City, 1689–1810" (Ph.D. diss., Columbia University, 1980) and Michael C. Scardaville's "Crime and the Urban Poor: Mexico City in the Late Colonial Period" (Ph.D. diss., University of Florida, 1977). All these works deal thoughtfully with the ambiguities inherent in the elite criminalization of lower-class "behaviors." So does Teresa Lozano Armendares's more narrowly focused but nonetheless extremely useful *La criminalidad en la ciudad de México, 1800–1821* (México: Universidad Nacional Autónoma de México, 1987), which examines the transition from colony to nation.

The major works on crime in the national period are equally good. Paul J. Vanderwood's *Disorder and Progress: Bandits, Police, and Mexican Development* (Lincoln: University of Nebraska Press, 1981) and Laurence J. Rohlfes's, "Police and Penal Correction in Mexico City, 1876–1911: A Study of Order and Progress in Porfirian Mexico" (Ph.D. diss., Tulane University, 1983) illuminate police practices in late-nineteenth-and early-twentieth-century Mexico. Pablo Piccato's pioneering work, especially "Criminals in Mexico City, 1900–1931: A Cultural History" (Ph.D. diss., University of Texas at Austin, 1997), explores the too-often ignored social dimensions of crime and criminality. The current shortage of work on the history of crime in Mexico appears temporary; the growing periodical literature is cited in appropriate chapters.

Historians of crime in Mexico benefit greatly from the important work of Latin Americanist colleagues. That literature is too extensive to include here, but interested readers should consult three volumes of collected essays: Carlos Aguirre and Robert Buffington, eds., *Reconstructing Criminality in Latin America* (Wilmington DE: Scholarly Resources, forthcoming); Ricardo D. Salvatore and Carlos Aguirre, eds., *The Birth of the Penitentiary in Latin America: Essays on Criminology, Prison Reform, and Social Control, 1830–1940* (Austin: University of Texas Press, 1996); and Lyman L. Johnson, ed., *The Problem of Order in Changing Societies: Essays on Crime and Policing in Argentina and Uruguay, 1750–1940* (Albuquerque: University of New Mexico Press, 1990). Carlos Aguirre's extensive bibliographical essay in *Reconstructing Criminality* is especially useful. Another collection—Daniel Balderston and Donna Guy, eds., *Sex and Sexuality in Latin America* (New York: New York University Press, 1997)—also includes several useful essays related to the history of crime in Latin America.

The present work deals primarily with elite visions of criminality as reflected in Mexican criminology, penology, and (to a lesser extent) anthropology. Thus most of the citations are published rather than archival sources. Professional journals were especially helpful, in particular *Criminalia* (for criminology and penology); *Quetzalcoatl, Ethnos, Revista Mexicana de Sociología* and *Anales del Instituto Nacional de Antropología, Historia y Etnografía* (for sociology and anthropology); and *Boletín de la Sociedad Mexicana de Geografía y Estadística* (for general attitudes). Of the many criminalogical and penological texts cited in the footnotes, the most important are: Manuel de Lardizábal y Uribe, *Discurso sobre las penas* (México: Editorial Porrúa, 1982); Rafael de Zayas Enríquez, *Fisiología del crimen: Estudio jurídico-sociológico*, 2 vols. (Veracruz: Imprenta de R. de Zayas, 1885); Francisco Martínez Baca and Manuel Vergara, *Estudios de antropología criminal* (Puebla: Imprenta, Litografía y Encuadernación de Benjamin Lara, 1892); Miguel S. Macedo, *La criminalidad en México: Medios de combatirla* (México: Oficina Tip. de la Secretaría de Fomento, 1897) and *Apuntes para la historia del Derecho Penal Mexicano* (México: Editorial "CULTURA," 1931); Julio Guerrero, *La génesis del crimen en México: Ensayo de psiquiatría social* (México: Imprenta de la Vda. de Ch. Bouret, 1901); Carlos Roumagnac, *Los criminales en México: Ensayo de psicología criminal* (México: Tipografía "El Fénix," 1904), *Crímenes sexuales y pasionales: Estudio de psicología morbosa* (México: Librería de Ch. Bouret, 1906), *La estadística criminal en México* (México: Imp. de Arturo García Cubas Sucesores Hermanos, 1907); Luis Lara y Pardo, *La prostitución en México* (México: Librería de la Vda. de Ch. Bouret, 1908); Luis Garrido, *Notas de un penalista* (México: Ediciones Bota, 1947).

The principal texts on the broader question of Mexican national identity— Manuel Gamio's *Forjando patria* (México: Editorial Porrúa, 1960), Samuel Ramos's *Profile of Man and Culture in Mexico*, trans. Peter G. Earle (New York: MacGraw-Hill, 1962), and Octavio Paz's *The Labyrinth of Solitude: Life and Thought in Mexico*, trans. Lysander Kemp (New York: Grove Press, 1961)—are classics and thus especially valuable for their canonic qualities. Another potentially canonic work, Roger Bartra's *The Cage of Melancholy: Identity and Metamorphosis in the Mexican Character*, trans. Christopher J. Hall (New Brunswick NJ: Rutgers University Press, 1992), provides a thought-provoking, sometimes whimsical critique of its predecessors.

It would be remiss not to mention some of the important "new" histories of Mexican social relations and nation-building that inspired this book. A necessarily incomplete list includes (in alphabetical order, by topic): On social relations: William Beezley, *Judas at the Jockey Club and Other Episodes of Porfirian Mexico* (Lincoln: University of Nebraska Press, 1987); William French, *A Peaceful and Working People: Manners, Morals, and Class Formation in Northern Mexico* (Albuquerque: University of New Mexico Press, 1996); Steve J. Stern, *The Secret History of Gender: Women, Men and Power in Late Colonial Mexico* (Chapel Hill: University of North Carolina Press, 1995). On nation building: Marjorie Becker, *Setting the Virgin on Fire: Lázaro Cárdenas, Michoacán Peasants and the Redemption of the Mexican Revolution* (Berkeley: University of California Press, 1995); William Beezley, Cheryl English Martin, and William French, eds., *Rituals of Rule, Rituals of Resistance: Popular Celebrations and Popular Culture in Mexico* (Wilmington DE: Scholarly Resources, 1994); Gilbert M. Joseph and Daniel Nugent, eds., *Everyday Forms of State Formation: Revolution and the Negotiation of Rule in Modern Mexico* (Durham NC: Duke University Press, 1994); Florencia E. Mallon, *Peasant and Nation: The Making of Postcolonial Mexico and Peru* (Berkeley: University of California Press, 1995); Mauricio Tenorio-Trillo, *Mexico at the World's Fair: Crafting a Modern Nation* (Berkeley: University of California Press, 1996); Alan Wells and Gilbert M. Joseph, *Summer of Discontent, Seasons of Upheaval: Elite Politics and Rural Insurgency in Yucatán, 1876–1915* (Stanford CA: Stanford University Press, 1996). A wealth of periodical literature, too voluminous to discuss here, appears in the endnotes for each chapter.

If the "new" Mexican history inspired this book, a distinguished tradition of Mexican intellectual history provided its foundation. Leopoldo Zea's volumes on positivism—*El positivismo en México* (México: El Colegio de México, 1943) and *Apogeo y decadencia del positivismo en México* (México: El Colegio de México, 1944)—are still essential reading. So too are the more recent works of David Brading, *The First America: The Spanish Monarchy, Creole Patriots, and the Liberal State, 1492–1867* (New York: Cambridge University Press, 1991); Arnaldo Córdova, *La ideología de la Revolución Mexicana: La formación del nuevo régimen* (México: Ediciones Era, 1973); Charles Hale, *Mexican Liberalism in the Age of Mora, 1821–1853* (New Haven CT: Yale University Press, 1968) and *The Transformation of Liberalism in Late Nineteenth-Century Mexico* (Princeton NJ: Princeton University Press, 1989); Annick Lempérière,

*Intellectuels, etats et société au Mexique: Les clercs de la nation* (1910–1968) (Paris: Editions L'Harmattan, 1992); Colin M. MacLachlan, *Spain's Empire in the New World: The Role of Ideas in Institutional and Social Change* (Berkeley: University of California Press, 1988); Jesús Reyes Heroles, *El liberalismo mexicano*, 3 vols. (México: Universidad Nacional Autónoma de México, 1957–1961); and Jesús Silva Herzog, *El pensamiento económico, social y político de México, 1810–1964* (México: Fondo de Cultura Económica, 1974). More extensive bibliographies of Mexican national identity, nationalism, liberalism, positivism, education, and so forth appear in various bibliographical endnotes. For general background, breadth of coverage, and inspiration, Daniel Cosío Villegas's multivolume *Historia moderna de México* and especially Moisés González Navarro's *El Porfiriato: La vida social*, vol. 4 (México: Editorial Hermes, 1957) remain indispensable.

My book has a theoretical bent, but "theory" serves here more as creative inspiration than as rigid dogma. Its huge debt to Michel Foucault—*The Archeology of Knowledge and the Discourse on Language*, trans. A. M. Sheridan Smith (New York: Harper Colophon Books, 1972), *The Birth of the Clinic: An Archeology of Medical Perception*, trans. A. M. Sheridan Smith (New York: Vintage, 1975), *Discipline and Punish: The Birth of the Prison*, trans. Alan Sheridan (New York: Vintage, 1979), *The History of Sexuality*, vol. 1, *An Introduction*, trans. Robert Hurley (New York: Vintage, 1978)—reflects an appreciation of his theoretical insights even as it rejects the rigidity of Foucauldian historical analysis. Equally pragmatic is its use of Benedict Anderson, *Imagined Communities: Reflections on the Origin and Spread of Nationalism*, rev. ed. (New York: Verso, 1991); Roland Barthes, *Image, Music, Text*, trans. Stephen Heath (New York: Noonday Press, 1977); Tony Bennet et al., eds., *Culture, Ideology and Social Process: A Reader* (London: Open University, 1981); Philip Corrigan and Derek Sayer, *The Great Arch: English State Formation as Cultural Revolution* (New York: Oxford University Press, 1985); Jürgen Habermas, *The Structural Transformation of the Public Sphere: An Inquiry into a Category of Bourgeois Society*, trans. Thomas Burger and Frederick Lawrence (Cambridge MA: MIT Press, 1989); Thomas S. Kuhn, *The Structure of Scientific Revolutions*, 2nd ed., enlarged (Chicago: University of Chicago Press, 1970); Edward Said, *Orientalism* (New York: Pantheon, 1978); Joan Wallach Scott, *Gender and the Politics of History* (New York: Columbia University Press, 1988); Tzvetan Todorov, *The Conquest of America: The Question of the Other*, trans. Richard Howard (New York: HarperPerennial, 1984); and Hayden White, *The Content of the Form: Narrative Discourse and Historical Representation* (Baltimore MD: Johns Hopkins University Press, 1987). While these distinguished theorists might not applaud the result, without their insights, this history could never have been written.

# Index